BY TRAIN TO SHANGHAI

A Journey on the Trans-Siberian Railway

WILLIAM J. GINGLES

Bloomington, IN   Milton Keynes, UK
authorHOUSE®

AuthorHouse™
1663 Liberty Drive, Suite 200
Bloomington, IN 47403
www.authorhouse.com
Phone: 1-800-839-8640

AuthorHouse™ UK Ltd.
500 Avebury Boulevard
Central Milton Keynes, MK9 2BE
www.authorhouse.co.uk
Phone: 08001974150

This book is a work of non-fiction. Unless otherwise noted, the author and the publisher make no explicit guarantees as to the accuracy of the information contained in this book and in some cases, names of people and places have been altered to protect their privacy.

© 2006 William J. Gingles. All rights reserved.

No part of this book may be reproduced, stored in a retrieval system, or transmitted by any means without the written permission of the author.

First published by AuthorHouse 9/26/2006

ISBN: 1-4259-5588-6 (sc)

Printed in the United States of America
Bloomington, Indiana

This book is printed on acid-free paper.

The Siberian railway now open for traffic stands as the first great enterprise of the 20th Century. Built by the order of the late Tsar Alexander, the Russians have rolled out its long ribbons of steel until they dropped the ends into the waters of the Pacific Ocean at Vladivostok, the ruler of the East. This railway will take its place amongst the most important works of the world ... Russia is awakening at last and moving forward.

> Michael Myers Shoemaker,
> 1903

Contents

Prologue ix

Chapter One
London to St. Petersburg 1

Chapter Two
Moscow 34

Chapter Three
Moscow to Irkursk 76

Chapter Four
Lake Baikal 115

Chapter Five
Mongolia 140

Chapter Six
Beijing 176

Chapter Seven
Xi'an 210

Chapter Eight
Shanghai 233

Epilogue 267

Prologue

My early morning call was for four o'clock (a most ungodly hour) to ensure I was ready for my 5am taxi, booked to take me to Heathrow Airport…the start of a journey that was conceived some decades go, but which passed into middle age without fulfilment, and only now was about to be realised.

This journey was on the Trans-Siberian Railway, the longest continuous track in the world on which trains are operated – the stretch from Moscow to Vladivostok alone is a staggering 9,289 kilometres. The name Trans-Siberian Railway is a purely English invention - to the Russians, it is the 'Great Siberian', and they define that section as the central part from Yekaterinburg in the Urals to Ulan Ude on the Mongolian border.

No one train is called the Trans-Siberian Express, but a series of trains running along its line - such as the Trans-Mongolian Railway - from Moscow onwards via Ulaan Baatar to Beijing - the Trans-Manchurian Railway - from Moscow to Beijing via Chita and Harbin, or the Far-East Railway from Moscow to Vladivostok on the Pacific coast.

I was embarking on a train journey from St Petersburg to Shanghai to visit my good friend, Chris, now living in that city and bringing new ideas to the Chinese after a successful, forty year career in the City of London. Chris was too trusting with some of his work colleagues, who in reality were a bunch of quislings, and the rest, as they say, is history. Being my employer, I suffered the same fate - which left me with plenty of spare time - so, with a little help from John McCririck during the winter months, the ideal time had arrived to fulfil my youthful ambition.

Another close friend, Kate, was also planning to be in Beijing around about the time of my arrival - so we plotted to meet up at the Beijing Railway Station when my Trans-Mongolian train arrived on 27th May. Initially, Kate was to be my companion, but instead was now travelling by aeroplane. She had scheduled a heavy load of business meetings with high-powered Chinese entrepreneurs and would need a large wardrobe for the various occasions. We both agreed - with the limited storage space on the train, she would probably require an extra compartment just for her luggage, which was out of the question - the plane it was for her!

Trains and railways have always given me a certain nostalgic feeling, ever since, more than fifty years ago, as a birthday treat, my late father took me on a train from Kells, more famous as the home town of that priceless, illuminated manuscript of the Four Gospels, The Book of Kells, across the rich rolling County Meath countryside, past the Hill of Tara, to Dublin. That journey was a mere 60 kilometres, visiting many stations *en route* - stopping for water for its steam engine, and taking two hours to reach its destination.

This special journey from St Petersburg to Shanghai will take me 25 days - allowing for stopovers on the way and will cover almost 10,000 kilometres. It will allow me to visit Russia, Mongolia and China before reaching my destination, Shanghai.

My soft-sleeper rail tickets have already been purchased, thus alleviating the need to join queues and negotiate purchases at ticket windows, from staff who may not speak English. So, I was finally ready to travel on the longest continuous track in the world, or at least part of it, in what constitutes the greatest single experience a tourist can have. Things may come and things may go, but the Trans-Siberian rolls on forever.

My odyssey will take me across the Urals, through the endless Siberian *tiaga*, for 200 kilometres around the shores of the beautiful Lake Baikal, through the wilderness of the Gobi Desert, and up to the Great Wall of China at Beijing. From the current Chinese capital it will then be on to Xi'an, the ancient capital to see Emperor Qin's mighty terra-cotta army, before reaching the great metropolis of Shanghai.

For one month, my drinking companions will by my fellow travellers, railway enthusiasts, back-packers, and an assortment of Russian, Mongolian, Korean, and Chinese that I shall meet along the way. For now- it will be goodbye to Happy Hour in my local bar, and I will miss the following, who are listed in no particular order: John the Fish and Maggie, Lady Patricia, Grumpy Frank, Posh Derek, (stockbroker), Gavin (money broker), Lord Bill, Lord Lloyd (occasional visitor from Cornwall) Scottish John, (retired boxer), Brian and Bob (chauffeurs), Jacko (an actor), Murphy - O'Connor (retired), Scottish George, (retired policeman) Larry, Don, Peter, The Colonel, Chris, Stan, Vivian, Jonnie… and not forgetting Malik the barman.

CHAPTER ONE
London to St. Petersburg
Monday, 9th May

My journey started from a block of flats in London, which was once the largest single block in Europe called Dolphin Square and wartime base for the French Government in Exile and their leader, General Charles de Gaulle. Had de Gaulle and the Allies not prevailed, then the Gestapo had earmarked this very same block as their future headquarters, which thankfully, did not occur.

Dawn was breaking as I opened my window to peep out and see if my taxi had arrived, as I was anxious not to get off to a bad start by being late. Just before 5am, saw a car arrive which was being driven very slowly and stopped outside my block, but had to wait another anxious five minutes for the driver to telephone confirmation of his arrival.

Finally, we were on the way and as the early morning traffic was light, we made good time and arrived at Heathrow at spot on 5.30 a.m. This gave me time to replenish my camera and buy extra film for the journey ahead. In no time, flight number KL1000 was on its way to Schiopol, Amsterdam. Leaving

Heathrow Airport on a beautiful, May morning, below, you could see the beauty of the English countryside, probably at its best this time of year.

The plane banked right to give a good view of the traffic build-up on the M25 motorway below (even at this early hour), and then the elegant buildings of the City of London before we headed off for the English Channel.

Flight KL1395 from Amsterdam to St Petersburg was completely full when it departed at 11 o'clock. On board was an assortment of passengers including some pretty Russian girls returning from holiday! They applauded loudly when the plane finally touched the runway as if in thanks for their safe arrival and were back in Russia - or perhaps they just remembered the bad old days of Russian aviation, when Aeroflot used to lose a Tupelov aircraft at least once a year - every year!

The airport building looked old and grey and not very inspiring, whilst the apron contained about a dozen aircraft of mixed nationalities. I got in line for passport control and a pretty girl in a smart brown uniform with two stars seemed to have a problem with my passport. She summoned another lady in a blue uniform, this time with three stars. She also examined my passport and consulted the computer, and eventually asked me to accompany her upstairs to a private office - to my great embarrassment, this required walking back past the line of my fellow travellers! At this stage, my mind reverted to the old Russia before 1991, with its Gulags and the Lubyanka prison run by the KGB. However, I was pleasantly surprised and delighted to be introduced to an elderly gentleman in civilian clothes, and more reassured that I was not heading for a Gulag – but would be going to Siberia in a few days time…totally voluntarily!

In about five minutes the whole matter was cleared up. I was travelling on my Irish passport but the Russian visa was showing my nationality as British. This was the reason - neither the computer nor the officials could handle the entry procedures. The polite gentleman merely asked me to confirm my nationality as Irish – and was on the way.

Outside the customs hall I was pleasantly surprised to see a man holding a name board with my name – spelt correctly! He introduced himself as Alexi and spoke little English. His taxi was a battered old Lada and we set off for my hotel, driving as if to impress on me that he was the fastest and best driver around. The object of his driving style seemed to be to get as close as he could to the car in front – without actually touching it, whilst at the same time appearing only interested in his car radio. "Slow down", I shouted to him, reminding Alexi that we had plenty of time, and did not want to arrive –dead!

Passing through the drab suburbs of St. Petersburg near the airport is not very attractive, having been largely destroyed during World War II. They have been re-built in Stalinist style, with ugly blocks of apartments for the workers and a large uninspiring war memorial set in municipal gardens. It was Stalin's plan to move the city centre away from its classical, crumbling grandeur because of its past links to the Romanovs, and relocate the centre here in the suburbs. We can all be grateful that Stalin died before he could implement this notion.

All along, I noticed thousands of red flags and emblems festooning the highway, celebrating the 60th Anniversary of something. Asking Alexi what this was all about, he explained in his best 'pidgin' English that this was a very special day…no ordinary Monday. I had not planned it this way, but had arrived in Russia on Victory Day – which marks a conflict they call the Great Patriotic War, during which the Soviet Union lost an estimated 27 million people, both military and civilian, and which ended 60 years ago, on 9th May, 1945.

As we approached the city centre, Alexi started to panic. I could not work out what his problem was as we turned into a side street, before mysteriously reversing out again. Finally, we arrived where some policemen were standing in the road and Alexi got out of his taxi in order to talk to them. The conversation was very brief and he received a firm "*nyet*". He then drove away and finally parked up, muttering something about a parade. He indicated we would have to walk the remainder of the journey to the hotel, and the reason would soon become apparent.

My hotel, The Neva, was situated on the north side of Nevsky Prospekt at No. 102. Unfortunately we were on the south side of this magnificent avenue, which runs east to west and is about four kilometres long. In the early master plan of St Petersburg, this was the "Great Perspective Road", which explains the term *prospekt*. The 60th anniversary parade was about to begin on Nevsky where we were, and the firm "*nyet*" which Alexi had received, was an order not to cross over, not even on foot. However, this left both of us in an excellent position to view the start of this memorable parade - which almost seemed to have been awaiting our arrival. The first line of the parade was lead by a group of octogenarians in military uniforms with countless medals and insignias. The leaders, I subsequently discovered were Captain Mikhail Moroz and a lady called Nina Ushakov, two veterans of the infamous blockade of Leningrad as the city was called during World War II, and numerous photographs of them appeared in the *St Petersburg Times* newspaper the following day.

Back then the German army besieged the city for 900 days causing nearly one million to die from starvation during two arctic winters in horrendous conditions but the city never surrendered. Therefore, emotions were running high as the bystanders on the pavements threw flowers as the parade passed by - as there are few greater honours in Russia than to be a veteran of the Leningrad blockade. After the veterans, there followed a variety of vehicles and bands playing patriotic music, then finally a few hundred of the current Russian army.

Back in 1900, Annette Meakin was the first English woman to travel the entire length of the Trans-Siberian Railway, and took her aged mother along for company on the journey. They travelled via Paris to see the Russian government display at the Paris Exhibition and immediately signed-up for the trip in March 1900.

After six weeks staying in Paris to perfect their French, the Meakins travelled by train to St. Petersburg, arriving on 7th May 1900, which happened to be the day that the Tsar held his annual military review. So, having just witnessed the parade of 2005 along Nevsky Prospekt, reflected on how Annette described the parade of 1900 in her book *"A Ribbon of Iron"*.

"The Nevsky, a bright and handsome street, at all times looked gay indeed as the mounted troops passed down it to the Russian Champs de Mars. Cuirassiers in white and gleaming gold were followed by a regiment all in what we call 'Prussian Blue', but far brighter than any blue worn by the Russian army. Then came a regiment in red and black, each man carrying a flag, followed by others equally striking. All St. Petersburg turned out to see the troops pass and the Nevsky, brilliant with flags and red draperies hung from the windows."

Now in 2005 the Tsar has long gone, as have the mounted troops and Prussians, although the flags and draperies, now emblazoned with the number sixty, were flowing in full glory, reflecting the significance of the day.

When the parade had all passed by, Alexi and I continued our journey on foot to the hotel, whose entrance was in a quiet courtyard, just off Nevsky Prospekt. At least I had my baggage with me, unlike Annette Meakin who complained that on arrival in St. Petersburg that it took four days to get her luggage through customs, as it had not been examined on the frontier. Growing impatient at the delay, her friends offered the following advice, "you cannot hurry a Russian, never show that you are cross, that only makes them worse. The safest thing to do is laugh. It helps you best in the end." So, Annette laughed and waited!

Boris Solkov, the young Russian manager at my hotel, spoke English with a strong German accent, and could easily have been a younger brother of Boris Becker. He received me with courtesy and admitted his hotel training was done in Germany, hence his accent. Having just checked in when I

By Train to Shanghai

received a telephone call from a young Russian called Jenya. He introduced himself as my guide for Tuesday when we were due to go on a three-hour walking tour of the city. He advised caution if going out later in the evening, because of the parade - a lot of alcohol was being consumed during the day with the resultant drunks wandering around the streets later.

Curiosity got the better of me, and after a shower decided to investigate what was happening on the streets outside. The parade had continued along the Nevsky Prospekt which had been pedestrianised for the day, and had ended two kilometres away on Palace Square, I decided to follow its route walking east to west. The Nevsky, as the locals call it, is the main thoroughfare as it was set out in the early plans for the city. Nikolai Gogol wrote some 150 years ago -"there is nothing finer than Nevsky Prospekt, not in St. Petersburg at any rate, for in St. Petersburg it is everything". It is difficult to disagree with Gogol, but then he did live at No. 17, and was possibly a tad biased. So, walking past some fine colourful, classical, if somewhat dishevelled edifices of 18th century Baroque, and after crossing two rivers and one canal, I arrived at the huge Palace Square where the parade had ended. There, a large stage had been erected for the orchestra, and various singers entertaining the large crowd. Not being able to get close, it was still possible to watch and listen as an enormous TV screen had been erected and was relaying the rich classical and Russian folk music.

The stage was set in front of the General Staff Building which is a three-storey circular building on which is mounted a bronze victory chariot commemorating the 1812 victory over Napoleon. Palace Square symbolises much of the city's past. It used to house the Tsar's residence; is a repository of art in the Hermitage nearby; Bloody Sunday occurred here in 1905 when troops shot demonstrating workers; and, in 1917 Kerensky's Provisional government was ousted from the Winter Palace leaving Lenin's Bolsheviks to take control of the city. Out of the turmoil, Lenin and his associates brought the biggest change in Russia's history since Peter the Great by replacing the Russian Empire with the Union of the Soviet Socialist Republics.

In the centre of the square is the Alexander Column, which stands some twenty-five metres high on a pedestal cut out of a single piece of granite. In 1832 it took several thousand soldiers to erect the column using an intricate system of ropes and pulleys, and now it stands without any additional support. On the west side of the square there is the Admiralty, built in both Baroque and Classical styles, to glorify Russian's navy. Its tapering gilded spire can be seen from many parts of the city and is one of St. Petersburg's main landmarks.

The party continued which turned into a marvellous atmosphere - the young were happy and mingled with the old veterans still proudly wearing their uniforms and medals. I walked back down the Nevsky which was now utilised like a motorway for people. Up and down they walked, but always on the right hand side. Over the River Neva, they performed a colourful pyrotechnic show, set to a selection of classical music, including an emotional rendition of *Shostakovich's 7th Symphony -,The Leningrad,* which the great composer wrote during the wartime blockade. As the light faded, the evening ended with a massive fireworks display. Later, making my way back to the hotel, I turned around and could see the gilded spire on the Admiralty building glisten in the low westerly sun as it faded over the horizon and the time approached eleven o'clock.

Tuesday, 10th
St. Petersburg

After a buffet breakfast, Jenya my guide duly arrived promptly at 10 o'clock and we set off on our three-hour walking tour. He was a student who spoke good English and started by explaining the history of St. Petersburg - its founding by Peter the Great in 1703, and its development from a marshy swamp to its grand design of European architecture. Although relatively a young city by European standards, by the 19th century it had been firmly established as a cultural centre, attracting famous talent like Pushkin, Gogol, Dostoyevsky, Tchaikovsky, Rachmaninov, and Borodin. Its name changed to Petrograd in 1914 and again to Leningrad in 1924 on the death of Lenin when the capital status moved to Moscow. In 1991, as the old Soviet Union collapsed its residents took the opportunity to have yet another change…this time back to its original name - St. Petersburg.

Built in a unique blend of Russian and European architectural styles, this beautiful maritime city on the shores of the Baltic on mainland, and with a delta made up of more than forty islands is a supreme monument to its founder. To the five million people who now live here, water plays a large part in their lives, although it is often in danger of flooding due to its low sea level. The River Neva and its tributaries plus canals which snake through the city freeze solid enough to allow people to walk on them from November to the beginning of April. Although St. Petersburg is on the same latitude as Moscow and the towns of South Alaska and Greenland, it enjoys higher temperatures because of its proximity to the sea. Summer has only brief twilights during the period known as "White Nights" when the average temperature rises to eighteen degrees.

Walking along Nevsky Prospekt, we shortly arrived at the Anichov Bridge of the Fontanka, a canal which meanders through the city centre. Memorable features of this bridge are the dramatic statues of four large bronze rearing horses at each of its four corners. Further long, we reached the famous Yeliseyev's food store, which was once St. Petersburg's most luxurious, with elaborate decorations, worthy of any European capital. Jenya pointed out the building with the largest single frontage along the Nevsky, called Gostinny Dvor. It was designed by the Italian Rastrelli and although now a department store, it was once one of the best and grandest shops in the Russian Empire.

From here we turned away from the Nevsky, passing the Grande Hotel Europe which occupies the complete side of the street, on our way to the Square of Arts. Here proudly stands the Museum of Russia designed by Rossi. It used to be known as the Michael Palace, after Grand Duke Michael, but was turned into a museum in 1896 to house priceless icons form the 12th century onwards as well as paintings by all of Russia's famous painters, including Kadinsky and Altman. The Italian - Rossi, spent fifteen years creating the whole square, which includes two small theatres and a fine statue of the poet, Pushkin.

By Train to Shanghai

The Emperor Paul used to live in the nearby Imperial Summer Palace, which is more like a fortress castle, surrounded by water on all sides for security. Because of a bad dream, Paul was paranoid about his safety, but in the end, his excessive security measures didn't protect him - he was strangled, in his palace, by one of his own servants.

In 1880 another Tsar, Alexander II, was assassinated in the Square of Arts by anarchists who blew him to pieces as he passed-by in his carriage. To commemorate this tragic event, his son commissioned the construction of the Cathedral of the Spilt Blood nearby, the blood being that of his father. This elaborate church with its crazy confusion of colours, and its onion-shaped domes, is a smaller imitation of St. Basil's Cathedral in Red Square.

Crossing the Moyka canal, our walk took us to a splendid panorama by the name of the Field of Mars, which used to be a parade ground for the military in Tsarist times. Although the military no longer use it, there is an eternal flame, burning in memory of the thousands of victims of the 1918 revolution, who are buried in a mass grave nearby. From here a spectacular vista across the Neva River opened up - with views of the Peter and Paul Fortress, the first building to be built in 1703 and regarded as the start of the city's establishment.

Jenya and I crossed the Troitsky Bridge and entered the hexagonal island fortress through the Neva Gate. It was midday and we were just in time to hear the daily cannons being fired. The St. Peter and St. Paul Cathedral dominates the island, with is golden spire rising high above the Neva. Used as the burial place for the Romanov Tsars, from Peter the

Great onwards, including the last Tsar, Nicholas II and his family who were re-interred here in the family vault - having originally been buried down a mine shaft in Yekaterinburg - following their murder in 1918. Later, the fortress served as a prison and over the years, held a variety of people, from Peter's son Alexis, to revolutionaries and terrorists, even Leon Trotsky and Maxim Gorky were incarcerated for some time.

A chill wind blew from the east as we crossed the Dvortsovy Bridge on to Vasilevsky Island on our way back towards the city centre. During the cold winter months Jenya explained he rarely walks across the bridges because it is just far too cold, and instead usually favoured the metro.

Vasilevsky Island is the largest in the Neva delta and is at a part known as Strelka and from here is a beautiful panoramic view of the city. On one side is the Winter Palace and Hermitage on the banks of the river, busy with ships and barges, whilst on the other is a splendid view across the Neva of St. Peter and St. Paul Fortress and its golden spire. We paused by the two Rostral columns erected as signal towers for ships, which also serve as an unmistakable city landmark. Opposite is the building known as the Central Naval Museum which houses all sorts of seafaring memorabilia including some of Peter's personal affects. Before it became a museum, it used to house the Stock Exchange but was closed down, like many other institutions, at the time of the Bolshevik Revolution in 1917.

Back on the mainland and past the Admiralty, we arrived at Decembrists Square so-called because, in December 1825, a group of aristocratic army officers called on the Tsar to implement reforms and make the life of the people better.

By Train to Shanghai

Nothing changed but the leaders of the short-lived coup were executed and the rest sent to Siberia. Later in my journey I was able to see how they resurrected their lives after imprisonment, becoming some of the earliest European travellers in Siberia. In this square stands the magnificent equestrian statue known as the Bronze Horseman. It shows Peter astride a rearing horse and trampling on a serpent. Its simple inscription reads *"To Peter the first from Catherine the second 1872"*.

The three hours were nearly up and it was approaching lunchtime but we had another must-see building to check out in Decembrists Square - on the southern side is St. Isaac's Cathedral, designed by a Frenchman named Montferrand. It took forty years to build and no expense was spared - one hundred kilos of gold went into gilding the dome and the interior designed to accommodate 14,000 worshippers. When Montferrand died his final request to be buried in his beloved cathedral was refused because he was a Roman Catholic and not the usual Russian Orthodox faith, and buried elsewhere. To improve our view of the city, Jenya and I climbed up the few hundred steps to the dome above. From this vantage point on top of the sombre magnificence of St. Isaac's I was reminded of the Pantheon of Rome. It was possible to view the entire splendour of the city with its many magnificently long and wide avenues, and squares, and, across the Neva, far grander than the Tiber, stood the fortress of St. Peter and St. Paul with its golden spire.

After this, it was time to thank Jenya for his educational tour, but not before showing me one of the houses where Russia's most famous writer, Fyodor Dostoyevsky, lived and where, in 1866, he wrote his best-known novel, *Crime and Punishment*

– set in the nearby streets surrounding Sennaya Ploshchad. Dostoyevsky's house was a simple building at the end of a row of small houses – it seems he always favoured living in the end house! Perhaps it was something to do with his dark brooding style, his pessimism and obsession with guilt?

Later in the afternoon as light rain was falling, I walked east along the Nevsky, past Uprising Square and the Moscow Railway Station to one of the great monuments of the city, the Alexander Nevsky Monastery, also founded by Peter the Great. It derives its name from Prince Nevsky who won a victory over the Swedes in 1241 on the exact spot. The whole monastery complex contains the Holy Trinity Cathedral, a seminary, and a smaller church. Religion, which was long suppressed and banned under Stalin, has now returned with a fervour and intensity, which was clearly evident, as I entered the cathedral.

Cavernous baritone intonations echoed out of the open doors. For an oppressed religion, the Orthodox Church had not done a bad job of surviving. The music was heavenly, and the faces in the congregation were Brueghelesque, medieval, candle-illuminated figures in old scarves and worn clothing. As the priests sang, I raised my head towards the startling gold-leaf mosaics in the vaulted ceiling, it was difficult not to shed a tear. It is certainly no surprise that today under President Putin, more than a decade and a half after the death of Communism, the Orthodox Church has once again seized all the national dominance it enjoyed under the Tsars.

The monastery area contains several cemeteries, so I paid my few roubles to enter one called the Tikhvin Cemetery - plus a few more to be allowed to use my camera! This cemetery is the Russian equivalent of Poets' Corner, and is the last resting-place of many of its great writers, artists and musician. In this quiet and damp place, among the tombstones of weeping angels and weather-beaten busts, are the graves of Tchaikovsky, Glinka, Borodin, and Rimsky-Korsakov. Borodin had left his most famous opera *"Prince Igor"*, containing the much loved *Polovtsian Dances*, unfinished when he died in 1887. It was completed by his friend Rimsky-Korsakov and now the two great composers lie side-by-side. Nearby I found the grave of Dostoyevsky, who may have died as long ago as 1881, but has obviously not been forgotten as someone had left a colourful display of flowers by his headstone. As I left this Slavonic Valhalla of the arts the heavens opened and the rain came down in torrents. 'It doesn't always rain in St. Petersburg' the receptionist tried to reassure me when I arrived back at the hotel - soaked to the skin!

Wednesday, 11th May

It had rained heavily throughout the night and was still pouring down in the morning, so it was the ideal time to stay dry indoors by visiting the Winter Palace collection. The Winter Palace situated on the banks of the Neva River is the former royal residence of the Romanov family with its staggering number of halls and rooms -1057 in all! Commissioned by Peter the Great (although he never lived there), the Italian architect Rastelli remodelled it on behalf of Catherine the Great. Catherine was a minor German princess, whose maiden name was Princess Sophie of Anhalt-Zerbst. She was brought to St. Petersburg in 1745 at the age of fourteen to marry the heir to the Russian throne, Emperor Peter III. The marriage was a disaster from the beginning. He was weak, stupid, ugly and sexually inadequate, so when he succeeded as Emperor in 1761, a plot developed to remove him and place Catherine on the throne. As part of the plot, the unfortunate husband was arrested outside St. Petersburg and placed in the custody of a couple of Guards officers, the Orlov brothers, who promptly strangled him in a drunken fight.

So, at the age of thirty-three, Catherine became the Empress of Russia and showed herself to be a superb politician and the most powerful woman of her age, whose achievements in all fields - military, political and cultural - were arguably greater than those of any woman ruler in history. She became the ruthless 18th Century Tsarina who stole the throne from her husband before he was 'accidentally' murdered. She was the self-made woman in a man's world, outwitting kings and prime ministers across the world. She had a reputation of a lustful lover between the sheets - which became the stuff of legend. The great love of her life was the victorious Marshall Grigory Potemkin, whom she secretly married. He became an effective co-Tsar with the title, Prince Potemkin, co-ruler, and on her orders was treated like a Romanov. Between them, their achievements were formidable, defeating Sweden and Turkey and extending the Russian Empire to Ukraine and the Black Sea, as well as founding the famous cities of Sebastapol and Odessa.

Catherine also won the favour of Voltaire, one of France's pre-eminent Enlightenment philosophers. Although they never met, the pair corresponded for many years until Voltaire's death. 26 of these letters changed hands at a 2006 Sotheby's

By Train to Shanghai

auction – in this case for a record £ 400,000 price. More than anyone has ever paid for 18th century correspondence - which is expected to return to Russia.

Catherine also scoured Europe for art creating the Hermitage Museum - which included an annex, which she filled with her personal collection and it became her private "Hermitage". Some of the artefacts were gifts from foreign governments or noblemen and it eventually became one of the most magnificent art collections in the world.

Buying works of art was an important sign to others of Russian dominance and power in the world, especially when she bought the entire collection of Horace Walpole, son of a former British prime minister, for £40,000, a fortune at current values. Today, her portrait hangs in the Walpole house in England.

A director of the Hermitage is reputed to have said, 'I can't say that the Hermitage is the number one museum in the world, but it's certainly not the second". With over three million works of art and treasures housed in its five connected buildings along the Neva, the museum cannot fail to impress. It has 1786 doors, 1945 windows, 117 staircases, 15,000 paintings, 12,000 sculptures, 600,000 drawings, 500,000 archaeological finds, and one million coins and medals. All, of course, are not on display at any given time - if they were - taking just one minute for each one of these, you would have to spend a solid five years in the Hermitage to view them all! Nancy Regan, widow of the late president, boasted of having seen it all in 45 minutes.

Having joined the queue of eager fellow tourists waiting to enter the palace, which on the outside, looks like a wedding cake, whilst inside, the collection is divided into seven major sections. The *first* covers Russian history and culture, and the *second* relates to prehistoric times. The *third* section concentrates on Asia, whilst the *fourth* holds items and artefacts from Egypt. Ancient Greece and Rome feature in the *fifth* section, whilst the *sixth* is devoted to European art. Russian medals and decorations have the entire *seventh* section to themselves.

With limited time my choice was to concentrate on European art which is sub-divided into a series of rooms, each devoted to the country of origin of the artists. All the rooms are connected by a series of corridors and watched-over by miserable, elderly female attendants, most of whom, looked as if they couldn't be less interested in the great art works they were guarding! The Spanish section had works by Goya, El Greco and Velazquez, is generally regarded as only second in importance to the Prado in Madrid. In the French rooms are works by Degas, Renoir, Claude Monet, Poussin and Cezanne, whilst the Flemish school is well represented. There are forty canvasses by Peter Paul Rubens, and twenty-five Rembrandts - in rooms devoted entirely to these two artists. English art is represented with works by Reynolds, Gainsborough, and William Morris. Titian has nine canvasses and there are other works by Leonardo Da Vinci, Picasso, Canaletto, and Van Gogh, as well as Michelangelo's sculpture, "Boy on a dolphin".

While Catherine was building up her collection, she also had time to order from Josiah Wedgwood a 900-piece dinner service decorated with views of England - which is also on display at the Hermitage. With all this priceless art available surely the invading German army would have loved to get their hands on it! However, during the siege, the Russians had already taken precautions against that eventuality by removing all canvasses from their frames and transporting them a thousand miles east to the Urals for safety. All that was left hanging - were empty frames! However, more than 250 shells bombarded the city every day, some of which damaged the many glass windows of the Hermitage, creating great difficulty for the staff when having to deal with the twin elements of snow and rain.

Also in this lavish setting is the Tsar's Throne Room, rich in marble and bronze as well as a ballroom, and, in between the two, is a military gallery of Russian Generals - commemorating victory over Napoleon. Here, hanging on the walls are a few hundred portraits of generals in their fine blue uniforms.

By lunchtime, the rain had finally stopped and having absorbed as much art as one could manage in one morning, it was time to continue with my city walk. I had heard that the Marinsky Theatre was holding a concert this evening, so went along to see if any tickets were still available. The Marinsky has been the principal home for Russian ballet and opera since the 1880s and all the famous Russian artists have performed here, whose resident conductor is the world famous Valery Gergiev. Sadly, as I'd half expected, no tickets were to be found for neither love nor money, but did sneak a glimpse inside to see its elegant blue and gold auditorium.

Heading back towards the Nevsky and after crossing the Moyka River I arrived at the green pastel-coloured - Stroganov Palace, which was also designed by Rastrelli. Built in Russian Baroque style, it was once the home of the Stroganoff Family. It now houses a restaurant in its courtyard, which is rather ironic given that the family's French chef, Olivier, is credited with creating that well-known dish of strips of beef cooked in a sauce containing sour cream. Nearby is one of St. Petersburg's finest buildings, the Kazan Cathedral which was built in 1800 as the Orthodox rival to St. Peter's in Rome, with a colonnade modelled on it, and a dome eighty metres high. It has massive bronze doors and a frontage of statues of various Russian saints. Stalin closed its doors as a church and used it for anti-religious propaganda, by re-naming it the Museum of the History of Religion and Atheism. In summer months its frontage gardens are used as café-bars.

After crossing the Griboedova Canal, arrived at Ostrovsky Square and there, found the National Library of Russia. This is another of Rossi's masterpieces with a façade adorned with statues of various Greek philosophers. The library's proud boast is a collection of 30 million items and retaining a copy of all books published in Russia since the earliest printing days.

The southern end of the square has the Pushkin Theatre with its six Corinthian columns which was built in 1830 and is one of Russia's most important theatres. Dominating a small garden nearby is a large statue of Catherine, surrounded by her lovers or associates from her reign, including Potemkin and Suvorov. Chess, very popular with Russians, was being played by many in the square - old and young.

From here, the final visit was to see the only Roman Catholic Church, of St. Catherine. Closed down and used as a warehouse during the Stalinist era, this beautiful church had recently suffered a fire. It is currently being re-furbished but lack of money is delaying the process. Trying to help I made a small contribution under the beady gaze of an elderly lady. In this rather sad place, lies the last King of Poland, and one of Catherine's lovers, Stanislaw Poniatowski, who is buried here.

This had been a long and tiring day - so where better to adjourn to than Mollie's Irish Bar. I walked down a street called Rubinshteyna, with its stately yet dishevelled row of elegant town houses, to the bar, whose marketing blurb claims credit from bringing Guinness to this city back in 1994. This I suspect was probably a very good idea, with all the warnings about not drinking the city's tap water! Inside, as well as the jaunty Irish music and the usual Irish memorabilia, was a wall clock - set to Dublin time! The bar was decorated with hundreds of different currency notes stuck all round the walls - obviously 'donated' by visiting internationals - the local clientele mixed and everyone was served by attractive Russian girls. I had a quick pint of the black stuff and headed back to the hotel.

Boris, the manager was the only member of staff around, so I instigated a conversation with him, and lubricated his vocal chords with a few beers. We talked for hours about the city's founder, Peter the Great, who became Tsar at the age of ten and ruled with his half-brother, Ivan. How Peter travelled extensively in Western Europe until the late 1690s and acquired knowledge of western technology and returned to Russia with western technicians who were to implement the modernisation programmes that marked his reign. Undaunted by the harsh climate and the marshy swamplands, he built this city and opened 'a window on Europe' by laying the foundation of this superb setting in which his successors, like his daughter, Elizabeth, and Catherine the Great, aided by their architects and builders created a fitting capital for the Russian Empire and which today, is habitually called "Peter". Later on, of course, it stood witness to the struggle against oppression, and the drive for justice. Tsars were assassinated and revolutions were kindled, first in 1825 by the Decembrists, then 1905 and finally in 1917, when Lenin arrived back from exile and gave his legendary speech atop an armoured car in front of the Finland Railway Station.

But the city's worst ordeal came during the blockade by the German army, for 872 days, from September 1941 until January 1944. In winter, the city residents had been kept alive by the food supplied across the frozen Lake Ladoga, the largest lake in Europe, on a makeshift road called the 'Road of Life', Across the ice came convoys of desperately needed supplies for the inhabitants of a starving city, their brave drivers having to run the gauntlet of German shelling. This continued even as the lake began to thaw, so that trucks would disappear beneath the ice. In recognition of the ordeal, St. Petersburg was awarded the status of "Hero City".

Long before anyone mentioned *"perestroika"*, a group of artists and writers calling themselves *"mitki"* were running their own anti-Soviet revolution in the bars and jazz clubs in the liberal safety of St. Petersburg. But today, with the Soviet Empire gone, this city is rapidly gaining a reputation of Europe's neo-Nazi capital. Nationalist sentiment is on the rise, and sensing the popular mood, the ultra-Right has begun to tap into the patriotic fervour sweeping the country. A recent opinion poll showed that almost sixty percent of the population had sympathy with the popular rallying call of the ultra-Right - "Russia for the Russians". According to the Moscow Bureau of Human Rights, fifty-nine people have been killed in attacks in Russia in the past two years. Russia is estimated to be home to more than 50,000 skinheads, with 10,000 in Moscow, and 5,000 in St. Petersburg alone. Critics argue that lethargic attitudes of the police in prosecuting racist attacks has encouraged neo-Nazi groups to flourish, whereby their numbers could rise to more than 100,000 within a few years.

With this in mind, public figures from St. Petersburg wrote an open letter to President Putin warning him of the rise of neo-Nazism in Russia, "You certainly know that in the last years along with traditional anti-Semitism and xenophobia, another kind of racism is thriving in Russia" they wrote. "The racism of Nazi nature is the ideological basis for crimes sweeping over our country".

Our conversation turned to architecture and I asked Boris about his favourite location in the city. He told me he prefers the non-touristy parts, where in some instances old buildings contain pre-Revolutionary signs on their façades as if frozen in time. He prefers the Kolomna area, in particular the Nikolsky Cathedral, where it is possible to discover old cafes, shops and other remnants of old Soviet times. Boris also likes walking along Vasilevsky Island and on the Petrograd side, where he sees beauty in the run-down façades, and this, in his view, is the city's real face. I told him I was also taken with the affects of time on the buildings and façades by use, abuse, neglect and the weather. There is a certain celebration in the beauty of decay, because it reminds one of the timeless human spirit.

Boris read modern history at university; so apart from the history of St. Petersburg, we went on to discuss the mad monk

- Rasputin. He confirmed that Grigori Rasputin was born of peasant stock in Siberia in the 1860s, and only arrived in St. Petersburg after having undergone a religious conversion by donning monks clothing, at the same time developing his own doctrine, based on mysticism and what appeared to be healing powers. His fame spread and by 1907 he had been invited to the Tsar's Palace. Almost immediately, the German born Tsarina, Alexandra, fell under his spell, and Rasputin demonstrated his power of healing by easing the pain of her haemophiliac son, something, a succession of doctors had failed to do. The impression grew amongst Russians that they were lovers, and that impression may have sealed the fate of the shaggy-haired monk. His fate was a grizzly end, and in December 1916, when his mutilated corpse was hauled out of a hole in the frozen River Neva it was found to have been battered, shot, bound and wrapped in cloth.

1916 was a year of crisis, with Russia fighting alongside Britain and France against Germany, in World War I, and suffering heavy casualties. Russia was a vital ally of Britain, who was well aware they could not win the war against Germany without Russian help. Boris explained that this religious charlatan - Rasputin threatened that alliance by influencing the German born Tsarina against the war, whilst there was no guarantee that the Tsar would be capable of asserting himself against the powerful forces that wanted Russia out of the war. Therefore, it was vital to assassinate Rasputin, and so began the plot against him, which was far from easy, because he was at the height of his influence with the Tsarina. At this period, she was ruling instead of the Tsar who was away at the Front, and by 1916, Rasputin had virtual carte blanche over the appointments to Church and State, many of whom were German sympathisers who would like to sabotage the military effort.

The British Government was fully aware of this and feared that if the Tsar had sued for peace, Britain faced defeat. The historian, Andrew Cook in his book *"To Kill Rasputin",* has revealed his theory that British intelligence was involved in the killing of Rasputin, by forcefully arguing that the bullet that felled him was British-made and could only have come from a British gun. But most astonishing of all is his suggestion that the future Prime Minister of Britain, David Lloyd George, at the time, Head of Military Intelligence, could have been behind the plot to murder Rasputin.

The assassination plot, hatched for 16th December, was that Prince Felix Yusupov, an Oxford educated and wealthy aristocrat should invite Rasputin to his palace to cure his wife of some unspecified illness. On his arrival, Rasputin would find no wife, but instead, four conspirators who would offer him cakes and wine laced with potassium cyanide. Alas, this seemingly simple plan didn't work because the cyanide had lost its potency, so the unfortunate Rasputin was subjected to a severe beating. The autopsy showed terrible wounds inflicted all over his body, with knives, fists, a sword and a truncheon - they had even torn out one of his eyes. The British connection relates to one of the four bullets recovered from the body and which probably delivered the *'coup de grace'*. This was an 'unjacketed' .45, and in 1916, Britain was virtually alone in using bullets without steel jackets, which meant they expanded on impact.

Oswald Rayner was a British officer, attached to the Secret Intelligence Service in St. Petersburg station. He was a friend of Yusupov from their days at Oxford and they remained close friends for the rest of their lives. He also had personal links to Lloyd George, having protected him behind the scenes from parliamentary censure over insider dealings in Marconi shares. Rayner confided to a friend he was most definitely in the Yusupov palace the night of Rasputin's demise, and he also carried a Webley service revolver which fires .45 bullets - the only man who carried that weapon that fateful night.

Rasputin's body was then bound and wrapped in cloth before being thrown through a hole in the ice of the frozen River Neva. When police with crowbars smashed the ice and hauled out the frozen, mutilated corpse, this semi-literate peasant mystic, who in 1916 was virtually dictating the fate of Russia, proved he was human after all. The Tsarina, Alexandra, was reported to be inconsolable with grief at his death. Yusupov survived the Russian revolution and died aged 80, and although Rayner had burned all his papers, he kept for himself, a 'souvenir' from the night of Rasputin's assassination - a bullet - Rayner had it made into a ring!

Thursday, 12th May

On my final day in St. Petersburg, and as it had at last, stopped raining, the sun was beckoning a trip to Petrodvorets. Built by Peter the Great as his county palace he commissioned a French architect, Jean Babtiste Le Blond to create a Versailles, this time by the sea. Located some thirty kilometres outside the centre of the city on the Gulf of Finland, it was the German

By Train to Shanghai

army headquarters during their blockade of St. Petersburg. Badly damaged then, today the whole complex is largely a reconstruction.

But first, there was a visit to the Railway Museum and a short journey on the metro system. Under a clear blue sky, I walked along the Fontanka River for half an hour before arriving at the museum that was established in 1809 and claims to be the oldest in the world. If that is the case no one will argue as that was twenty-eight years before the first working railway in Russia ... or anywhere else for that matter. Again paying the mandatory few roubles to an old lady in the kiosk, I entered. Sadly, there was no English translation to assist, but I joined a group of school children for a demonstration of a model railway in operation. This was the ideal place for any railway enthusiast young or old, to visit, with its large collection of locomotives, big and small, as well as railway bridges, even a model of the ship used to ferry passengers and trains across Lake Baikal before the railway lines joined up. The school children listened intently to the guide and observing their concentration, it was obvious they take great pride in their railway system.

On leaving the museum I joined the underground system at Sadovya which was a couple of stops to the Baltic Station. The St. Petersburg metro system was completed in 1955, has 100 kilometres of track, and is reputed to be the deepest in the world. The original transport in the city was by rivers and canals, so building an underground system meant it was necessary to excavate very deep because of the high water table. Having always been fascinated by Hampstead, London's deepest station, I was amazed to discover that St. Petersburg's system is twice the distance down. In fact from the top of the escalator it is difficult to see the bottom and it moves twice as fast. The world's longest escalator is also here at the Ploshchad Lenina with its 729 steps, and a vertical rise of 60 metres. What a difficult construction job this must have been, and what a walk back up should the escalator break down!

At Baltic Station, the guidebook told me to take bus number 849 which would get me to Petrodvorets. Whilst queuing for the bus, I overheard a pretty young Russian girl explain in English to an elderly couple that the bus to Petrodvorets was number 404 and that she would be travelling on it as well. I got into conversation with the couple, who were of Chinese origin, now resident in Vancouver and were also travelling around Europe by train, but today were heading for Peter's Palace, the same as myself.

On the bus, I sat beside the Russian girl who said her name was Anna and 22 years old. Whilst at university she was studying mathematics from an English text, and also English literature. She then proceeded to show me the English book she was reading as part of her education, and which had been recommended by her tutor - *Lady Chatterley's Lover* by D. H. Lawrence. I was surprised by the choice and told her that back in the United Kingdom, in 1960, this book and its publishers, Penguin Books, were subject to a criminal prosecution - a most significant event - the trial of a book by a long-dead author, to determine if it was obscene and likely to deprave or corrupt.

Lined up for the defence to attest that there was a distinction between pornography and literature, were various distinguished witnesses like the novelists, E. M. Forster and

Rebecca West, the poet Cecil Day-Lewis whilst T.S. Eliot waited outside Court No. 1 to be called - but fruitlessly. The prosecution searched high and low for witnesses, but had found no one to denounce the book, so the jury found Penguin Books not guilty which was to become a bonanza for them as every reader in the land now wanted to buy it. Huge queue began to form outside bookshops. Three printers worked together to mass-produce copies of the book in batches of 300,000, and within twelve months, three million copies were sold.

Anna was very surprised by this as she felt it was realistic literature and evoked relations between men and women, but her greatest difficulty with the book was to understand the local Derbyshire dialect, which Lawrence used.

We finally arrived at Petrodvorets after a pleasant journey through the suburbs and past the odd German tank kept as a souvenir and said goodbye to Anna. From the bus stop, it was possible to see in the distance and appearing on the horizon, what is usually described as Russian's answer to Versailles. The original Peter's Palace as it was know, was built between 1709 and 1724, using 5,000 soldiers and slaves, but was largely destroyed in the Second World War. Its painstaking reconstruction took place in the 1950s, using photographs and old maps. For some unknown reason, the only room to survive intact was Peters' study, which is a very ordinary room indeed. The Chinese and myself entered the grounds through the upper gardens, walking past manicured lawns and several water fountains. On each side of the palace stood two golden-domed buildings with religious crosses on their tops, which glistened magnificently in the midday sun.

The Lower Park contains the major attraction of the Grand Cascade, with its 144 fountains and three waterfalls, as well as thirty-five bronze statues. Below the Grand Palace features a golden statue of Samson gripping the jaws of a lion from which water spurts into the air. This represents the Russian victory over the Swedes on St. Samson's day. Water is brought here from a great distance by a series of ducts and pipes without the need of a pumping station, and the water then flows downhill into a canal and on into the nearby Gulf of Finland. Rashly, I dipped my toe into the icy waters and promptly decided the next time I'd test the temperature would not be until the warm China Sea!

Looking towards the sea from the Grand Palace the view is breathtaking. The extensive gardens are laid out in French style and contain more fountains and cascades, as well as attractive 18th century buildings such as the Hermitage Pavilion and Marly Palace. This restored Grand Palace sits in splendour on top of the hill overlooking everything. Inside is a large Throne Room, which used to be used for official ceremonies and receptions and the Partridge Drawing Room with its silk covered walls adorned with the birds that give their name to the room.

After arriving back at the metro station - Gostiny Dvor, just below the department store, care was taken to avoid the pickpockets who operate in this area during the hectic rush hours when there is a lot of pushing and shoving. Setting off down the Nevsky for my final walk and passing the Grand Hotel Europe I noticed the whole street called Mikhaylovskaya closed off to the public from top to bottom. On the street pavement outside the hotel was one very long table and all set up for dinner. Significantly, it was set for 130 people, I was told, represented the 130 years since the hotel was built, in 1875. A gigantic birthday party was about to begin and it was amusing watching the waiters struggling to prevent the tablecloths from flying away in the gusty wind. This Grand Hotel is Russia's first five star hotel, with a beautiful façade and striking Art Nouveau décor. Bill Clinton's recent stay probably helped its star rating!

Continuing my final wander along Nevsky I reflected on my first visit to St. Petersburg and slightly regretted that I hadn't had more contact with ordinary Russian folk due to my limited Russian, In four days I had seen only part of the city, but even that was a revelation, with its unsurpassed blend of Russian and European architecture and art, which thankfully survived the German blockade. Colour was clearly an essential part of the planning, which was reflected not only in the spectacular gardens, but also importantly in the multi-colour painted façades on the magnificent buildings.

After the war, the money for rebuilding work was directed at factories and housing, and as a result, the grand houses were allowed to fall into disrepair - still there, still elegant, but in a rather crumbling grandeur. Today, it is clearly less resplendent than in the 19th century, when ladies paraded, either in horse-drawn carriages or on foot, along the fine avenue, Nevsky Prospect.

The present Russian government would like to reinvigorate Russia as a viable superpower again, but it's currently experiencing the twin demographic scourges of a falling birth rate and HIV/Aids. For instance, in the first six months of

2005, Russian's population fell by half a million, and the huge public health crisis is being worsened by Aids, a problem turned into a disaster because the authorities are in Soviet-style denial about the deadly affliction. In Irkutsk, in eastern Siberia, one in five of the population has HIV/Aids, which will have long-term catastrophic consequences. There is a popular saying; "freedom is an illusion - when Communism collapsed, so did the health of the nation". It is hard to argue against that, with the staggering drop in male life expectancy to a mere fifty-eight years. Currently, abortions outnumber live births, so if this trend continues, by 2050, the population of Russia could have halved!

Russia has an enormous 87,500 kilometres of railway track, spread over ten time zones, but all long-distance trains run exclusively on Moscow time. I arrived at the ornate Moscow Railway Station in good time for the 23.14, Train No. 19, which was going to take me, non-stop, to the capital, some 650 kilometres away. My reservation was for carriage number one, which meant a very long walk along the length of the platform. On the opposite track, a blue coloured train waited and at each carriage door of both trains, attractive female *provodnitsas,* in smart grey uniforms, were standing to attention by each open door, patiently awaiting the arrival of their passengers. This was quite a sight, and walking down the platform to my carriage, couldn't help thinking it was like having a guard of honour.

Frequent travellers confirm that the Moscow train from St. Petersburg is the best in Russian and there was no disappointment - this one was new and modern. Handing my rail ticket to the *provodnitsa* in exchange for clean sheets and bedding and soon discovered that on this overnight journey,

By Train to Shanghai

I was to share with two Russians and Guy a South African from Cape Town. We exchanged greetings and the Russians immediately retired to their upper bunks. At precisely fourteen minutes past eleven, the train pulled slowly out of the station, as the South African and myself went off to find the restaurant car for a night-cap.

Chapter Two
Moscow

Friday, 13th May

For whatever reason, known only to Russian Railways, all passengers received an early morning wake-up call at 5.15 a.m. - a good hour and a half before our scheduled arrival time! But at least the smiling *provodnitsa* brought us some tea by way of compensation. Looking out of the window I glimpsed the rising sun as the train made its way through a forest. It was raining as train number 19 pulled into Leningrad Railway Station. Our journey had taken just over seven hours and pleased to see my driver, armed with a name board, waiting on the platform, and were quickly on our way through the rain-sodden streets of Moscow. We passed a large white building on the banks of the Moscow River, which the driver confirmed was the White House - best remembered as the building at the centre of the famous 1991 stand-off between Boris Yeltsin and the Russian army. Yeltsin won, and grabbed power in the political vacuum.

My hotel was set in a green-forested location about five kilometres to the west of the city centre. After checking in, I received a message to say that my guide would arrive at 10.am for a walking tour of the city and as the hotel was close to the metro, we would start by taking a train to the Kremlin, and walk on from there.

Lena, my fifty year old guide, duly arrived, introduced herself and explained that although she is a teacher by profession, she has to supplement her income because salaries for teachers are very low. So low, in fact, that her government employers arrange her work schedule around her guide work!

The metro station Filevsky Park was seven stops to the end of the line which was close to the Kremlin Wall. It all looked very confusing but at least Lena gave me a map of the system with the station names in Roman letters and after fifteen minutes our train finished at Borovitskay Station, right by the Kremlin.

We walked along the Alexander Gardens, which was bedecked with red tulips and reached the Tomb of the Unknown Soldier still surrounded by many wreaths and flowers following Moscow's huge parade in Red Square to mark the 60th anniversary of the end of World War II. The event had been attended by Russian President, Vladimir Putin and sixty presidents and prime ministers from around the world and had taken place the previous Monday.

A short walk up the hill and we entered Red Square. I had seen it on television many times before, usually showing military parades, but in reality looked so much smaller than I had imagined. Dominating the Square, is possibly the best recognised building in Russia, with its crazy confusion of colours and shapes, is the Cathedral of the Intercession of the Mother of God at the Moat - or as its better known - St. Basil's.

Built in 1555 by decree of Ivan the Terrible to celebrate his victory over the Khanate of Kazan, the cathedral is constructed of nine individual churches. To represent their individuality, each is crowned with a differently designed, coloured and sized onion-shaped dome.

The central spire represents the supremacy of the Mother of God over the church and the people. Each of the other spires is named after the Saints whose day it was when the main battle of the Kazan campaign took place. St. Basil is buried here, hence the nickname given to the building. Lena explained the popular legend that Ivan was so impressed with the building that afterwards he ordered the architect, Postnik Yakovlev, (nicknamed Barma), be blinded, so that he could never again create anything as good. Over the years, the cathedral has been saved from destruction on at least four occasions - the first being Napoleon's order that it should be burnt down as he retreated from Moscow: luckily it started raining. The second being the Russian Revolution - the archpriest, Ioann Vostorgov, was shot and the cathedral turned into a war museum instead. The third - a plan was put to Stalin to remove the cathedral so that Communist parades in Red Square would run more smoothly - it was declined. And finally, during World War II, Moscow was heavily bombed - but luckily the Germans 'missed'. How lucky we all are!

The main focus of Red Square is the Lenin Mausoleum, sited beside the Kremlin Wall between the Spassky and Nikolsky Towers. Facing it, is the attractive GUM department store on the north-eastern side, which was built in the 19th century to house over 1,000 little shops, and business appeared brisk as we strolled through.

Our walk continued up to the Lubyanka, a grim looking building which used to be the headquarters of the notorious K.G.B., the feared and fearful organisation of enforcers of political repression. Still not open to the public, I wondered what dark secrets this building will tell when its doors are finally opened? Nearby is an area known as Theatreland and includes the famous façade of the Bolshoi Theatre, home of Moscow's opera and ballet companies. Due to neglect and lack of any recent maintenance work, it has fallen into disrepair and will shortly close its doors for a five-year renovation programme. After almost a decade of post-Soviet neglect the building's colonnaded façade is crumbling, the foundations sinking, and its antiquated back-stage machinery often grinds to a halt.

Built in 1824 when only Russian works were performed, the Bolshoi Theatre was the setting for the premier of Tchaikovsky's *Swan Lake* in 1877. Lena told me that already the re-building project is faltering, as President Putin is cutting the renovation budget. It is supposed to be the mother of all makeovers, costing half a billion pounds, to put it on a par with La Scala and Covent Garden. However, the present Russian government has got cold feet, accusing the theatre's management of extravagance, and has ordered the budget to be drastically reduced. So, the Bolshoi continues to have its problems, just as last year when one of its leading ballerinas, Anastasia Volochkova sued the theatre after she was dismissed for being overweight and too heavy for other dancers to lift - she lost her case in court. During the Bolshoi Theatre's sabbatical, dedicated fans will still be able to visit a smaller theatre opposite.

Continuing down the Tverskoy Boulevard, a lovely tree lined park, and past the Pushkin Theatre, we arrived at the Gorky House Museum. Then the final visit was to the Cathedral of Christ the Saviour, standing on the banks of the Moscow River. It has recently been totally rebuilt at an estimated cost of three hundred and sixty million dollars by the Mayor of Moscow, Yuri Luzhkov - or his wealthy wife - who happens to be the only female billionaire in Forbes Magazine. According to this magazine, Elena Baturina is worth £ 1.3 billion – making her Russia's richest woman! Stalin demolished the original church and the site was turned into the world's largest swimming pool, until President Yeltsin persuaded the Luzhkovs to dig deep into their pockets and the Moscow skyline has benefited accordingly.

It was now lunchtime, and Lena suggested we walk back to Arbat Street, a pedestrian only thoroughfare, which is sometimes, called "Moscow's Covent Garden". We went to the eastern end, which houses various ethnic restaurants, and Lena recommended some Uzbekistan food. As we walked, she told me she had a twenty-five year old daughter, who is equally as dark skinned as herself, which causes her problems, because when she travels around Moscow is frequently stopped by the police - she now carries her passport at all times. It seems it is all because of Chechnya and the recent dreadful atrocity at the Moscow Theatre. There, some female Chechins arrived at the theatre strapped with explosives and during the siege; the Moscow police botched a hostage rescue attempt using gas - consequently a few hundred people died. As a result, all non-Caucasians are likely to attract suspicion from the police, she told me.

By Train to Shanghai

Lena was old enough to remember the bad old Soviet times when nothing was available in the shops, and the lengthy queues that built up when items became available. To obtain basic household goods, such as a bed or fridge could take up to a year, and that was after joining a waiting list and queuing again, every week, just to maintain your name on the list! Being first in the queue was often the only way of getting what you want - and sometimes not even then.

Lena continued by telling a popular anecdote circulating at the time: A long queue was forming at a shop, an hour before opening time. At 9 o'clock, the shop manager came out and asked if there were any Jews in the queue. Five or six people raised their hands and the manager told them to go away - we are not serving Jews today. Muttering protests, they left and the manager went back into the shop. An hour later, the manager reappeared and asked if there were any Georgians in the queue. Three raised their hands and they too were told they would not be served and he disappeared back into the shop. At 11 o'clock, he re-emerged and asked about Armenians - they too had to leave. And so it went on each hour with Latvians, Estonians and Chechins being dismissed, until only Russians were left waiting. The manager came out and announced that the shop was not opening that day. "You see," said one Russian to the other, "the Jews always get the best of everything".

So, life was tedious and tough, but at the same time, Lena was aware that in the West, where everything was available, often wondered why it was so bad in the Soviet Union – a country rich in oil and mineral wealth? It seems Stalin's agricultural collectivisation policy had failed: otherwise, why would Muscovites have to queue for hours to buy potatoes imported from distant Cuba? During those awful years, for entertainment, she listened to the BBC or Voice of America radio programmes – that is, when they were not being jammed by the authorities. But what inspired her and others most of all, was the stand taken by the dissidents, in particular Dr. Andre Sakharov, the 1975 Nobel Peace Prize winner.

Sakharov, a physicist and member of the Academy of Sciences, was the ultimate emblem of dissent in the Soviet Union, who had once been called "the father of the Soviet hydrogen bomb", but who then became the country's greatest critic. As a result, he was sent into internal exile, to Gorky in 1980. There he was to live, isolated and under constant police surveillance, until a phone call from Mikhail Gorbachev called him back to Moscow in December 1986.

Unknown to Lena at the time of Sakharov's exile and just two years before in 1978, the Party Secretary from Stavropol, Mikhail Sergeyevich Gorbachev had arrived in Moscow.

One thing is certain and on which we both agreed - the world today would look very different without Gorbachev, who was instrumental in driving through the restructuring of the old Soviet Union. He, it was who made the words *perestroika* (reform) and *glasnost* (opening), familiar in every language in the world. Ultimately, he was to become the most admired and respected head of state –anywhere.

"This is a man I can do business with", was the announcement made to the waiting press by Britain's Prime Minister, Margaret Thatcher on 16th December 1984, following her meeting at Chequers with Mikhail Gorbachev, a hitherto obscure Soviet Agriculture Minister. When Konstantin

Chernenko, the Soviet leader died in 1985, it was by no means certain that Gorbachev would succeed him. His backers who were by not all means supporters of democratisation, but they saw in him a man with modern policies. Also, the triumphant success of his visit to England the year before - proved him to be a man who could successfully represent the Soviet Union in the outside world.

On 10th March 1985, the Politburo elected Gorbachev as Party leader at the age of 54 years. This was a remarkable achievement for a man born in a small village in the Caucasus, to a genuine peasant family in 1931.This fact distinguished him from all other Soviet leaders, who all arrived with their experience in cities or industrial districts. Gorbachev was the first major political figure in Soviet history, who spent his youth in a village and in the fields, before rising through the Party apparatus.

His maternal grandfather was of Cossack stock whilst his mother worked in the fields and his father was responsible for the repair and upkeep of agricultural machinery. Young Gorbachev was ten years old when the German army invaded Russia, occupying and laying waste much of the western Soviet Union and occupying the village of Privolnoye where the family lived.

After liberation, village life gradually returned to normal, but young Mischa, as his family called him was absent from class. Life had become hard. His father had been wounded in the war and hospitalised in Cracow, Poland. One winter he had no clothes to wear to school and for three months had to stay at home. This fact was confirmed by his mother in an interview with a Soviet television journalist, but never broadcast. She finally resolved the problem by selling the family sheep to raise some money.

In 1950, Gorbachev made the two day journey to Moscow to study law at Moscow University with a wooden suitcase and a few provisions. However, he always returned to his native village, even when General Secretary, to visit his mother, even dispensing with his bodyguards.

"Mr Gorbachev, tear down this Wall": these were the words of American President Ronald Regan when he visited the Brandenburg Gate in Berlin in 1987. Within two years it had actually happened when Gorbachev refused the pleas of East Germany's dinosaur President, Erick Honecker to intervene and use Soviet troops based near East Berlin to quell the mounting protests. On 9th November 1989, the East German Politburo opened the Wall and the crowds surged through peacefully.

Communism had also crumbled in the other satellite states of Hungary, Poland and Czechoslovakia whilst Gorbachev continued with his reform programme. However, during his summer holiday of 1991 in the Crimea, an eight-man Communist junta, led by Gennady Yanayev, staged a coup. Boris Yeltsin, who had been elected The President of the reconstituted Russian Federation in 1990, had stood on a tank in front of twenty thousand people opposite the White House, his parliament building, calling for "mass resistance".

Gorbachev arrived back in Moscow with the help of loyal forces but his fate was now in the hands of Yeltsin. His price for restoring him to the presidency of the Soviet Union, was Gorbachev's signature on an edict, suspending the very Communist Party of which he was the boss.

On Christmas Day 1991, Mikhail Gorbachev submitted his resignation. He really had no alternative: he no longer had a country to govern. Later, he stood as a candidate in the subsequent presidential elections for Russia itself and received a derisory half of one per cent. It had been a long road to the top, from the fields of Privolnoye – so this was the ultimate humiliation for a man who had, perhaps unwittingly, changed the world. Worse was to follow: when in 1999 his beloved wife, Raisa, whom he had married as a law student in Moscow, died from leukaemia

Yeltsin was now in charge and at first the Russian economy performed well, but then went into free-fall, with hyperinflation and the usual food shortages. Yeltsin toured the world seeking economic aid, but on terms seriously detrimental to the Russians. This resulted in the "sale of the century"- when oil and gas, plus gold mines and other natural resources wee sold off for a pittance to a few oligarchs, who included Roman Abramovich, the present owner of Chelsea Football Club.

Towards the end of his presidency in 1999, Yeltsin was in poor health from heavy drinking, and the final year of his presidency was wobbly - both literally and figuratively. Russia was being run by what became known as "The Family" - a mixture of oligarchs and Yeltsin's family, principally his daughter and son-in-law. They started looking around for a tame successor, and after shuffling the pack, the unknown Vladimir Putin came to the top as Yeltsin's heir apparent. Putin, who was from St.

Petersburg, was an obscure former lieutenant colonel in the KGB, who still had to be elected and only stood a measly three per cent in the polls. However, with clever manipulation of his image by the main TV station (owned by the oligarch, Boris Berezovsky), against a background of the Chechin conflict, Putin raced up the opinion polls and succeeded in being elected president in 2000, and re-elected in 2004. His first act was to offer Yeltsin and his family, immunity from prosecution for any wrongdoing committed whilst in office, whilst Berezovsky fled to the U.K. and was granted political refugee status.

Over lunch, Lena explained that living standards are higher in Moscow because salaries are double those of St. Petersburg, and sometimes up to ten times higher than those in the remote areas of Siberia are. The feuding and wrangling over which city is better has continued for the past 300 years. Petersburgers accuse Muscovites of being a common lot who do not speak properly, whilst Muscovites accuse Petersburgers of being intellectual snobs. In general, most Russians living outside Moscow do not like it because it is the capital and responsible for framing laws and collecting taxes. The headquarters of Russian TV is in Moscow and their national channels cover all ten time zones, so that viewers in Vladivostok will be watching "Breakfast Time" shows on TV whilst they sit down to dinner on the Pacific Ocean. Equally, advertising, goods and services are aimed at the Moscow wealthy, having no relevance to someone living in Siberia and earning a pittance.

After the excellent lunch of chicken shashlyk it was thanks to Lena for the information and her educational walking tour and we said goodbye. This was just the start of her busy tourist season and she complained that not many visitors brave the

By Train to Shanghai

chill Moscow winter, when the river freezes and temperature plunges. Although life is still hard now and she needs to do two jobs, she would never want to return to a Communist state again.

Taking the metro back to my hotel as it was Friday 13th, and although far from superstitious, decided not to tempt fate in a strange city and settled for a quiet evening indoors. Walking around Moscow with its heavy emphasis on security - there seemed to be big, burly, bald-headed security men in dark glasses and black suits, everywhere - including by the hotel entrance. Not to mention the numerous and sinister-looking chauffeurs of large, tinted window limousines, that sped around everywhere.

Another noteworthy observation - one of convenience, or shall I say the sorry lack of…conveniences, around the city. There are some, but of a mobile, portable-type where you pay a few roubles for the privilege. All I can tell you is - don't ever look down and don't, whatever you do, fall in.

Later in the evening, I went to the hotel bar for a night-cap and got into conversation with Vladimir, the barman. He spoke excellent English and told me he used to be in the Soviet army. Noticing that he walked with difficulty and had only one eye he explained that these injuries were the result of his time spent in Afghanistan, where he was wounded. In spite of this he was glad to get out alive considering how many of his countrymen were killed. He complained how the Russians fought a lone battle against the *mujhedin* who were supported by the Americans, Saudia Arabia, Pakistan and of course were assisted by Osama bin Laden. The situation became so absurd, that Soviet military targets by 1985, were being lined up on American satellites and the information fed straight to the increasingly high-tech equipment, by then in the hands of the *mujhedin*.

It seems that in 1979, when the Soviet army invaded Afghanistan in support of their puppet regime, the Saudi royal family were encouraged by the CIA to provide an Arab legion to lead a guerrilla war against the Russians. After much prevaricating, up stepped Bin Laden, a Saudi billionaire, and with his construction background in the family business, he decided to get involved, as he felt the Afghan Muslims had been humiliated by the Soviets. With his money, he set off on his own personal *jihad* and brought machinery as well as men, to blast massive tunnels in the mountains for hospitals and arms dumps, as well as cutting a dirt trail across Afghanistan to within a few kilometre of the capital, Kabul. Vladimir, agreed it was a bloody and brutal ten year guerrilla war in which five million Afghans fled the country and left 15,000 Russians dead with 35,000 wounded.

He agreed that eventual victory went to the *mujhedin* guerrillas and Bin Laden's Arab legion, resulting in humiliation for the mighty Soviet army, who were finally driven out of Afghanistan in 1989. Almost simultaneously, the Berlin Wall came crumbling down - and the rest they say - is history. The barman did admit that being in a conscript army was no match for dedicated fighters, who idolised their charismatic leader, who was portrayed in so heroic and influential a role. Also, he did express resignation of how difficult it is fighting an enemy who is not afraid of death, as Muslims are, and who believe that when they die, they go straight to heaven.

Our conversation turned to alcohol and Vladimir confessed to having been an alcoholic, having slithered into his darkest drinking days during the turmoil of *perestroika*. "Perfume, brake fluid, meths, toilet cleaner, nail varnish remover - I drank them all", he said. "After that, I went on to the hard stuff, and only survived because I got poisoned by some chemical cleaning agent and could not drink it any more. After that, I stuck to cologne!" However, with the help of a twelve-step recovery programme, he is now in control of his illness, but alcohol remains "Russia's curse", and millions remain trapped by the alcoholism.

Whilst in most of the western world, life expectancy is on the increase, in Russia it is actually falling, and is already down to fifty-eight years for males. An estimated 500,000 Russians die each year from alcohol-related causes, a figure that covers about thirty per cent of all male deaths. Vodka, which only costs thirty roubles a bottle, is the drink of choice - taking up almost three-quarters of official consumption. Production of over-proof moonshine vodka called samogon is rife, and nearly fifty per cent of alcohol consumed is clandestinely made - the police simply turn a blind-eye in exchange for their own supply. As a result, alcohol-poisoning kills 40,000 people a year - and despite the size of Russia, it only has 300 Alcoholics Anonymous groups.

Saturday, 14th May

The idea of having gone to bed early on Friday night was a good one - as I awoke feeling thoroughly refreshed and ready for a full day's sightseeing. On entering the breakfast buffet room an elderly English gentleman greeted me. Without hesitation he enquired whether I was working in Moscow, or on holiday and without waiting for a reply, he introduced himself as George. He had just arrived in Moscow having travelled east to west by train from China, describing his China holiday as more a splendid five star affair - dressing for dinner etc, which he'd arranged through a discerning travel agent. In his wisdom he had decided to try the low life and return home by train.

Giving me a run-down on what to expect - the weather was very hot in China, but very cold in Mongolia - this I found rather surprising for mid-May. Also, that Lake Baikal was still frozen as he had walked on the ice. He proceeded to tell me all about his experience so far on the railway journey, including his travelling companions; what he'd eaten; his toilet arrangements; and how he generally survived on the trains. His worst scenario was the border crossing between China and Mongolia. For some unknown reason, all foreigners were put into the last carriage - which was then locked! Then the train pulled out of the sidings - leaving his carriage in situ! Eventually the train reversed back down the line and was re-connected. "Total border crossing time of twelve hours is not very convenient when one is locked in one's carriage, with no access to the loos!" I couldn't help feeling sorry for the other passengers being locked up with George for twelve hours!

Trying to change the subject, away from railways and, as George was from Manchester, told him that Manchester United was about to be bought by an American Group. This was the only piece of news I had heard since starting my journey last Monday. George couldn't have been less interested about my revelation and simply continued with his tales of life on the trains. He told me about the dozens and dozens of eggs he'd found under the table in his compartment - which he discovered were the property of a young Mongolian boy on his way home from China. Dying for breakfast (and a bit of peace) I said goodbye to George and wished him all the best - but not before he told me his flight arrangements including his departure and arrival times! I pondered, was he just another of those boring people who are only interested in themselves, or had he just been travelling too long, on his own, and without speaking to anyone in English? Either way, luckily for him, I appeared at the right time!

The metro was not very crowded on this Saturday morning and arriving at the terminus walked through the Alexander Gardens, just outside the Kremlin Wall. From the direction of Red Square, I could hear music and discovered it was a military ceremony in front of a very large bronze statue of a military man aboard an enormous horse, and both mounted on a fine marble plinth. The rider's sword was drawn, and one of the horse's fore-hooves was crushing a Nazi emblem. The military man was one General Georgi Zhukov, a Marshall of the Soviet Union, and the hero of Stalingrad. His leadership in the defence of that city during the winter of 1942-43 was one of the two biggest turning points in World War II; the other was the success of the enigma code breakers at Bletchley Park. It was obvious to me from the respectful way the wreath laying ceremony was carried out, that there is no greater hero in Russian history.

Zhukov, who was a peasant from the Kaluga region south of Moscow was heavily involved in the Battle of Moscow during the vicious winter of 1941. Moscow was the biggest battle in history. Seven million soldiers fought for the Russian capital across an area the size of France. 925,000 soldiers on the Soviet side died – more than the combined casualties of the U.K. and U.S. during World War II.

The triumphant progress of the Wehrmacht was finally halted at the gates of Moscow which was a major turning point. Patriotism, Orthodox Christianity, the intense bond between a people and its land were just some of the qualities that helped turn the invader back. The senior commanders who channelled this energy, including Zhukov, were brilliant soldiers, ruthlessly committed to victory. The violinist David Oistrakh and the pianist Emil Gilels joined the Eight Volunteer Division that was to be almost annihilated at Vyazma. Battalions of writers, scientists, historians, academics and others joined them. Genuine volunteers oversubscribed an Air Force regiment composed entirely of women, from mechanics, up to the commanding officer, Marina Raskova.

When the ceremony had finished there was a headlong rush of people up the hill to the entrance of Red Square. First, one security check, and then another - to relieve you of any video recorders or cameras - as they are not allowed into the Lenin Mausoleum, but possible to deposit in the nearby History Museum. Entrance to the mausoleum was down twenty steps, and there lying in a glass floodlit cage, is the embalmed body of Vladimir Ilyich Lenin, Russian revolutionary and first leader of Communist Russia. Lenin, who practised as a lawyer in St.Petersburg, but was imprisoned and sent to Siberia in the year 1895.

After the failure of the 1905 Revolution, he went into exile in Zurich where he wrote various anti-capitalist books. Returning

By Train to Shanghai

to Russia in April 1917, he again had to flee, this time to Finland. Finally he arrived back for the last time in October 1917 to lead the Bolshevik Revolution, which overthrew the Provisional Government, and established the Soviet of People's Commissars. He died prematurely in 1924 at the age of fifty-four and has remained here ever since - guarded over by Russian soldiers. Rumour has it that after all these years, it is merely a wax work model, but with little more than a glimpse of the body, because of a fast moving queue, it is impossible to say if I think there is any validity in this theory!

On exiting the mausoleum and following the crowd back down Red Square to the cemetery where the remains of former Soviet leaders lie. Stalin, Brezhnev, Kosygin, Andropov and Chernenko are buried here in front of the Kremlin Wall, which contains a few hundred urns set in the wall including Gorky, Kirov, and the cosmonaut Yuri Gagarin, the first Soviet man in space. In 1961, in Vostok 1, his flight lasted just one hour and eight minutes, but was a milestone in the space race that developed between the then super powers. This was on the 12th April, and just a few weeks before the Americans achieved it. He became a real Soviet icon, but sadly he was killed in a mysterious air crash in 1968 - when he was just thirty-four.

What intrigued me most about the urns - were two with distinctly English and Irish names - William Haywood and Arthur McManus, whose deaths were in 1928. I wondered - who were these gentlemen and what did they do to have the honour of being interred in the Kremlin Wall?

All the Soviet Premiers, except the disgraced Nikita Khruschev, lay buried here in what is called the Tombs of Heroes. It is ironic that Khruschev has been excluded and buried elsewhere, when all he did was expose the past wrongs of Stalin. He was born Josif Dzhugashvili in Georgia, and after education in a religious seminary, adopted the pseudo-name Stalin (man of steel) to avoid being caught by the authorities who were looking for him for his role in bank robberies used to finance the Communist Party. They never caught up with him and instead he seized power when Lenin died in 1924.

Stalin arranged for Lenin's body to be embalmed and put on public display as it is today, but Lenin would have preferred a normal funeral, and so, eighty years later, it is still on view to the public, in the nearby mausoleum. Stalin, also had a wish to have his last resting place, lying beside his hero Lenin, but was disinterred in 1961 and his embalmed remains removed from the mausoleum and buried in an ordinary grave outside with the other leaders. What Khruschev tried to expose was the disastrous policies of Stalin, obtain justice of the victims or relatives, and allow displaced people to return to their homes from forced exile. This policy was not acceptable to the hard line military who removed Khruschev from power in a *coup d'etat*.

Stalin was a megalomaniac who was responsible for the 1930s purges, which saw intellectuals arrested on trumped up charges and had millions sent to labour camps in Siberia. In 1932 he organised a collective system of agricultural reforms, but this was steadfastly refused by the peasant farmers who refused to accept collectivisation. The result was death for ten million, either by execution or starvation. Stalin, also signed a secret non-aggression pact with Hitler, had most of the top military men shot and left his country totally unprepared and undefended against the *blitzkrieg* that Hitler was about to unleash.

In total, over twenty-seven million in the USSR died during the Second World War and not all on the battlefield. A lot of these were caused needlessly as a direct result of death marches, execution or where whole populations of ethnic minorities like Chechens and Tatars were sent to certain death. He saw enemies everywhere, doubted their loyalty against Hitler, and had them transported to the Siberian wilderness away from towns or cities, often dumping them straight off trains in freezing winter conditions.

One of Stalin's most insane policies was to build a tunnel to Japan through which he could attack the Japanese. Less than one mile was ever built for the loss of one hundred thousand lives under the sea.

Stalin had caused man-made famines on a biblical scale and under his authoritarian rule, the Soviet Union had become one giant prison, where border guards were rewarded as heroes, but no-one knew exactly where the borders were. Only his death prevented the liquidation of leading members of the Politburo, which would have unleashed another mass persecution throughout the country. It only became known later about the so-called "gulag archipelago", which held about seven million prisoners, matched by an equal number working for – the secret police. Stalin, who said, one death was a tragedy, millions a statistic!

The exact number of Stalin's victims will never be known. The USSR was victorious in World War II, but one quarter of its male population was dead, and the country was an economic disaster zone. Stalin died of natural causes, in his own bed, in 1953 and is buried here in a simple grave.

From here, it was time to join the queue for entry tickets to go inside the Kremlin, for centuries the site of the palaces of the Tsars and which occupies a triangular plot of land on a hill on the north bank of the Moscow River. It is enclosed by red-brick battlement walls, some two and a half kilometres in circumference. The walls are reinforced by twenty towers, five of which are used as gates and this situation has remained unchanged for five hundred years. The walls are more than sixty metres high and in places four metre thick. The word Kremlin means fortress and it would indeed have been one when Ivan the Great supervised its construction in 1500. Thereafter, Napoleon entered through one of its gates, the Kutafa Tower which was left open, and proceeded to blow up part of the old city and trash it before retreating from the conflagration in 1812. The Bolsheviks stormed it in 1917, presumably using the pretext that it was home to the Tsars, who used its churches for coronations, weddings, christenings and funerals. The Armoury, which houses the expensive and priceless treasures, has limited numbers, and with no tickets available, I proceeded to the ancient churches, These are actually three enormous cathedrals, each built in old Russian style and form a frame around the paved square called, the Square of Cathedrals.

The Archangel Cathedral is a five-domed edifice, built by an Italian architect, Aleviso Novi, which with its ornate decorations has distinct elements of the Italian Renaissance. Between 1540 and 1700 this was the burial ground of the Russian princes and Tsars: their likenesses are painted on the walls above each of the 46 tombs, including Ivan the Terrible. Inside, I joined the many tourists as well as worshippers and admired the large carved wooden iconostasis.

By Train to Shanghai

On the opposite side of the square is the Annunciation Cathedral whose foundations were laid in the 14th century and which contains beautiful iconostasis, painted by famous Russian artists like Rublev and the master painter, Theophanes, the Greek. This cathedral also served as the private chapel of the Tsars.

The third church in the square is the single-steeple, Church of the Deposition of the Robe. Built in 1484 on the north-western corner, it is the smallest, and was used as the personal church of the Patriarchs of Moscow. Rebuilt several times, it is home to many brilliant frescos from the 17th century, covering all its walls, pillars and vaults.

A little further along is the Assumption Cathedral, one of the oldest and most magnificent edifices with its five golden helmet domes. It was once Russia's principal church where the Tsars were crowned, and also used as a burial ground for the leaders of the Russian Orthodox Church. Built in 1475 by an Italian architect, Fiorovanti, it contains icons from the 12th and 14th centuries and behind it is the Patriarch's Palace. Built in 1655, it served as the Patriarch's private church, and is now a museum of books and religious clothing.

The tallest building in the Kremlin is the Ivan the Great Bell Tower, with its 329 steps, and, in accordance with tradition, is the tallest building in Moscow. First erected in 1500, it was re-built in 1600 with an onion-shaped dome, which was used as a watchtower. It holds fifty bells, the largest of which weighs seventy tons, which may appear tiny, when compared to its two hundred and two-ton bell which never rang and just sits on a stone pedestal nearby.

Known as the Tsar's Bell, it is a massive seven metres high, eight metres in diameter and was cast in the Kremlin over two hundred years ago, and is reputed to be the biggest bell in the world. Near this bell is the Tsar's Cannon, the largest calibre of any gun made in the world. Cast in bronze in 1586, it weights forty tons, is over five metres in length - an absolute monster!

Apart from the churches, the rest of the Kremlin contains an amazing Arsenal - surrounded by eight hundred canons, captured from Napoleon which is confirmed by the monogrammed "N" on each. Finally, there is the Senate which houses the offices of the President of Russia, Supreme Soviet and the Poteshny Palace where Stalin lived. Walking through the Kutafya Tower with some chattering Japanese tourists, I reflected on the beauty of what I had seen, and wondered what history these Kremlin walls could tell!

During our walk yesterday, Lena had mentioned that for Saturday night's performance of *Swan Lake* at the Bolshoi, one of Russia's leading ballerinas would be in the principal role. She enquired my interest in securing a ticket but as they are usually sold out months in advance, especially for the final few performances before refurbishment, it could be difficult and pricey. Giving her a budget of fifty pounds - Lena would call if successful - alas - no call, so I decided to visit the Bolshoi myself to see what was going on.

The theatre staff confirmed the situation and advised me to watch out for ticket touts operating nearby as they usually control the supply of surplus tickets and are a particularly nasty bunch of individual. I watched an elderly American couple chatting with one. The tout was selling a pair of middle row

By Train to Shanghai

tickets and was asking a mere five hundred dollars for both. The American man tried to negotiate a price reduction, whilst his wife tried a dose of pleading "we are now retirees, we are now both retired". She was probably more worried how the cost of the tickets was going to affect their finances for the remainder of their holiday. Neither the negotiating nor the pleading had any effect, and the American paid up. His dollars were well dispersed throughout his clothing, obviously for security, as he kept taking twenty-dollar bills out of various pockets. At this stage, other touts had arrived and formed a circle round them - they could smell money like a pride of lions smell blood.

Only after handing over the full sum, were the Americans given their tickets, and went on their way, hopefully to enjoy the evening of ballet. The successful tout shared out his spoils with his accomplices - so they had a good evening and wondered what the Americans will think of their visit to Mos-Cow, as they pronounce it. So, with no reasonably priced tickets in sight, I decided to abandon the ballet and retrace my walk of the previous day.

In Moscow, it is prudent to use the subway when crossing roads, and particularly Teatralny, the road in front of the Bolshoi. This is a one-way, eight-lane speed-track. As I left the theatre, the Moscow elite in their designer finery was arriving in American style stretch limos, for a night at the Bolshoi.

One level below ground - an entirely different life style was manifesting itself - utterly oblivious to what was going on above the subway. The space under Revolution Place was home to a very different Moscow life. There were dozens and dozens of small cramped kiosks, usually manned by women selling everything from cigarettes, beer, clothes, flowers and jewellery to DVDs and lottery tickets. This was a bustling market, totally unseen by the patrons of the Bolshoi above. Below that again was the huge Moscow Metro system, which has one hundred and twenty stations and two hundred and fifty kilometre of track - which is used daily by ten million Muscovites – paying a mere 30 pence to any station. Built in 1935, it is considered one of the city's marvels with its many ornate stations.

On the grapevine I had heard that there was a good Rosie O'Grady's Irish bar nearby which dispensed some decent Guinness. I used to know the brothers who, some years ago, established their chain of pubs in Paris, and hoped that just maybe one of them would be in Moscow. It was located in a small side street, just off Gogolevsky Boulevard - another six-lane, one-way, downhill, speed-track that had to be crossed with extreme caution, especially in the fading light. Inside, it had a distinct Russian feel about it, and all the staff happened to be Russian - not Irish which for some reason, I'd half been expecting. Enquiries regarding the whereabouts of my friend, Brian led to a firm *"nyet"*. The music and singing was also Russian, although intriguingly, in one corner there was a pretty young girl all dressed up in a Jonnie Walker outfit including a top hat. I realised she was there to dispense free shots of the famous red to whomsoever wanted it - for free. There was no rush! Perhaps Russians prefer their cheap vodka at two pounds a bottle!

At the other end of the bar, there was a group of men watching TV - a live rugby match from Twickenham, and I joined them. I was introduced to Sid and Wally, both English, who had lived in Moscow for some time. Looking at their girths, it was obvious that life for them was very agreeable and that visits to the gym, didn't feature in their daily routines. The third man introduced himself as an Irishman, called Seamus Burke from Limerick.

Sid and Wally worked in construction, but were very evasive about why, or how, they had arrived in Moscow. Sid explained that there were now boom-times for their business, but getting the right workers was a problem and promptly gave me a quick history lesson on the changed nature of work in Russia's capital. The most difficult, dangerous and least appealing jobs are no longer done by Slavs, but are mainly performed by workers from Azerbaijan, Tajikistan and Georgia. Official estimates suggest that there are twelve to sixteen million illegal immigrants living in Russia, representing up to ten per cent of the entire population, and therefore accounting for a large proportion of the workforce.

Wally said that for all the city's inequities, Moscow is awash with cash - making it a magnet for migrant workers from impoverished corners of the former Soviet Union. There are Tajiks, Uzbeks, Moldavians, Azerbaijanis, Georgians, Ukrainians, Armenians and Kyrgyz - and of course, poor migrant labourers from Russia's impoverished regions, who are legally Russian, but because of their non-Slavic ethnicity are treated as outsides in their own land. Drawn by a bustling consumer economy and a blur of new construction, they work in low-paying and physically draining jobs that many Russians do not want. They toil on Moscow's buildings sites summer and winter, sell fruit in its market, and clear snow from the streets in sub-zero temperatures. These migrant workers earn as little as fifteen dollars a day, and after a back-breaking twelve-hour shift - head off into a city that seems not to welcome them.

The Irishman did not have any such problems, as he had a successful building company, and had married a Russian girl - who only spoke Russian, and although he could understand his wife, he could not converse with her. I mentioned to Burke that he was not the first Limerick person to come and live in Moscow, and reminded him of the infamous Sean Burke who arrived forty years earlier. This Burke, whose main claim to fame was his imprisonment in Wormwood Scrubs prison in London at the same time as George Blake. Blake was the notorious Russian spy, then serving a forty-two year sentence. That was the stretch imposed on him by the Lord Chief Justice of England and was meant to represent one year for each of the forty-two agents whose deaths, Blake was deemed responsible. After his release, and with the help of others, Burke organised Blake's escape by throwing a rope ladder over the prison wall and both managed to get to Moscow.

Blake stayed, as he had no other option, but Burke, disillusioned with life in Moscow and the grim austerity of the time, returned to Ireland, where he died shortly afterwards - mainly due to alcohol abuse. That was 1966 - perhaps he might have found the Moscow of 2005 much more to his liking! At least he would have had a plentiful supply of Guinness to drink here in Rosie O'Grady's, and all paid for by a grateful KGB,

He would also have had a good supply of attractive young ladies - out of the corner of my eye, I noticed a tall, good-looking young woman, dressed all in black and with hair to match. She kept making eye contact and seemed to be anxious to join our table, as she was standing on her own. Wally told me she was a regular in this bar and her name was Olga. He added that if I had a spare two hundred dollars that would do nicely for her and she would happily relieve me of it! She came highly recommended and with advice from this seasoned professional, that whilst in Russia, I really should experience the pleasures of a Russian woman.

Finally, Wally invited Olga to join us. She spoke perfect English and said she worked in tourism. She was young, attractive and tempting…however I was just at the start of a long journey and could not take a risk. I had heard stories of visitors; not just being 'relieved', but also relieved of their wallets … and clothes, leaving them stranded in their underpants! In the words of that well-known journalistic cliché, I made my excuses and said good night.

Sunday, 15th May

It bucketed down during the night, and by the time I surfaced it was time to get an early start on my last day in Moscow. Breakfast was with Guy, the South African I'd shared the compartment with on the St. Petersburg-Moscow leg. He was an accountant but had decided to take a year off to do some travelling – ending his journey in South America. After an excellent Russian breakfast and a good chat about his country, said goodbye – I was going back to the Kremlin - he was catching a train to Yekaterinburg, after which he'd be going to China. Alas, we couldn't arrange to meet again as our schedules didn't tally.

As it was Sunday morning, the metro had few passengers and was lucky this time, and bought an entrance ticket for the Armoury - so called because of the rigid security guarding all those priceless treasures collected over centuries by the state and church. Housed inside the Great Kremlin Palace, it has seven hundred rooms, and is also the official residence of the Russian President.

The Armoury houses nearly 4,000 exhibits, which date from the 12th century, right up to the end of Romanov rule. Divided into several Halls – there are displays of Russian arms and armour including the helmet of Ivan the Terrible's son - Prince Ivan. Also, numerous glass cases with displays of ancient battleaxes, maces, sabres, suits of armour, pistols, muskets, etc. – in *Hall I*.

Halls II and III have the work of goldsmiths and silversmith, including a collection of Russian and foreign clocks, watches and various items of jewellery. *Hall* IV has many vestments of silk and velvet, worn by the Tsars, whilst *Hall* V contains foreign gold and silver objects given as presents by ambassadors.

Hall VI holds royal regalia, and several thrones - including one made entirely of carved ivory, and was said to have belonged to Ivan the Terrible. Pride of place is the joint coronation throne of the young Tsars, Peter the Great and his half-brother, Ivan. This throne actually has a secret compartment at the back, where their elder sister, Sophia sat - and prompted the young boys into giving the correct answers to ambassadors' questions!

Hall VIII was the most interesting, containing twenty court carriages originating from several different European

By Train to Shanghai

countries, the oldest being an English one, reputed to have been presented by Queen Elizabeth I to Boris Godunov, the Lord Protector and Tsar. Despite their great ages, all were in good repair and looked spectacular. My favourite had to be a large snow carriage belonging to the Empress Elizabeth. It needed twenty-eight horses to move it - what a sight that must have been as they trotted their way through the snow-covered streets of St. Petersburg.

Within the confines of the Armoury is a separate museum called the State Diamond Fund. After paying a few more roubles and passing yet more security, I entered a vault that guards two priceless Fabergé eggs. Fabergé was a Russian goldsmith who is best known for his gem-encrusted eggs, containing surprise gifts, which were given to the Tsarinas by the Tsars each Easter. In 2004, nine of these eggs were bought for the eye-watering figure of a £ 60 million price tag by the oligarch, Victor Vekselberg a gesture that brought back part of Russia's rich cultural legacy to the Rodina or Motherland. Amongst this opulent collection is the world's largest sapphire - including the monster one hundred and ninety carat Orlov Diamond.

Emerging into daylight, and on the corner of Red Square I noticed a little Orthodox Church called Kazan Cathedral and decided to join the congregation as it was Sunday morning. Packed with worshippers all praying with the same deep fervour I'd noticed amongst other Russians and on entering, my greeting was by sacred songs echoing down the aisles and incense filling the air above gilded icons. This tiny Kazan Cathedral seemed a haven of religious harmony.

After lunch as the temperature started to rise, a sight-seeing trip on the Moscow River seemed in order - reason one: to cool down, and reason two: a chance to see the city from another angle. Walking from Red Square, past the re-built Christ the Saviour Church and towards the river, I had a good look at one of the tallest skyscrapers from the Stalin era. It is now the Foreign Ministry and as much part of the city as the Eiffel Tower is to Paris. The riverboat started at Kievskaya and finished at Novospassky, so it was possible to see much of central Moscow en route as it meandered past parks, and under bridges, and made frequent stops at numerous jetties for embarking and disembarking passengers. Officially considered public transport, river cruise fares are cheap, which probably explains why our boat was very crowded with families on a day out.

Passing south of the high, redbrick old Tatar Wall of the Kremlin is a good vantage point to view the splendour of its campanile domes and palaces, glittering with gold and many colours, high above the parapet. Sitting in the sun on the upper deck, I overheard a young Irish couple speaking to their children who were sitting beside me, so promptly introduced myself. The husband worked in the oil business and although he enjoyed life here, confirmed that surviving Russian winters can test one's endurance! His wife said she'd survived two winters so far, and although money was likely to dictate her plans, she'd had enough of the cold! Being young and educated people, they were making good money, and with oil prices continuing to rise, there was a great rush to extract as much as possible, as quickly as possible - and oil workers were in much demand - in a the city that is awash in oil money as the price of "black gold" hovers at record levels.

By Train to Shanghai

As the boat passed the Kremlin I couldn't help wondering about what happened in 1812. The old city was well protected by its mighty sixty-metre high wall, perched way up on the highest hill around, which in turn was protected by the wide expanse of the Moscow River - so why on earth did the Russian army not stand to defend the city? Historians tell us their forces were withdrawn to defend the then capital, St. Petersburg – but it was just a clever Russian trick, engineered by the Russian general, Kutusov, which "allowed" Napoleon to enter the city, unopposed?

The story that emerges about Napoleon's desire to invade Russia, having been lured slowly, by bluff and counter-bluff, into arguing with himself that to achieve peace in Europe, he had to defeat, decisively, the Tsar, as he had done in 1807. His *Grand Armée* had rarely fought outside Europe and the Battle of Smolensk on the Polish border had drained its powers, but yielded a partial victory - although at enormous cost. In August 1812, they were now cast into the trackless wilderness of Russia, and Napoleon should clearly have withdrawn his army back west. Instead, Kutusov led them on into Russia by a policy of non-engagement. Napoleon now made the fatal decision to press on into the inhospitable, under-populated, friendless Russian countryside before engaging with the courageous Russian army at the battle of Borodino. Both sides suffered vast losses, and although Russia did not win - it did not lose either.

The Russian army now retreated back towards Moscow with Napoleonic forces following some ten miles behind. The Russians passed through Moscow without stopping, whilst the military governor, Count Fyodor Vasilievich Rostopchin, set fire to the city - and the army of Napoleon arrived to see Moscow in a sea of flames, without food or forage for their horses and with winter about to set in. Here, Napoleon made his second fatal mistake. He should have left and returned home by now, but in his folly, he waited until 20th October. This poor decision guaranteed that his return journey would be hampered not only by ceaseless harrying Cossack forces, but also the onset of a harsh Russian winter.

By the time Napoleon had reached the River Berezina he had became detached from the rest of his army, and barely managed to get across it. But, having done so, he then managed to make it back to Paris is just four days. For the rest of his army, it was utter chaos and carnage, in temperatures as low as minus forty degrees - the soldiers were forced to eat all their horses, and many were frozen to death in their sleep.

Meanwhile in Paris, Napoleon acted as if matters were normal, but of the original *Grande Armée* of 500,000 men, a staggering 400,000 perished in a brutal winter retreat, and the aura of his invincibility was shattered. Tchaikovsky wrote his famous *1812 Overture* as a celebration of this Russian victory.

Unlike St. Petersburg, which was built to a plan, Moscow was a medieval city that grew naturally from its centre, the Kremlin. Today its basic plan consists of three concentric circles bordered by the main boulevards. The first circle contains nearly all the important visitor attractions, and the others are just outside this circle and are within easy walking distance. The other two circles act as wide freeways, which keep Moscow traffic on the move - and at quite a pace - as I'd witnessed!

By Train to Shanghai

At the end of the boat trip, I walked back along the banks of the river and past the Rossiya hotel - one of the biggest hotels in the world. It was built on the orders of Stalin - quite simply to out-do the Americans with its size. It has 3,150 rooms with accommodation for 6,000 people, and a concert hall seating 3,000. From the 21st floor restaurant, diners have an excellent view over the Kremlin.

The year 2006, will see the Rossiya being demolished and most people will rejoice that one of the Soviet era's most hideous landmarks will disappear. The iconic British architect, Lord Norman Foster has been commissioned to play a leading role in rejuvenating the 13-acre riverside site, regarded as one of the most desirable pieces of development land in the world.

The revised plan is to build a town-within-a-town, having pastel-coloured re-creations of 18th and 19th century Moscow mansions so as not to jar with the Kremlin next door and will include a terminal for boats on the adjacent Moscow River - which is the only European capital to name its river after the city, and is a mere sub-tributary of the Volga. An entire pre-revolutionary street called Velikaya Ulitsa will be re-created, a church painstakingly resurrected and the old walls rebuilt. That Foster is co-ordinating the project is unusual in the extreme, since such prestigious and quintessentially Russian ventures are not usually entrusted to non-Russians.

With my love of trains and everything to do with them, Lena had recommended that I investigate the ornate stations of the metro system. Some are spectacular and each one has its own style of design - usually commemorating some region or city, and most were built under Stalin's dictatorship. Like

London, the metro lines are identified by different colours, and as I was now near the green line, which has two must-see stations. Firstly, the Mayakovskaya built in 1938 and grand prize winner at the 1938 World's Fair in New York - secondly, the Novokuznetskaya built in 1943, and again went down into the bowels of Moscow. Travelling along this line, it was possible to see both without risking the possibility of getting lost on Moscow's notoriously confusing system, and also thus saving some precious time.

Mayakovskaya has its central hall all decorated in stainless steel and marble, having 36 oval ceiling mosaics with their theme on sport and aviation. Novokuznetskaya's elegant marble benches hail from the original Church of Christ the Saviour, which were rescued before Stalin's demolition workers had started. The ceiling mosaics have a military theme. During my short journey, I noticed that passengers rarely speak when travelling and when they do, they keep their voices down. Foreign visitors can be recognised by their talking!

Unfortunately, these ornate stations were not matched by the green-line trains, which looked as if they were the original ones from the days of the line's construction - 1938! As in London, the stations were used as bomb shelters during World War II when the German aerial bombardment was in full flow. It is rumoured that there is a secret metro line which was built in 1967 for the sole purpose of evacuating the government of the day in the event of nuclear attack. Unfortunately, if this is true, it is not open to the public.

On this lovely May evening, as the sun was disappearing, I walked for the final time along the Alexander Gardens, bedecked with rows and rows of beautiful pink tulips - the whole place seemed to buzz with happiness. Muscovites, young and old, were out in force and thoroughly enjoying themselves - and needless to say, the fast food restaurants had lengthy queues, patiently awaiting their fare.

Sitting down for a breather, I chuckled on overhearing two German men trying to chat up a couple of Russian girls - through the medium of English - I have a funny feeling there was a happy foursome that evening! I scanned the scene and noticed a little square, where a uniformed band was standing and playing some jolly music. This had attracted a large group of dancers including an elderly man in military uniform with medals, who spun his equally elderly female partner round with youthful, gay abandon. Realising how late it was getting I reluctantly left and headed back to the hotel.

After collecting my baggage and checking out, the taxi to take me right across Moscow to the Yaroslavl Railway Station had arrived, and thus away from a most enjoyable three days in the city - without any major mishaps.

This departure from Moscow did not compare to the one from St. Petersburg with its uniformed staff lining the platform, but was no less a pleasure. The taxi parked near the station and the driver offered to come with me and happily carried my bags. This station is a rather open place with small shops doing brisk business as people stocked up with food and water for the journey ahead. My rail ticket had already been delivered to the hotel, so luckily I didn't have to join the very lengthy queue. The kindly taxi driver walked all the way down the platform to the spot where he anticipated my carriage was due. We both waited in anticipation along with other carriage number five passengers, until, out of the stillness of the evening, our train slowly reversed into its position along the platform. Before the train had even come to a standstill, there was the usual scramble of impatient travellers. We waited until the jostling crowd had finished their battle before the driver helped me find my berth. I thanked and tipped him, said goodbye and he left with a grateful smile.

In exchange for my ticket, the blond *provodnitsa* gave me clean sheets, told me the other three travellers would be arriving soon, and that they would be very close companions as we were about to endure four days together! The first to arrive was a young Russian chap who introduced himself as Sasha, and promptly disappeared to his allocated upper berth. Then the *provodnitsa* returned, and this time with Bridgette and Sidonie, two French ladies. My French isn't too bad and I could have managed some conversation but luckily both spoke excellent English. They were somewhat surprised to have been berthed with two men until I explained that the Russian railways never allocate by sex - it's just a pot-luck arrangement! Although both were experienced travellers, they too were undertaking a 'first' in travelling to China by train.

As train No. 10 with its eighteen carriages slowly pulled out of the station at precisely 23.25, I disappeared to the restaurant car, which was conveniently placed in carriage six, so that Bridgette and Sidonie could get ready for bed in some privacy. Others obviously had the same idea and the bar soon filled up with Russians, and the German and Dutch travellers I'd seen on the platform. Other than the Russians who had to travel this way for convenience or economic reason, most of the other passengers were on a special journey - either because they were railway enthusiasts, or backpackers at the start of their world trips. For certain, they had chosen this route, not for an economy fact, but out of choice - for the unique experience of travelling the longest train journey in the world. We all quickly became friends and enjoyed a few beers together as the train moved smoothly past the drab and dreary Moscow suburbs. We were on our way to Irkutsk, capital of eastern Siberia - a mere 5,133 kilometres from Moscow, and this train hauled by a powerful, Czech locomotive, would be my home for the next four days.

The first Russian railway, built in 1836, was a private line from the Tsar Nicholas I summer palace at Tsarkoye Selo to St. Petersburg - a distance of only twenty kilometres. The next fifty years saw a massive expansion of the railway system, linking the towns and cities in western Russia to the Ural Mountains. To the east lay Siberia, an inhospitable land where people only went if they had been forced into exile. Siberia, whose name comes from a Tatar word meaning "sleeping land", comprises the eastern and greatest part of Russia – itself the biggest country in the world. Indeed, Siberia – stretching from the Ural Mountains to the Pacific – is so vast that, were it a sovereign country, it would still be the largest in the world.

Before the railway was built, people had to travel along a rough track, known as the Great Post Road, along which were many stations where they could hire horses, carts, sledges or carriages - depending on which season it was. This route had been firmly established over two hundred years earlier by the Cossacks, who established a thriving fur trade, and were very much a law unto themselves. For those early travellers, life could be extremely uncomfortable and rather dangerous - wolves and bears roamed around and didn't discriminate when it came to attacking horses or men.

One popular mode of transport was the *tarantass*. This had a large boat-shaped body where travellers stored their belongings on the floor, covered them with straw and mattresses, which they lay on. It was pulled by a *troika* along atrocious roads, between the various post stations, and driven by the *yamshchik* who was invariably drunk. For these early travellers, the idea of a railway would have appealed greatly!

Before finalisation of the exact route, there were many eccentric suggestions put forward, and one in particularly has gone down in history. During his travels in Siberia, an English engineer named Duff noticed a large number of wild horses roaming around and suggested to the relevant authorities in St. Petersburg that a railway line with carriages pulled by wild horses would be a good idea. Needless to say, his proposal was politely declined. Finally, after much prevarication, official sanction to build the line was given in 1891 by Tsar Alexander III, shortly after he became Tsar. It was seen as a way of developing the vast wilderness east of the Urals and also facilitated the swift and easy movement of troops, and thus countering any aggression from the Japanese and Chinese in the Amur region. The railway was to be built as cheaply as possible and in various sections simultaneously, and the Tsarevich, Nicholas laid the first stone at Vladivostok the same year.

The overall project was given to Sergie Witte, a former station master, who quickly set about organising the finance.

By Train to Shanghai

Rothschild's Bank pulled out because of anti-Semitic legislation and pogroms, so in an effort to raise the necessary funds, Witte simply printed more banknotes, issued bonds, and raised taxes. Instead of the long and expensive, 2,000 kilometre section along the Amur River in the east, he persuaded the bankrupt Chinese government to allow a short cut across the Manchurian Plains. He offered a soft loan in return for the creation of a new entity called the East Chinese Railway Company, plus an eighty-year lease on this line.

There was no heavy machinery, and the men built the greater part of the Trans-Siberian Railway with little more than wooden shovels. Many of the workers were imported from as far away as Turkey and Italy. On the east Siberian, Ussuri Line, Chinese coolies were employed, but were unreliable and fearful of the Amur tigers that roamed the area. Soon, to relieve the shortage of labour, the Government had to turn to the prisons - and gangs of convicts were put to work. The inveigle them to stay and work hard, a system of remission was worked out - eight months work equalled one year's imprisonment. Cutting through the trees of the *taiga* proved particularly difficult, and in some places, the building season lasted only five months, due to the frozen ground in winter, and the swampy conditions in spring.

For the workers, life was extremely hard. Winters were long and cold, and their log cabin accommodation was poor protection from the weather. And summer was no respite due to plagues of flies, and mosquitoes in the swamps. There were outbreaks of bubonic plague and cholera, whilst in the Amur region, the world's largest tigers were a constant danger. There was a major set-back when severe flooding washed away two hundred kilometres of track near Lake Baikal.

Gradually, as the sections were completed, the first trains began to run, but in having tried to keep the cost as low as possible, the folly of that economy soon became apparent. Frequent derailments resulted in a speed restriction of a measly fifteen kilometres an hour being imposed. As rails bent and buckled, these and numerous other unsuitable materials, had to be replaced. In spite of these difficulties, the builders managed to construct three huge stone bridges - each spanning almost one kilometre - over the Rivers Irtysh, Ob, and Yenisey.

By 1900, travel across Siberia was possible, although largely supplemented by water transport on Lake Baikal and the Amur River. The Russian government decided that the Paris Exhibition of the same year, would be a good platform to show-off their great engineering masterpiece. Set against a Siberian landscape, several carriages were exhibited including a restaurant car, and spacious sleeping carriages furnished in sumptuous style. Other carriages contained a music saloon with piano, a library, a gymnasium, and a marble and brass bath. These carriages were to be operated by the Belgian company, International Des Wagons-Lits.

The marketing literature advised that the Trans-Siberian would knock ten days off the current travel time of five weeks from London to Shanghai. Visitors to the exhibition were intrigued and impressed and many signed up and immediately set off on their epic journeys. Sadly, disappointment soon set in, as the reality was very different from the blurb. However, grim as it was in parts, it was now a way to circumnavigate the globe by rail and ship, via Japan and America - and many wealthy people opted for the whole experience.

In 1904, the Circumbaikal loop-line around Lake Baikal, was completed. This was a world-class engineering feat, as it was carved out of rock, necessitating the building of over one hundred bridges and viaducts, and blasting thirty-three tunnels out of the rocks around the shores of the lake. However, its completion made the ferries redundant, but troops could be moved east in greater numbers to confront the Imperialist Japanese army, which had landed in Vladivostok. The decision was then taken to restart work on the Amur Line, which had earlier been abandoned due to cost. It took until 1916 to complete because of numerous problems, including permafrost, disease, and insects, also the necessity of building complicated bridges including a massive one at Khabarovsky, with a span two kilometres across the Amur River.

The Trans-Siberian Railway was now complete. It had cost one billion gold roubles, and now employed 750,000 workers - had 1,500 locomotives - and 30,000 wagons. When the Bolsheviks took power in 1918, they needed to gain access to the raw materials that were in plentiful supply in Siberia, so they invested heavily in upgrading the line. A second track was built alongside the original single track, but using heavier steel rails, whilst wooden bridges were replaced with iron and steel.

During the Second World War, the Trans-Siberian line served as a lifeline for Soviet survival. It was used to supply their Front with necessary supplies and reinforcements. Today it is one of the busiest railway lines in the world, and is still a vital lifeline for the people of Siberia.

Chapter Three
Moscow to Irkursk

Monday – 16th May

So I was finally on my way through the hinterland of this vast country Russia, or to give it its correct title of the Russian Federation. Comprising 75 per cent of the former USSR, but is still the largest country in the world with 17 million square kilometres. It is twice as large as America and the United Kingdom could fit into it 69 times. It covers 14 per cent of the earth's dry land and is the sixth most populous with 150 million people, which includes, 100 nationalities, all with their own language. Ten time zones cross its 10,000 kilometre expanse, a quarter of the globes. It borders Finland in the north-west and North Korea in the south-east and in between, adjoining Ukraine and Estonia, Iran and Afghanistan, Mongolia and China. Japan is a mere 160 kilometres by sea from the mainland and 20 kilometres from the southernmost of the Kuril Islands. The United States is a mere 60 kilometres away across the Bering Sea.

Morning arrived with a clear blue sky, and as we slowly came to life, this proved to be a better time to get more formally acquainted with my fellow passengers. I had hoped that my

By Train to Shanghai

Olympic standard snoring hadn't disturbed anyone as the train, unbeknown to me, had passed by Nizhny Novgorod - the third largest city in Russia, where the main station is still called Gorky - a hangover from its Soviet era.

In 1980, Nizhny Novgorod was the closed city of Gorky, where the dissident, Dr. Andrei Sakharov was exiled. He was the Soviet physicist who, having helped develop the hydrogen bomb, spoke out in the 1960s against nuclear weapons, and the need for free speech in the Soviet Union. His exile to Gorky in 1980 roused international protest, staging a series of hunger strikes in order to obtain medical treatment overseas for his sick wife, Yelena Bonner. He was finally freed in 1986 on the orders of Mikhail Gorbachev.

Our train arrived at the mighty Volga River and we crossed via an incredible bridge, whose span at this point is one kilometre. The Russians affectionately call the Volga, *Matushka* – "Dear Little Mother", which is quite a contradiction since it is the longest river in Europe. It flows from the Valday Hills, north of Moscow and meanders for 3,700 kilometres to the Caspian Sea. On its way, it drains an area a million square miles and linking five oceans and seas with Moscow through a series of canals.

Navigable for most of its length, it grows stronger and wider after looping past Nizhny Novgorod, then flows on to Kazan further east. Dams built decades ago have tamed the once-wild waters, turning long stretches into placid lakes – some reaching a width of twenty-four kilometres, before narrowing again. After Kazan, the Volga flows south to Volvograd – which - then called Stalingrad, was the site of one of the bloodiest battles of World War II. Here the Red army stopped the Nazi onslaught on the river's western bank and this epic battle is memorialised with an 85 metre steel-reinforced concrete statue of "Mother Russia" – a woman raising a sword and calling out for the defence of the homeland. Here at least 600,000 soldiers on each side died in the six months of fighting during the autumn and winter of 1942-43.

From here the Volga divides into eighty branches at its vast delta at Astrakhan – a port city on the salty waters of the landlocked Caspian Sea. Mother Volga, a river of history, folklore, song and art, maybe Russia's most famous and the longest in European Russia, but it is only the country's fifth longest and is much shorter than the great rivers east of the Urals : The Ob-Irtysh is 5,400 kilometres long, followed by the Amur, Lena, Yenisei, in that order.

Russia's southwards expansion also relied on rivers. Catherine the Great sent troops – followed by colonists – down the Rivers, Volga, Dnieper and Don, in a campaign based on forts on the river bank, gradually winning a great new province reaching to the Black Sea and the Caspian. To view her newly-won lands, the Empress and her entourage journeyed down the Volga in richly-furnished galley and 80 accompanying ships, carrying 3,000 courtiers and nobles as well as thousands of troops.

I met our blonde *provodnitsa,* who came from Nizhny Novgorod, in the corridor, and on discovering she spoke a little English, asked her more about the river. She explained that life without the Volga would be unimaginable, "It provides everything - work, pleasure, food. It is incredibly beautiful, and it defines Russia's spiritual heartland".

By Train to Shanghai

Thereafter, the landscape became a mixture of farmland with many smallholdings nestled between the spruce and fir trees of the *taiga*. We were now in this enormous coniferous forest, more than twice the size of the Amazon rainforest, stretching 6,400 kilometres across northern Russia – from the Finnish border to the Pacific.

This is the *taiga*, the largest forest in the world, where one in three of the world's trees grow and by far, Russia's largest habitat: a 2,500 kilometre wide belt, across the entire country, between the tundra to the north and the *steppe* to the south. From west to east, the tree cover of the *taiga* varies dramatically. Spruce is the dominant tree to the Urals, then mainly pine, spruce and fir to the Central Siberian Plateau, thereafter, larches, particularly the Daurian larch. Usually the *taiga* is silent and is the realm of many animals, including the great brown bear, lynx, sable and a profusion of birds and rodents.

All the rivers we crossed were in heavy flood, following recent heavy rains and melting snow. Arriving at the restaurant car for breakfast, the same attractive waitress from last night smiled and greeted me warmly. It was busy, and as to be expected, the Germans were the first to arrive! At the end of the car and near the kitchen sat a middle-aged lady peeling potatoes. She looked the typical matriarchal Russian woman with her hair coiled into a large bun. The TV video was noisily blaring away with some ghastly music programme - I wondered if it would have been more appropriate to show *Doctor Zhivago,* with its long train journey.

We stopped at Kirov for a twenty-minute break, giving an opportunity to get off the train and stretch my legs - even my muscles object to days of total inactivity. Everywhere *babushkas* or hawkers were out in force, selling goods from dried fish, bread and fruit to oodles of cheap beer and vodka. Kirov obtained its name in 1934 in honour of the assassinated communist leader of the same name who needless to say was one of Stalin's associates. Previously called Vyatka after the river that flows through it, the city used to be at the centre of the fur trade which had depended on the river for transport. The death of Kirov gave Stalin just the excuse to unleash one of his great purges, resulting in the death of millions.

South of Kirov, and on the alternative Urals route from Moscow, is the famous city of Kazan, capital of Tatarstan. It is the old Tatar city which dates from the 14th Century which has a population over one million. Tatars are Turkic people who used to rule parts of Russia with a strong nationalistic fervour. Built on the eastern bank of the Volga, Kazan was at one time capital of the Kazan Khanate. Ivan the Terrible paid a visit in 1552 and in his inimitable way, destroyed the city, and forced the Khan to become a Christian – because Khan feared further attacks if he did not conform to Moscow's wishes, Ivan got his way. To celebrate its capture he had St. Basils Cathedral in Moscow built and was able to send a handsome present of sable pelts to Elizabeth I of England in 1567. These days, the old city centre of Kazan is dominated by its Kremlin - now declared a Unesco World Heritage Site - which houses the Annunciation Cathedral designed by the same architect as St. Basils as well as the large Kul Sharif Mosque with its four minarets.

Former old boys of Kazan University include Leo Tolstoy and Lenin who lived in Ulyanov Street with his family from 1888 after his return from exile – today the house is a museum. During the same period, Maxim Gorky worked here as a bakers assistant.

When the train finally set-off again, Sasha, who had so far had spent the entire time in his upper bunk, came down and joined us. Bridgette and Sidonie my French cabin-mates, were already preparing lunch. They laid out on our small table a large chunk of Italian cheese, bread and some sausages. Sasha then produced a dozen boiled eggs, plus tomatoes and cucumber - my contribution was merely to enjoy eating it! Together we ate our impromptu feast while, the train rolled on to the next stop at Yar. Despite the close confinement in the compartment, we were all getting on well, which I hoped would be a good omen for the rest of the journey.

Yar is 1126 kilometres from Moscow and one hour ahead. This used to be in the Udmurt Republic, and is home to the Udmurts, who are one of the four major groups of Finno-Ugric people - being much more Asiatic - with different features. The stop at Yar was for twenty minutes and as soon as I stepped off the train, a Russian who was drunk, insisted on having a conversation with me. He spoke little English but through his thick guttural accent I kept hearing the word capitalism, and got the distinct impression he was blaming us Europeans for all the ills and problems of Russia. With him were two other men; one who kindly saved me from the accusations and who also found himself acting as interpreter. The third man said nothing and just observed.

Earlier in the day I had explored the layout of our mighty train. We were travelling in a 2nd class compartment which has two upper and two lower berths with good storage under the lower berths and in the large overhead bay. 1st class compartments are the same except there are no upper berths and shared by two people only. So, paying double, there is considerably more privacy. Third Class is essentially a dorm! These carriages sleep a mere fifty-four people – therefore – next to no privacy!

The 2nd class carriage is by far the most popular with tourists. Each carriage has 9 compartments for passengers, plus one half-sized compartment occupied by the *provodnitsa* or carriage attendant. There are two WC's at each end, plus a *samovar*, which provides a constant supply of boiling water. Our *provodnitsa* was a tall blonde Russian lady in an ill-fitting, blue uniform – she could have used a larger size! My first introduction to her was the previous night when she handed out the bed linen and checked the tickets – they are responsible for opening the train doors at station stops as well as ensuring all passengers are back on board on time. This morning she was busy vacuuming the corridor and compartments carpets.

At 8p.m. local time the train traversed the Kama River and stopped at the industrial city of Perm, a densely wooded, mineral rich area and the train had now climbed to 500 metres above sea level. This city is 1,432 kilometres from Moscow and made a name for itself in ballet, ever since the Kirov Company was evacuated there from St. Petersburg during the last war. So that today, Perm supplies the Bolshoi and Kirov ballets with promising young dancers. Catherine the Great decreed it a provincial capital in 1780 when it became a major trading station, ideally situated on the Rivers, Kama and Chusovi for the transporting of salt caravans and wheat. With the arrival of the railway and also the discovery of oil, helped it develop its industrial base. Today, its most famous product is the Kama bicycle and its most famous tourist attraction is the Kungur Ice Caves, the largest in the region. Their total length is six kilometres although not all is open to the public, but it includes beautiful grottoes and lakes. Also here near is the last surviving gulag camp – now a museum as well as the only preserved salt-mining operation – again as a museum.

Perm is also the setting for Chekhov's masterpiece, *The Three Sisters,* who dreamt of escaping this grubby provincial town [Perm] and going to the capital [Moscow]. In the play, the three Prozorov sisters, Olga, Masha, and Irina really inhabit Moscow in their hearts, where the spring comes early and there is love and fame. In the flesh, they find themselves resident in this dull town [Perm], where winter lingers and no one has ever heard of it. Chekhov wrote his play whilst recuperating in Yalta, from consumption, which was eventually to kill him aged 44 years. Whilst living there, he complained of the heat and cold and like the Prozorov sisters, longed for Moscow.

We are now deep in the foothills of the Ural Mountains, which stretch all the way from Kazakhstan to the Kara Sea in the Arctic Ocean, traditionally dividing Europe from Asia. Kazakhstan lies south of here, which up until 1991 was one of the Soviet Central Asian republics and home to the Aral Sea along with Uzbekistan. Without doubt, the demise of the Aral Sea has been the greatest ecological disaster of the 20th century and the biggest man-made catastrophe in history.

For 35 million years the Aral Sea has existed but since the late 1960s it has faced the gravest challenges to its survival, due to the work of Soviet engineers. It's two sole tributaries, two giant rivers, the Amu Darya and Syr Darya have been used for irrigation across millennia. From the 1960s a major expansion of irrigation, virtually doubled the water extracted, primarily for the cultivation of a cotton crop. Half the rivers flow was used for irrigation and for twelve years the Syr Darya did not reach the Aral Sea at all. Similarly, the Amu Darya failed for five years.

The Aral Sea used to be the fourth largest amongst the world's inland waterbody, covering an area the size of Belgium and the Netherlands combined. During the second half of the 20th century, the water receded to a 10th of its natural volume and the sea's area fell three-quarters. The water retreated – up to 150 kilometres from the former southern port of Muynak – leaving hundreds of fishing boats apparently beached in the middle of a desert and vast areas of its bed have now totally dried up, exposing huge amounts of salt. Every year, dust from the dried-out sea bed, contaminated by salt and pesticides such as DDT – long ago washed there from farmland, are blown over the surrounding land, vast tracts of which are now salty deserts. Even the wells that provide drinking water have turned salty too.

The effect on the region's population and wildlife is incalculable. It's 3.5 million people living around it have suffered poverty, disease and death. For the past 15 years, chronic bronchitis has increased by 3,000 per cent and arthritic disease by 6,000 per cent. Life expectancy has slumped from 64 years to 51, whilst the majority of babies are born with anaemic conditions to mothers suffering from anaemia. The Aral Sea used to produce a plentiful supply of sturgeon, pike and roach - now there is no fishing harvest and all 24 specie of endemic freshwater fish are extinct. Sadly, the big fish canneries at what were once ports, have become obsolete.

By Train to Shanghai

But there is a glimmer of light on the horizon. After the break-up of the Soviet Union, the new state of Kazakhstan, home of the North Aral Sea, decided to try and rescue it. Two attempts failed, but the World Bank finally agreed to help. Firstly by financing a dam across its narrow connection with the southern sea, doubling the flow of the Syr Darya and trying to fill it. Optimists thought it would take many years - pessimists said it could never happen. By early 2006, the dam has filled and waters are now flowing back towards the main port in the north, Aralsk, having previously retreated as far as 80 kilometres. Fishermen in the surrounding villages are going to sea again and there are plans to release 30 million young fish stock to restock the North Aral Sea. Sadly, the much bigger southern sea and the Amu Darya is controlled by Uzbekistan, which shows little interest in a similar recovery, but at least the springing to life again of the north, has the potential to be the greatest environmental comeback ever.

I had extended an invite to Bridgette and Sidonie to join me in the restaurant car for dinner but they declined as they had already organised their evening meal from food already prepared, perhaps they did not trust Russian cooking. Earlier, as we shared a coffee, Sasha told us an amusing story about the President of the Democratic People's Republic of Korea whose name was Kim Jong Il. It appears there are plans to extend the Trans-Siberian line from Vladivostok into South Korea, passing through Kim's secretive and inaccessible country. To discuss the project with President Putin of Russian, he travelled all the way from Pyongyang to Moscow by train in 2001 as he refuses to fly. Kim is paranoid about his security and rightly so, in view of his nuclear standoff with the Americans, so he set off for Moscow in his own twenty-carriage, armoured train.

With his entourage of 200 officials and bodyguards his train caused massive disruption as stations were closed along the Trans-Siberian route, trains being re-routed, even the main arrival station in Moscow was closed during rush hour which happened to coincide with Kim's arrival.

There was still daylight when I reached the restaurant car and ordered beef stroganoff from the waitress as the daylight slowly faded and the train climbed slowly through the Urals *taiga*. About half an hour later and with no food served I noticed that the waitress was sitting at the far end of the dining car - in an amorous embrace with a young man! When I went in search of my beef stroganoff I discovered that this young man was indeed the chef and as long as he was distracted by the waitress, forget food or anything else; After remonstrating with the waitress, she re-adjusted her clothing, apologised, and the chef moved off to cook my dinner.

At the far end of the carriage I noticed Yuri, the young Russian musician who had earlier acted as interpreter when the inebriated Russian was insulting me on the platform at Yar. He was on his own, and when he'd finished eating, came and joined me at my table. He now formally introduced himself: Yuri Poliakov, a cellist with the Musica Viva, a well-known Moscow orchestra, and was on his way to play in a concert at Yekaterinburg.

Yuri then proceeded to tell me an amusing story about his musical instrument, which was not just an ordinary cello, but a Stradivarius. So, much to my astonishment, a Stradivarius was also on board the train as well as the passengers. Just one of the estimated 650 violins and cellos that remain intact throughout the world and made by the genius, Antonio Stradivari and his two sons in Cremona, Italy in the 18th century - who signed his instruments with the Latin form of his name, Stradivarius.

This instrument is so valuable that when it leaves Moscow, an insurance requirement is for it to have an armed guard, protection against getting into the wrong hands. This is where the third man on the platform at Yar comes into the picture. He was the armed guard. So, whilst Yuri could come to the dining car for dinner the security man had to remain in his compartment, with the cello for company. Security of his musical instrument was not Yuri's problem - he merely had to play it at the concert in two days time.

To understand the value of a Stradivarius can be gauged by the £ 3.5 million price tag recently paid by the Royal Academy of Music in London, for one known as the so-called "Viotti violin". Giovanni Viotti dazzled audiences when he first played it in Paris in 1782 and later in London. This instrument was made by the great master, Antonio Stradivari, which first alerted listeners to the genius of his craft. The tone and expressiveness was completely new at the time and led to the recognition of the Stradivarius violin. Before Viotti - Stradivari was just one violin-maker among many. After him, everyone wanted to play a Stradivarius.

As we sipped a few Russian beers, Yuri continued his story about buying his rail tickets. As his cello is rather bulky it was necessary to purchase two tickets at Yaroslavl Station. Russian bureaucracy has not changed that much since Soviet times! It also requires people travelling around their large country, to show their identity card when buying long distance railway tickets. Yuri purchased his two tickets - one in his name, and one in the name of Antonio Stradivari! His explanation to the ticket clerk was that his travelling companion was delayed and would arrive later. The clerk had reluctantly accepted the situation but Yuri had to apply more persuasion when boarding the train.

Usually, the *provodnitsa* checks the tickets before boarding, so when Yuri showed her his two tickets, she enquired as to the whereabouts of Mr Stradivari. He explained that the second ticket belonged to the cello, but it took much convincing – she had trouble comprehending that someone would buy an expensive ticket for a musical instrument when the train had perfectly adequate storage for bulky luggage – which was free.

As the train headed east towards Yekaterinburg, Yuri and I enjoyed our beers, whilst the Stradivarius cello was safely lying in its case, in upper berth 35 of carriage 8, and watched over by its armed guard. We chatted about life in general in present day Russia, and how it compares with the old Soviet days. He complained that the people were still not free, or at least, not economically free. Life was very tough for the majority, particularly those living and working in Moscow – with a population of ten million - it was far too overcrowded. Having travelled on the Moscow metro, I wholeheartedly agreed with him – remembering the crowded carriages and seriously glum faces of the unfortunate Muscovites.

Yuri lived with his parents and complained that to buy a small apartment could cost him up to half a million dollars, depending on location – how on earth does an average Russian like him buy a decent property at a reasonable price? It seems he missed out on the big *property handout* when the Soviet Union started to fall apart in 1991. Back then; most people lived in property owned by the "state"- which was once the epitome of cheap, state-subsidised living. Overnight when the government collapsed, tenants inherited the property they lived-in - for free. Yuri told me that nowadays many young Muscovites are desperate to get a foot on the property ladder and sometimes resort to desperate measures; the media often carries stories of contract killers hired to bump off flat owners, of elderly people tricked out of their city centre apartments, and of apartment blocks burnt down "accidentally" to force people to sell.

It was now past mid-night local time and the waitress announced that she was closing the bar, so we ordered a few more beers and happily repaired to the corridor to continue our chat and swig beer. At precisely 1.37 a.m. the train pulled into Yekaterinburg and it was time to end our happy evening. We said goodbye and I wished Yuri all the best with his career. He was talented enough to have been a pupil of the great master, Mstislav Rostropovich and he was still only twenty-six. Maybe one day, I'll see his name up in lights - The Last Night of The Proms at the Royal Albert Hall - World Famous, Yuri Poliakov plays Elgar's Cello Concerto!

So, this is the famous, or is it infamous, Yekaterinburg? Famous, because it was named in honour of Catherine, the new wife of Peter the Great, and infamous, because the last Romanov family including Tsar Nicholas II, his wife and children, who had abdicated in 1917, were imprisoned in a house here in May 1918, before being murdered by the Bolsheviks at midnight on July 16th. This had been the last ruling dynasty of Russia - they had transformed their country into a large empire from the time of the first Romanov Tsar, Michael, in 1613. Their most famous successors were Peter the Great, Catherine the Great, Alexander I, Nicholas I and Alexander II.

With the executions of Tsar Nicholas II and his family, Romanov rule ended and their bodies were ignominiously thrown down a mineshaft. The party official and leading Bolshevik responsible for the executions, Yacob Sverdlov had the city of Yekaterinburg, renamed Sverdlov in his own honour! It was changed back again in 1991, but the railway station still carries his name. It was not until 1998 that the Romanovs finally received a state funeral - when their remains were authenticated by DNA match, and at a cost of only one million dollars, they were re-interred in the family vault alongside their ancestors, in the Peter and Paul Fortress in St. Petersburg.

As far as the train journey was concerned we had crossed the Europe / Asia border obelisk and were now 1,814 kilometres from Moscow. Even for me, it was now quite late and time to call it a day. Everyone else was sound asleep as the train slowly pulled out of the deserted station. We were now officially in Asia, but at least we were rumbling agreeably along at about forty kilometres an hour aboard the Trans-Siberian. As I headed for bed I pondered - few travel experiences can be more heartening and I will long remember that marvellous definition of conviviality: trundling along on the Trans-Siberian; watching a Monday evening drift past outside, chatting with an entertaining bunch of fellow-travellers, especially a star in the making - and all in the company of a priceless Stradivarius!

Tuesday 17th May

Yekaterinburg is Russia's fourth largest city which was firmly established in the 18th century when gold was discovered nearby. The main road east from Moscow passed through it and the builders of the Trans-Siberian Railway followed the route of the old Great Post Road. It has always been a major military city with its regiments supplying the backbone of the Imperial and the Red armies. One of its most famous engineering graduates, Boris Yeltsin, served as the mayor here. Apart from his time at the Kremlin during his presidency, he is famous for two little events – one, the stand-off outside the White House in Moscow when he jumped on a tank to confront the military, and two, for keeping the entire Irish cabinet waiting on the tarmac at Shannon Airport for five hours, whilst he slept on his aeroplane suffering from a hangover, much to the embarrassment of his Russian entourage.

Apart from Boris Yeltsin, who dismantled the Soviet myth, and the murder of the Romanovs setting the way for the socialist era in 1918, Yekaterinburg also had a hand in the Cold War, when the American spy plane U2 was shot down nearby in 1960. The pilot, Gary Powers parachuted to safety, and to be eventually exchanged for another spy. Now, with a population approaching two million, it has become an important industrial city for engineering, chemical production and iron ore. It is well served with schools and educational institutes such as the Belinski Library, reputed to hold fifteen million books.

Our next scheduled stop was at Tyumen, which we reached at 8.30 a.m. We were now 2,138 kilometres from Moscow but the station clock showed "06.30" local time, as all long-distance trains run on Moscow time. Officially, we were now in Siberia, also known as "Sebiyr" which means the sleeping land in the Tatar language. With the train coming to a halt, it seemed everyone else was still sleeping as very few got off for a platform walk On this beautiful, warm spring morning. watching the train driver of maybe it was his assistant, wash the front window of his train - although it was obviously not to enjoy the beauty of Tyumen Station – it may be the oldest city in Siberia, and be its oil capital - but the station was the least attractive so far – somewhat uninspiring.

Then it was back on board and on to Tobolsk, which used to be the old capital of Siberia. Very little remains of the original settlement, but it has the only Kremlin in Siberia and for some totally unexplained reason the train now detours off the official Trans-Siberian line. As the train trundled on, the landscape became a mixture of lakes and *taiga* of pine, fir and larch trees.

The Cossacks founded Tobolsk in 1582 having defeated the Tatars. Cossacks were shaggy haired cowboys who were fugitives from justice but free men who eventually swore allegiance to the Tsar, and as cavalry, were at the vanguard of the Russian expansion into Siberia and elsewhere. Before the Gold Rush they established the Fur Rush, enabling a plentiful supply of furs and pelts for the Tsar - which also ensured their continuing freedom. Well-known for their horsemanship, as long ago as 1689 the Cossacks reached the Pacific Ocean and founded the town of Okhotsk, and from then on Alaska became the eastern outpost of the Russian Empire. Alaska was sold to the Americans in 1867 for a few roubles… and what happened in 1868 - gold was discovered there!

By Train to Shanghai

Napoleon once said "Give me 20,000 Cossacks and I will conquer the whole of Europe and even the whole world." In present day Russia, even President Putin is enlisting the help of the Cossack ethnic minority to keep order in Russia's volatile southern regions. The President has personally introduced to the Duma, (the Russian Parliament) a Bill that would create special Cossack security units to preserve law and order and fight terrorism.

About 600,000 Cossacks would be eligible to join the units, a move that would mean Cossacks returning, after a 90-year hiatus, to their traditional role as tough defenders of Russia's border regions. Cossacks now want to pick up their long tradition of military service to the Russian state, but critics of the move fear that because Cossacks now are indivisible from nationalists, they concede that the plan could be very dangerous!

The Rivers Tobol and Irtysh meet at Tobolsk and the centrepiece of the city is the Kremlin and its twin cathedrals - the St. Sofia and Intercession. The 19th century prison where Dostoyevsky was imprisoned en-route to his exile has recently been restored as a museum. In the old town, some dilapidated wooden houses still survive and an old mosque to cater for the minority Tatar population. The last Tsar, Nicholas and his family are remembered by a small museum, which commemorates their brief stay here on their way to execution.

Down from hills and mountains, through *steppe*, desert, forest and tundra, they flow: the Tobol River is just one of nearly three million streams and rivers, draining the huge land mass of the world's largest country. They flow out north into the seas of the Arctic Ocean: west into the Baltic, south into the Black Sea and east into the three seas of the Pacific. Into eleven seas in all - but excluding the Caspian and Aral – which are lakes.

As the train pulled out of the station, Sasha, who up to now had been quiet and almost invisible since our feast yesterday, came down from his upper bunk to prepare his food. Again, he offered to share his boiled eggs and bread with us and as we ate breakfast, the train rounded a wide bend and slowed down. Rounding this switchback, a beautiful view emerged and it was possible to see the remainder of the train following behind whilst travelling through the forest. A little later as the line straightened out we rejoined the main Trans-Siberian line and I decided to visit the other carriages and meet some more of my fellow travellers.

The nearby *platskartny*, or 3rd class carriage, was crowded, with bodies everywhere, but was much better than I expected, and all the occupants appeared Russian or Mongolian, both male and female. The price of tickets for this area cost about a quarter of the 2nd class fare, but privacy is totally non-existent and is essentially a dormitory on wheels for 54 people. It is said that if you want to meet real Russians and enjoy their hospitality this is one way to do it - travel *platskartny* class. I could vouch for this, because when moving through - a Russian offered me a beer.

Having viewed the realities of this modern train, including the *platskartny* accommodation, it was interesting to compare it with Annette Meakin's description of the first luxury train, 105 years earlier. She and her mother found their accommodation "entirely satisfactory", even if a few of the luxurious items they had seen in the carriages of the Siberian exhibition in Paris were missing. Annette described the train as a kind of "liberty hall" where you can shut your door and sleep all day if you prefer it, or eat and drink, or smoke and play cards if you liked that better. She explained how an electric bell summons a serving man to make your bed or sweep your floor, as the case may be, whilst a bell on the other side summons a waiter from the buffet. She also remarked how time passes very pleasantly on such a train, and that distances, like time, counts for nothing in Siberia.

Sadly, long gone are the electric bells, even in first class, but time still passes pleasantly.

Annette wrote that for entertainment at the end of their cheerful dining car was a Bechstein piano, and opposite it, a bookcase stocked only with Russian novels. The Meakins were travelling on the weekly train de-luxe, non-stop stage, to Omsk via Samara. Their journey would take four days and four nights, travelling at an average speed 25 kilometres per hour. On the 4th day, they had an agreeable concert and amongst the performers, were a gentleman with a good tenor voice and two lady pianists of no ordinary merit.

My train was shortly to arrive in Omsk after just 38 hours and travelling at an average speed of 70 kilometres per hour and powered by a whopping 126-ton engine.

Later I wandered down to the restaurant car and where by now our waitress whose name was Yanetskia, recognised me and showed me to my table. The large German party of eight women and four men had already arrived for lunch and had clearly pre-arranged everything. With them was Alexi, their Russian guide who seemed to be permanently inebriated and who had joined their party in Moscow. I met him on the first night when he was arguing with the matriarchal lady, presumably about prices or his commission. This lady seemed to be in charge of the restaurant, giving instructions and generally bossing everyone around, and always managing to position herself at 'her' place on 'her' table.

Since Soviet times, Russians have developed an effective safety valve, the joke, and especially the political joke which is one of their most endearing characteristics. Back then, jokes used to cover everything, especially the party leadership and the system is general. Most played on official slogans and turned a common cliché back to front, making an opposite point. Others were more topical and swirled around within days of a particular event – like the party congress. As I sipped a beer with Alexi, he related to me two contradictory jokes about a congress back in the 1980s.

In one, the party delegate returns to his small town and presents his report to a workers meeting. He begins: "Comrades, in the next five-year plan we shall have more to eat. We shall have better cars. We shall get better medical treatment. We shall see our living standards rise...."Finally, one of the workers puts his hand up and asks: "And what about us"?

In the other joke, the party official returns home with a bleak report: "Comrades, there will be difficult times ahead. There will be shortages of food. We shall have to spend money helping our socialist neighbours. Our industry is facing problems….." He is interrupted by two men who call out: "We shall work

By Train to Shanghai

double shifts". Continuing, he has more news of bad times ahead, and they call out: "We shall work round the clock". After he has finished, he enquires where these keen men work. Back comes a flat reply: "At the morgue".

As we finished lunch, we arrived in Omsk at 13.50 p.m. as scheduled, having crossed a six-span bridge over the Irtysh River, which was in heavy flood. During the civil war, Omsk served as the White Russian government's capital until the Red army overran it in 1919. We were now 2,676 kilometres from Moscow and had advanced three hours ahead of its time. This is a very busy section of the line, reputed to be the busiest freight line in the world, mostly with coal from Novosibirsk, heading for the Urals smelting plants. Omsk was put on the international stage in 1938 when Howard Hughes landed here with his four crewmen in his Lockheed Model 14 twin-engine transport plane. Having managed to avoid the Lufwaffe who were trying to shoot him down over Germany because he did not have permission to fly through German air space, he landed at Omsk. The Russians offered him caviar and vodka but Hughes rejected it politely, explaining through an interpreter that he had to keep a clear head for the journey ahead. From 10th to 14th, July 1938 he continued around the world in the then record time of 3 days, 19 hours and 17 minutes.

In 1849 the writer, Fyodor Dostoyevsky was exiled here, having narrowly escaped the firing squad in his native St. Petersburg, while in more recent times, Alexander Solzhenitsyn, the man described as "Russia's greatest living writer," stopped here on his way to forced exile in Kazakhstan. Dostoyevsky, spent four years doing hard labour in Omsk, which included two floggings – once, for complaining about a lump of dirt in his soup, and once for saving the life of a drowning prisoner, when told by his guards to let him drown So much for the Russian penal system of the time!

These experiences are poignantly recorded in his novel, *"Buried Alive in Siberia."* So what was it about "being sent to Siberia" as we usually referred to a form of purgatory or as a punishment? In Victorian England and Tsarist Russia it meant one thing, an inhospitable land where criminals paid for their crimes by working in the gold, silver and coal mines or for early arrivals - salt mines.

By 1900 over one million were exiled and kept in squalid and horrific conditions. Today, these jails have all gone, and Omsk which was established in 1716 as a Cossack outpost, now has a population over one million and a prosperous economy. One of the most impressive sections of this region is the forest zone, dividing the land into sections, and covering many thousand of square kilometres. Vast, gloomy, and unbroken, these forests stretch away to the north, until, growing thinner and thinner, they dwindle away, finally vanishing into the frozen land, which in turn, gives way to the Arctic Ocean. This is the tundra, where the sunlight never penetrates and the soil is perpetually frozen. Many of the stories of horror and death which one associates with Siberia are connected with these forests. Lost therein, there is no possible hope. The silence is forever unbroken, except for the sighing of the branches and an occasional howl of a wolf.

North of the *taiga* lies the belt of tundra, seemingly empty and desolate with no trees higher than dwarf shrubs. The word "tundra" comes from the Finnish *tunturi*, meaning treeless heights, which rings the northernmost land masses from the Finnish border to the Bering Straits, some 7,000 kilometres east. Below lies permafrost up to 1,000 metres deep, ground which may have been permanently frozen since the last ice age. This is an endless space, empty, except for the hordes of polar foxes, wolves, reindeer and vast numbers of waterfowl and other birds. But everywhere rivers, lakes, pools and bogs: This is the wettest landscape on earth because there is virtually no evaporation or absorption into the frozen subsoil. For nine months of the year it is covered in snow suffering ferocious blizzards and the average temperature down to minus 35C.

In the 1960s, oil and gas were found in the tundra just east of the Urals with the resultant arrival of men, machinery and vehicles. The consequences were disruption and environmental degradation as well as decline of migratory birds caused by the overhead electric power lines. The construction of pipelines across the tundra has brought problems. Unfortunately, some were built across reindeer migration routes, so that when the reindeer encountered these barriers it caused confusion and thousands of reindeer died from lack of fodder. Since then, sections of pipelines across their traditional routes have been raised to allow the reindeer to pass beneath. Gradually, they re-adjusted to this change.

On this mammoth train journey the most popular book people take to read is Tolstoy's masterpiece *War and Peace* which took him four years to write. Declining this, and instead brought along a book I had bought in a London junk shop. *My Manor*, by Charlie Richardson is the autobiography of a notorious London villain, who, back in the 1960s, was convicted of grievous bodily harm for which he received a 25 year stretch.

Richardson sets out his side of the affair and laments how both the English legal and class systems let him down, and on reading his story one has to feel sorry for him. By pure coincidence, chapter nine is called *Crime and Punishment*, the same as Dostoyevsky's most famous novel. Richardson goes on to explain the hellhole of prison life with three men sharing a cell, with a bucket as a toilet, in a cell the size of a toilet. On this journey our compartment is small with four people sharing its space, but at least we can move around and walk down the corridor to the bar or the toilet even if it means having to queue!

By the time we reached Barabinsk we had travelled 3,000 kilometres. This area of boggy grassland was once inhabited by the nomadic Kirghiz people before they moved to a mountainous area bordering on China called Kyrgystan. The station platform had the odd *babushkas* selling their wares - as usual - food and water and at nine o'clock, as daylight slipped away, the train pulled out heading for Novosibirsk

The dining car is favoured more for its makeshift role as a social centre than for its gastronomic qualities, therefore it was with some trepidation that I extended an invitation to Bridgette and Sidonie to join me for dinner. Quality apart, the restaurant car was doing a roaring business, but we managed to get the last table. The Dutch party of fourteen from our carriage - and, of course, the German group with Alexi, their drunken guide - had taken all but one of the other tables. At the corner table, sat two armed policemen who had been on the train since Moscow, and as far as I was aware, they hadn't spoken with any of the passengers.

The written menu was extensive, but very limited in what was actually available, but not too surprising, considering we are now almost three days into our journey. We all settled for beef stroganoff, which was available, but declined the French wine as it was over-priced according to the French ladies. Sidonie, who was in her early thirties, told me she worked in a chocolate factory just outside of Paris, but needed a break and was taking a six-month sabbatical. When she reached China, she planned to go on to Australia and New Zealand. Bridgette, on the other hand was in her fifties, and twice married with one daughter. She owned a small art gallery outside Paris, but business was poor and would sell-out at the right price. The French economy was struggling and she would definitely be voting *"non,* in the forthcoming referendum on European enlargement.

Sidonie and Bridgette were old friends but had not holidayed together before. Sidonie had been the instigator of this trip but did not relish the idea of being a lone female on a train journey like this - and who could blame her? It took quite a bit of persuasion and arm-twisting for Bridgette to agree to come along for company and protection. However, when I related the story about Annette Meakin and her train journey over a hundred years ago, and how she too befriended a French woman with whom the question of personal security was discussed. Sidonie was amused when told that Annette had remarked that her French friend thought she was bold, if not, rash to travel without a revolver. "I always carry two" the French woman replied. "Oh, how times have changed" Sidonie said with a laugh!

Coming from a country with a reputation for the world's best cuisine, I wondered what their opinion would be on this dish originally concocted by a French chef for the Stroganoff family - to which Bridgette politely replied, "There is a French saying to the effect that one should always leave the table wanting more. That is why French women don't get fat - they take their time about eating". From that reply I could not work out whether the food was good or bad but it was a diplomatic one!

The girls retired to their respective bunks and I stayed on for a night-cap. Nearly everyone else had departed, and the staff all settled down at one of the tables. The middle-aged woman with her hair coiled in a bun, appeared to be in charge as she gave orders or instructions from time to time. Sitting beside her was an unshaven man, who I'd never seen doing very much – I suspect he could have been the lady's husband. The tall trolley girl, who could have been their daughter, had finished for the day and sat with them. She had a pretty face but was at least five stone overweight and wore an ill-fitting uniform – perhaps they don't make uniforms for her physique! The chef and his girl friend, Yanetskia the waitress, sat smoking cigarettes, which is permitted in the dining car and corridors but not in any compartment.

I discovered later that they were not employees of Russian Rail, as the catering part of railway system is privatised and operates independently. I wondered if, and where, they would replenish their stocks? This train was going all the way to Vladivostok on the Sea of Japan, which would not be reached until next Sunday, and although this was only Tuesday night, they were already short of supplies!

By Train to Shanghai

Thinking about the train driver, his assistant, the mechanics, and the eighteen *provodnitsas* - what is their work schedule? Later, I found out they work for fourteen consecutive days and then get the next fourteen off. In other words the train driver and crew take this train to Vladivostok without a break, and after a short stay, take it back to Moscow which means a round trip of 18,578 kilometres. If they do it twelve times per annum, that equates to an awful lot of kilometres, maybe not compared to an airline pilot, but the equivalent to quite a few times round the globe!

Walking back along the corridor towards my cabin, I noticed that the Dutch had displayed a map on the door of compartment number four. This showed the rail route to Irkutsk and someone had highlighted our current position on it, which confirmed that we were shortly to arrive in the city of Novosibirsk.

During the night we crossed over the seven-span, 870 metre-long, Ob River Bridge. This mighty river flows for 5,400 kilometres from its source in the Altai Mountains all the way north, before its confluence with the River Irtysh and then flowing into the Arctic Ocean. The Ob-Irtysh is the world's fourth longest river, after the Nile, Amazon and Yangtze. The Ob River creates a major problem with flooding – because whilst its lower reaches remain frozen the upper lengths will have already thawed in spring - resulting in vast areas being flooded, which in turn creates large areas of permanent and impassable marshes.

The now defunct Siberian river diversion scheme is a classic example of man's until recently unchallenged belief in his right to meddle with nature with impunity. Plans were developed in the 1970s for an expensive system of dams and canals. These would divert water from the north-flowing rivers, Ob and Irtysh, flowing "wastefully in the Arctic Ocean," south instead, to the parched republics in Central Asia. The so called "project of the century" was due to begin in the late 1980s but was halted, largely by scientific protest and attacked in the media for its unfeasibility, huge cost and enormous environmental damage. In view of the ecological disaster area around the Aral Sea, perhaps it is not surprising.

Novosibirsk is a city on the Ob River, which didn't exist at all until the arrival of the Trans-Siberian Railway. A small settlement sprung up in 1891 for the workers building the mighty bridge and from that, a large city has emerged of nearly two million people, which was renamed Novosibirsk or "New Siberia" in 1925. Thereafter the population increased as the factories and furnaces were built for the iron ore and coal that was mined nearby. During the Second World War, civilians and factories were moved here away from European Russia and today it is the major industrial city of Siberia.

At this stage we were 3,343 kilometres from Moscow and here is the junction where trains branch off to Kazakhstan, an alternative route into Urumqi in China. Recently it was announced that a new Siberia to China highway was in the planning stage. The plan is to build a road via Tuva into West Mongolia, then on to its capital Ulaan Baatar, to join up with the highway into Beijing. If that materialises, I wonder what effect will it have on this railway line?

Sometimes you forget the extraordinary achievements of thousands of men who carved this track through a hostile environment, using only the technology of the 19th century!

By Train to Shanghai

Wednesday 18th May

The platform at Marlinsk was deserted of *babushkas* as the train pulled into our next stop. Not surprising perhaps because it was 7a.m. local time – which meant we were now four hours ahead of Moscow time and the distance travelled was 3,680 kilometres. Shortly after we stopped, a green commuter train arrived on the opposite track. Its passengers alighted and quickly dispersed in all directions – as happens during rush hour all over the world.

It was the start of another beautiful day and enjoyed stretching my legs in the sunshine with a few lengths of the platform. So far I seem able to manage with very little sleep, no more than five hours at a time, whereas my fellow travellers, particularly Sasha, seem to need a lot more. At times during the night, it can be difficult to sleep when the train is travelling at full speed as we get tossed around in our bunks. This morning however, Bridgette also was up early – she was complaining that the air in the compartment was foul - perhaps not surprising after last nights beef stroganoff!

Walking up and down the platform, I noticed the train had become much smaller and was now down to ten carriages. During the night, probably at Novosibirsk up to eight carriages had been un-coupled. Two men, who I presume were our travelling mechanics, walked along on either side of the train, banging iron bars against the bogies. I assumed it was some sort of safety check for any possible damage and the ding-dong, ding-dong noise this made sounded as if from a smithy's forge.

This was a fifteen-minute stop and on rejoining the train I walked along the corridor towards the *samover* to get some boiling water to make a cup of tea. One of the compartment doors had opened and coming from within, I heard some very noisy snoring, which sounded like the dawn chorus. Looking in I saw the three corpulent Dutch men snoring away in harmony. They were so well orchestrated the noise sounded like a Wagnerian overture and was truly world class!

At 3,932 kilometres the train passed the white obelisk marking the halfway point between Moscow and Beijing on the route via Ulaan Baatar. The landscape had also changed. Gone was the greenery of the Urals, and the terrain had become much browner from being covered in snow for many months, and which had only recently melted with the late arrival of spring in this part of the world. We were now deep in the Siberian *steppe*, which varies according to the time of year. With the exception of a few solitary birch trees, some grass and a few herbaceous plants of a sturdy nature, nothing much grows here – there is just too much salt in the soil, and the lakes.

Nikolai Gogol who was born in Ukraine of Cossack parents wrote eloquently about the green virgin wilderness of the *steppe* and its millions of different coloured flowers in his story *"Taras Bulba"*. That was in the 19th century but much has changed since then – the flowers have become extinct and now the human population is dense, particularly in the west.

The endless *steppe*, is a flat and treeless plain, an enormous expanse of grassland, nearly 1,000 kilometres wide in places that lies south of the *taiga*. It stretches uninterruptedly all the way from the lower Danube basin, through the Ukraine

By Train to Shanghai

and the south of European Russia and on eastwards across Kazakhstan to the Altai hills of southern Siberia. Further east is the Mongolian *steppe* and isolated patches along the Chinese border. It has its own totally different wildlife, its own land use, history, peoples, cultures, settlement patterns and environmental problems.

From time immemorial, nomadic tribes have wandered the *steppe*, seeking pastures for their flocks, whilst the Cossacks developed their renowned horsemanship here on these flat plains. 1929 saw Stalin begin the forced collectivisation of agriculture, which merged 25 million peasants across the country into about 200,000 enormous collective farms. The peasants rebelled and millions of them were dispossessed and sent to distant labour camps whilst millions more died from the consequent famine. Considering that the great mass of the Ukraine *steppe* is *chernozen*, the black earth, some of the richest topsoil in the world, the folly of Stalin's policy can be viewed.

It was then on to the industrialised and not very attractive city of Krasnoyarsk. Apart from the railway station with its colourful mural of Lenin, and a small but beautiful gold-domed church, sandwiched between hideous blocks of flats – there is little to admire. On leaving Krasnoyarsk, the train crosses the mighty Yeniseh Bridge, over the Yeniseh River which is reputed to be a full kilometres wide. This new bridge is a recent replacement for the original award winning structure built in 1898.

There was just not enough time to break my journey here but had I done, then the delights of a trip north on the Yeniseh would have been possible. In summer months it is possible to travel all the way to the Arctic Ocean, on passenger boats that ply the river, which Anton Chekhov believed was the most beautiful he had ever seen in the world.

This amazing journey north is through an almost impenetrable *taiga* wilderness of spruce and larch trees. Multitude of wildlife nest along its banks, whilst in the forest, bears, sables, wolves and Siberian polecat roam. Halfway along its course is the Central Siberian Nature Reserve, a totally uninhabited reserve of crystal clear rivers, where mammals and birds live a protected existence.

The Meakins also stopped here and travelled south on the river. With the aid of horses, they proceeded to Lake Tschuro, which was famed for the medicinal qualities of its water. A Russian lady recommended the Meakins go there, as thousands of Siberians do every year for their health, and thousands of Siberians can't be wrong!

Their return journey to Krasnoyarsk was to remind them of Britain, because here, in the middle of central Russia, was a vessel called the "Scotia". Built in Scotland, it was originally, a sea-going pleasure yacht, and was described as a tough little ship. It was one of the two that made their way the thousands of miles from England, down the mighty Yenisey River from the Arctic Ocean.

Whilst in the area, the Meakins also had time to visit the Alexandrovsk prison, which was an eighty-kilometre journey by *tarantass*. Their journey took 7 hour with a change of horses three times. Before the arrival of the railway, the *tarantass* was not exactly the most comfortable way to travel. Annette

By Train to Shanghai

described the jolting of a *tarantass* as something that must be experienced in order to be understood and that the first hour or so brings one to the conclusion that, by the end of the journey, the body will be a mass of bruises. However, she soon discovered that the art of *tarantass* travel was to sit with your chin resting on your knees, which means the spine, is least affected by the motion.

During the prison visit, the governor announced that one of the inmates was an Englishman, and he came at once when called. Annette chatted briefly with the chap and discovered he originally hailed from Glasgow but had spent some years in the Whitechapel district of London. He was rather dour and said there was no one to whom he wanted a message sent. Apparently he had been a soldier in Riga and therefore thought he could never return to England. He said he was reasonably comfortable at the prison, confirmed that she was the first English woman he had seen for ten years and then promptly asked her for some money. Annette gave him a trifle, was much impressed by what she had seen, and left.

The 4,000 kilometres Yeniseh marks the boundary between the great western plain and the Central Siberian Plateau. West of the river the winter climate is moderated by the warmer weather systems of the Atlantic, but still very cold. The plateau prevents the moderating air reaching the area east, where high pressure lasts for most of the winter. As a result, east of the river, winter temperatures can be as low as minus 70C, whilst during the short hot summer, rise to 30C. In harsh conditions like this, which also sees a change of animals as well - the Daurian larch dominates where few other trees could survive. These trees are deciduous with shallow spreading roots, shedding their leaves in winter to prevent any water loss, which helps their survival.

To the north of Krasnoyarsk is the Russian space centre but, for obvious reasons, it's off-limits to the public. To the south is the Tuva Republic, formerly part of the Chinese Empire in the 19th century - it is inhabited by the Tuvans who are Turkic speaking people of Tibetan Buddhist origin and closely related to the Mongols.

At Ilanskaya, there was a fifteen-minute stop but the guidebook recommends that 'no photographs be taken because of a recent bad experience by a tourist'. Caught snapping the water-tower and commemorative plaque, he was promptly arrested and accused of spying and then watched as his train left, without him, but with his luggage! The police eventually released him without charge, but the next train consisted entirely of *platskartny* carriages.

Continuing our journey, the landscape changed to rolling hills and scattered green-roofed houses, whose occupants seemed totally oblivious to passing trains and more interested in their farm animals - but without the normal joyousness which is usually apparent with most people when the day's work is done. At this point the train speed slowed considerably because of the twisting bends making its familiar rhythmic clackety-clack sound. It was early afternoon and the time had advanced five hours ahead of Moscow time, and by the time we arrived at Tayshet, we had travelled 4,483 kilometres.

This is the westernmost junction with the BAM line. Passengers can change here for the BAM line or Baikal-Amur-Mainline, to give it its correct title. The BAM train travels east from here for 2,500 kilometres, north of Lake Baikal and many consider it a more scenic route as it climbs over densely forested, mountainous terrain along switchbacks and through many tunnels. At one stage the train actually crosses the top of a gigantic one kilometre-long dam on the Angara River with spectacular views from both sides.

Tayshet was established in 1897 when the railway arrived and was infamous as a transit point for Gulag prisoners. Already abolished at the start of the 20th century, Stalin brought the system back with a vengeance. This was when Siberia became synonymous with death and an estimated 20 million died in these Gulags. It was not difficult to become an inmate of the Gulag, even association could send you to a life of cutting trees, digging canals, working in factories, or laying railway track in remote areas of Siberia. This was a full-blown, home-grown slave trade.

The rest of the day passed quite quickly. Sasha, as usual remained in his upper bunk, and Bridgette read a book. By now everyone just waited for the morning and arrival at Irkutsk - and a much-needed shower! The French girls politely declined my invitation to the restaurant car and as I walked along the corridor, the map outside compartment four was updated to show our arrival at Nizhneudinsk, some 4,678 kilometres from Moscow.

The dining car had an air of the last nights of the Proms about it. As was to be expected for this last dinner, there was very little to choose from the menu and I opted for the borsch. The three corpulent Dutch men seemed to be enjoying their beef stroganoff – and I couldn't help thinking they were welcome to it! I have re-named them the front-row, as they would make a formidable trio in a game of rugby. Alexi joined me and as usual, was well inebriated having spent the entire day boozing. He boasted about his ability to speak fluent German, Polish and Danish, but as became apparent, his English was rather limited - so we drank instead. Alexi was typical of those Russians whose character few people can sum-up, as it seems to be a mass of contradictions.

A Russian can at the same time be warm-hearted and cruel, fearful, yet also reckless, hospitable and xenophobic, emotional and inhibited. They themselves speak of their broad nature and admit they are a blend of Oriental and European. By nature they are conservative and believe the way laid down in earlier days is best. In Russia, almost every conceivable thing a man might do is regulated by the written law. This Russian idea of governing the people is in direct opposition to the conceptions of the West.

With us, everything that the law does not expressly forbid is permitted. Whereas in Russia, everything is forbidden that the law does not expressly grant - which means next to nothing. As the light faded outside, apart from myself the only people left in the dining carriage were Russians including the dining car staff as well as the trolley girl who had finished for the day and was busy checking her list of unsold items and completing her inventory.

I watched one goods train after another pass by, some with up to a hundred wagons. This was indeed an important commercial line, as well as carrying an assortment of some five hundred passengers on this train along towards Irkutsk. We were still travelling through Siberia. The very name inspires awe and dread and with its vast expanses of tundra and virgin forests, its mountains, deserts and *steppe* has some of the richest fauna and flora in the world. It is also a land of enormous natural wealth, a vast unexploited reserve of oil, coal, gold, iron ore and every other natural resource. Siberia has been isolated for thousands of years but its inhabitants have a tough frontier spirit about them, and are proud of their enduring approach.

They have a saying "minus thirty is no frost, two hundred kilometres is no distance". Russians take pride in the fact that their harsh winters defeated both Napoleon and Hitler and believe they are better equipped physically to survive extreme cold than foreigners. They even have a popular dark anecdote about it - What is good for a Russian spells death for a German!

Finally, it was time to say good night and goodbye to everyone, starting with the matriarchal lady who was still perched imperiously in the same seat. Then I made my way round the rest of the catering staff, - I had enjoyed very much their dining car and the pleasant hours spent in this social centre, even if its gastronomic qualities were still in question. My last farewell was for Alexi – he may be a drunk, our conversation may have been limited by language difficulties – but he was an amusing man!

As I retired to my bunk for the last time, the train continued making its familiar clackety-clack sound and I was reminded of Robert Louis Stevenson's famous few lines: The speed is so easy, and the train disturbs so little the scenes through which it takes us, that our heart becomes full of the placidity and stillness of the country: and while the body is borne forward in the flying chain of carriages, the thoughts alight, as the humour moves them, at unfrequented stations: they make haste up the poplar alley that leads towards the town: they are left behind with the signalman as, shading his eyes with his hand, he watches the long train sweep away into the golden distance.

Chapter Four
Lake Baikal

Thursday, 19th May

During the night we passed the foothills of the Sayan Mountains with its endless pine forests of the *taiga*, and the train slowed down as it swept round bend after bend. Dawn was breaking when we arrived at our last major stop, Zima, which means winter. Again, I had been the last to retire and was again the first to arise this morning, and in the company of just one fellow traveller, went for a walk along the deserted platform with not one *babushka* in sight. The same ritual was taking place with the mechanics checking the bogies and in the calm of the early morning their banging noise created its own echo while the *provodnitsas* washed the white door handles as they do at most major stops. Then it was off again, this time shadowing the Angara River. As the train approached Irkutsk, it crossed the River Irkut from which it derives its name. There was a buzz of excitement.

Our seemingly 'tired' Russian companion, Sasha, an air force officer, was excited to be returning home, while Bridgette and Sidonie made themselves beautiful and packed up their luggage. After four nights cramped together, we had got on well, shared food and stories but it was now time to move on. We all looked forward to more space and a good shower but I definitely had nostalgic feelings about leaving the train, but coming to my senses realized that if I'd stayed on board, it would mean another three day's travelling as it was heading for Vladivostock on the Sea of Japan.

I said thanks and *dosvi danie* to our blond *provodnitsa*, and *au revoir* to Bridgette and Sidonie as I hoped to meet them later on in Mongolia. This train number 10 had travelled 5,185 kilometres and arrived at precisely 9.30a.m. local time – precisely as the Russian timetable stated, travelling at an average speed of 63 kilometres per hour and no - unscheduled stops. I couldn't help thinking British railway companies might learn a thing or two from the Russians! Our journey was slightly faster than Michael Myers Shoemaker's in 1902, who wrote "all day long at a dog trot. Certainly no more than ten miles an hour". R. L. Jefferson wrote that at meal times, the train would stop at a convenient station and all passengers including the train driver would get off for a meal at the station. These early travellers experienced all too frequent breakdowns including twenty-four hour waits for a new engine - but this had not been regarded as a long delay.

Annette Meakin recorded an incident outside Kansk where the train had stopped and a Russian sailor commented in broken English, "She is sixty years old and was made in Glasgow. She is no use any more." Then the poor old engine was towed to her last berth and Annette whipped out her "Kodak" and took a photograph. Because the original line was so badly laid, sometimes it was rough and uncomfortable and the train speed had to be restricted. She complained of the frequent stopping at a great many stations on some parts of the route, getting into a chronic state of stopping. Over some sections it was reported that as the train went so slowly, passengers could get out and pick flowers as they walked along beside it. However, these delays meant some respite and time to catch up on current affairs as Annette observed whilst delayed for four hours at Taiga Station. She writes, "As we sat waiting in the station the good news was brought that Mafeking had been relieved."!

In 1898, Irkutsk was connected to European Russia when the Trans-Siberian Railway arrived here. This was a big improvement from travelling on the Old Post Road in wooden *tarantasses* and the discomfort that entailed. The city was founded as a military outpost by a tax collector who tried to squeeze taxes from the local fur traders. Being on the caravan route from China it quickly established itself as the capital of Siberia and a number of famous exiles re-located here, which helped its development.

Gold was discovered in 1800 and this produced the usual boomtown effect - the usual boom and bust associated with this phenomena. Later, in the century a major fire destroyed most of the city but in spite of this, Irkutsk still maintained itself as the cultural and financial centre of Siberia, whose population now included fur traders, gold prospectors, tea merchants and exiles as well as ex-convicts.

My guide Tatyana was on hand to meet me at the end of the platform and we headed for the village of Listvyanka, some sixty kilometres away on the edge of Lake Baikal. Irkutsk used to be described as the Paris of eastern Siberia, but from what I had seen of it so far, I could not understand how it could possibly have earned that reputation - but I would have an opportunity to review my opinion in a few days time. Right now I was on my way to see the " Pearl of Siberia "- Lake Baikal.

As we drove along the road, Tatyana asked me what I thought of the highway and, slightly perplexed said it was excellent. She then explained how this famous highway came about and related its history. In 1960 when Dwight D. Eisenhower was President of America, it was rumoured that he had found relatives living in Irkutsk. The road at the time had merely been no more than a dirt track, so if the American President were to come here it was natural that he would want to visit Lake Baikal – and at a greater speed than a couple of kilometres an hour. In anticipation, of his visit, the locals built a new highway - however fate intervened when an American airman, Gary Powers who was doing a little spying in his U.2 Aircraft, was shot down by the Russians. Eventually exchanged for another spy the Americans had been holding but the whole incident soured relationships between America and Russia. As a result, Eisenhower's visit proposed or otherwise never took place but the compensation for the locals was a brand new highway. However, I could not find anyone else to verify the truth of this tale!

Tatyana was forty years old and also a schoolteacher. She had two children and had been doing this work for thirteen years to earn some extra money. In winter, when tourists are few and far between, she takes part in cross-country skiing, which is very popular here with plenty of snow. After travelling for an hour through endless forest, there appeared over the horizon a seemingly endless vista to reveal a huge lake glistening in the mid-day sun. This was an impressive sight with snow-capped mountain ranges on the east side looking more like a mirage than reality. There was no sign of the ice on which George had said he had walked on just a few weeks ago. Perhaps it had melted in the meantime.

Lake Baikal is called the "Blue Eye of Siberia" or as the Russian song describes it "majestic ocean, holy Baikal", is the largest lake in the world and shaped like a banana. It is over one mile deep on the western side, 630 kilometres from north to south but only 60 kilometres wide. It is twenty million years old and contains one-fifth of the world's fresh water. Formed by a collision of two tectonic plates, scientists predict it will eventually become the earth's fifth ocean, when the plates separate thus splitting the Asian continent. But they do not predict when this is likely to happen.

We arrived in the small tourist village of Listvyanka on the shores of the crystal clear waters of Lake Baikal. A lone ferry was arriving at the small ferry port as we went to find number 16, Sudzeilovskogo Road in a picturesque area called Krestovka which was to be my home for the next couple of days. Zoya, who owns the house is a charming widow of Buryat extraction who had children and grandchildren living nearby. Buryats are the largest native Asiatic peoples of Siberia and ethnically connected to the Mongolians. They are also descended from the Huns whose infamous leader, Attila, pillaged his way across Europe as far as Paris.

Zoya prepared an excellent lunch of omul fish, which is white, one of the salmon specie and Baikal's main "delicacy". After lunch, Tatyana and I set off on a tour of the village, where most of the buildings were of wooden construction, although there are some new concrete structures along the shore road, and in between these are other buildings of exotic Russian design. We paid the mandatory visit to the local St. Nicholas Orthodox Church and luckily there was a religious ceremony taking place at the time.

I did not know very much about the Russian Orthodox Church so I asked Tatyana about its origin. Explaining that God is never far from a Russian's life and everyday expressions mentioning God are as common in Russia as they are in English. To trace its history she said it was necessary to go back to Prince Vladimir of Kiev, who embraced the religion of Byzantium in Constantinople in 988, just over one thousand years ago and established Christian Orthodoxy as the religion of the Russian-speaking people. An offshoot of the Greek Orthodox Church, it thrived until a few centuries later when the Mongols changed everything as Russia came under Mongol influence before Ivan the Terrible threw off the "Mongol yoke" with the capture of Kazan and forced the Khan to become a Christian in 1552. During the 15th century, connections with the Greek parent church were severed and in the 18th century the Church fell increasingly under state control. Everything changed after the 1917 revolution when the communists denounced religion and therefore the political influence of the Russian Orthodox Church.

The Bolsheviks confronted the Church and inaugurated a period of unparalleled persecution because of its close identification with the old Tsarist regime, accusing it of siding with the ruling classes In Tsarist days, there were 60,000 priests plus 100,000 monks and nuns serving nearly 60,000 churches and monasteries but today, as a result of purges by Stalin and Khrushchev, who between them had thousands of priests executed, the number was down to a few thousand. There was a similar fate for the churches and monasteries - they were closed down and left to decay. The more famous churches including St. Isaac's Cathedral in St. Petersburg and the ancient churches in Moscow's Kremlin became museums. But the Second World War brought a sudden change, when Stalin used the Church to help rally support against the Nazi invaders. Churches were re-opened and new regulations were drawn up defining the legal position of churchgoers thus giving the Church a better basis on which to exist.

Yet all this did not break the will of the people and since *perestroika* the Church is now witnessing an extraordinary revival. It is coming back from the abyss and thousands are now returning to the religion of their forefathers, and Russian Orthodoxy is one of the world's largest and most influential divisions of Christianity. Tatyana explained, that to be in this church today, during the ceremony, gave her a sense of eternal Russia, and with its beauty and ritual a sense of history, a great spiritual fulfilment. One other ritual that did not change after the revolution was the date of Christmas Day, which still remains January 6th, unlike the rest of the secular calendar, which reverted to December 25th.

Also, back in Tsarist days when the first trains began to run on the Trans-Siberian line, the train themselves carried a peculiar carriage behind the baggage car, which was known as the church car. This was the Russian Orthodox Church on wheels, complete with icons and candelabra, church bells, and even a cross on the roof, and of course, a travelling priest who dispensed blessings along the journey. It also provided the spiritual wellbeing for railway workers and their families, as the carriage was detached at stations and settlements, where churches had not yet been built.

Walking further along the lake we arrived at the Baikal Limnological Institute, which also houses a museum. This institute studies the lake ecosystems and the fifty or so different fish in the lake, some living at the bottom, over a mile down. The museum also houses an extensive section dealing with the history of the lake as well as having two live mother and daughter freshwater seals happily swimming around in their tank. There are around 60,000 seals in the lake and rarely seen except on the ice in winter in the remote Ushkany Islands. They are believed to have migrated to Baikal in the ice age, swimming up the river systems from the Arctic.

The whole area around Lake Baikal is designated a National Park but it is not on the international tourist route, mainly because of its inaccessibility, but other than travellers on the Trans-Siberian Railway who frequently visit here, Russians themselves do use this gem of a place for their holidays. Arriving at Listvyanka and travelling a few kilometres north, there is a place called Bolshie Koty - which roughly translates as "big boots". Here, visitors can hike along the lakeshore, or walk around rocky cliffs above the lake which gives spectacular views of the water below. A further 80 kilometres north is the village of Bukhta Peschanaya, which means sandy bay, and it really is one. It is served by a hydrofoil service out of Irkutsk during the summer months.

One hundred and fifty kilometres along the western shore from Bukhta is the large island of Olkhon, which is seventy kilometres long. This narrow island has only one permanent settlement, a fishing village and to arrive here by road, it is a tough eight-hour bus trip over pot-holed roads to Sakhyurta, and then a ferry crossing to the island. But for those who suffer it, they will find a beautiful island, filled with lakes in the centre and a dramatic coastline of cliffs. In places the ancient silver and spruce firs are thirty metres tall forming a fine stretch of *taiga* sweeping down from the mountains to the edge of the lake.

On the eastern shore of Lake Baikal is the Selenga River, which is the longest of the 336 rivers that flow into the lake. The Selenga rises in Mongolia, and after crossing the frontier, waters the most fertile valleys along its journey and forms a waterway between Russia and China. It was also used extensively for transporting tea from China in the 20th century. From here, the remainder of the eastern shore is relatively virgin territory, uninhabited even by the Buryats in their own republic, and is the least explored. However, in the Barguzin Reserve, which was established in 1916, sables survive. These animals are an almost exclusively Siberian animal with dark brown fur, which were almost extinct due to relentless trapping. Thanks to the reserve, several thousand now thrive both within and outside as well as being home to bears and the elegant flying squirrels. Beyond the reserve, the shoreline continues for another few hundred kilometres until it reaches the city of Severobaikalsk at the top of the northern end of the lake. This city did not exist until the arrival of the BAM Railway in 1970, linking it up with Irkutsk. The crossing of the hydroelectric station at Bratsk is a marvel of Russian engineering, notwithstanding the effects on the environment, which has been exasperated by local factories dumping their waste into the pristine lake. It is to be hoped that recent conservation measures will preserve this priceless jewel, albeit not in its former beauty.

As if this dumping of waste wasn't bad enough, I have heard that Russia is poised to ignore ecologists complaints and construct what will be the world's longest oil pipeline along the northern shore of Lake Baikal, a distance of over 4,000 kilometres from Tayshet in eastern Siberia to the Sea of Japan. Tatyana told me that environmentalists have warned that an oil spill would pour 4,000 tons of oil into the lake in just twenty minutes, causing irreparable damage. But the Russian government is impatient for construction to begin and has given the environmentalists concerns short shrift. It seems the lucrative prospect of hundreds of millions of pounds going to the Russian treasury for supplying oil to China, Japan and South Korea, far outweighs the sanctity of a Unesco World Heritage Site.

The plan is to lay a stretch of the pipeline close to Lake Baikal in order to follow the Baikal-Amur railway line which skirts the northern shore, making the construction work cheaper but Green groups have warned that this puts the lake's protected status at risk. These groups have warned that the pipeline is a catastrophe waiting to happen to a lake holding twenty per cent of the planet's fresh water, and a rich store of bio-diversity, with many animal and plant species, many of them endemic.

Commenting on the beauty of Lake Baikal and the danger of pollution, Annette Meakin wrote in 1900 that, as a lover of nature, she had herself seen the desolation wrought by naphtha wells on the Caspian Sea, a region that was producing more than 50 per cent of the globe's oil at the time. She shuddered at the thought that one day, the beautiful shores of the Baikal might be polluted by the presence of a "black town" and the sweet country air rendered noxious by the smell of petroleum. How ironic - that 105 years later, her warnings are again being repeated by modern-day ecologists.

Finally, it was time to return to the house and I discovered Zoya had prepared a *banya*, especially for me. *Banyas* are very traditional in Siberia and hers was situated at the end of the garden. Similar to a sauna, this was now a good opportunity to remove four days of face stubble, thoroughly relax, and then have a good nights sleep on terra firma - in a comfortable bed and far away from clattering trains.

Friday 20th May

Zoya was up early to prepare my breakfast whilst enjoying a leisurely lie-in. Today, there was a choice of leisure activities - either a fishing trip on the lake, or a trek in the forest - I plumped for the latter. The travel people who had arranged my overall itinerary prefer to arrange homestays, as it helps the local economy in remote places like eastern Siberia and it is difficult to argue against this. It also gives you an insight into the living conditions of these people and how they live - particularly during the winter months. Although it was late spring and the snow had melted, I tried to anticipate what it would be like next January when the white stuff would return again, and the temperature could possibly plunge to minus 40 -degrees, as it did in the year 2000.

Eating a typical Buryat breakfast, I studied the layout of Zoya's wooden house. It was heated by a large stove in the centre of the house where she burned wood, as there's a plentiful supply. The stove was not only for cooking and heating it also provided a central brick column support for the roof. The remainder of the house was, quite literally, built around it and hanging on to the brick column! The windows were certainly well insulated and the house had a double door entrance through a small hallway. Presumably, one door is opened at a time in order to exclude the chill Siberian air from getting inside the house. This style of house is called an *izba*, a traditional log-timbered type, which was brought to Siberia by the Russians.

Slava, my guide for the day arrived promptly at 10.30 a.m. He had come from Irkutsk where he lived and worked as a teacher in mathematics. He was about forty years old and spoke English in a slow deliberate way as if searching for words. In his spare time he acted as a mountain guide and told me that two more English people would be joining us for our trek in the forest. A young Geordie couple, David and Helen, duly arrived with heavy rucksacks in tow.

I soon discovered they were staying with Olga at number 11, and had rented out their flat in London E.7, given up their well-paid jobs, and were at the beginning of a six-month sabbatical ending somewhere is Asia. I had come well prepared against mosquitoes but was slightly surprised when Slava told me there was no mosquito problem during the month of May, but there was a major *tick* problem during the months of May and June. To me, tick is getting extended credit from your pub landlord! However, here in Siberia, *tick* has a much more sinister meaning. It is a dreadful little, blood-sucking parasite, which is responsible for transmitting a wide range of diseases including typhus, to mammals. If it settles on your skin it implodes its own blood into your system. Encephalitis results if not treated quickly, and it eventually affects the whole nervous system of the body.

So we all prepared meticulously against this *tick* menace, which meant covering up all exposed body parts other than the face and hands, and spraying all our clothing and exposed flesh with *anti-tick* spray. Slava, was carrying a huge rucksack and later discovered that it included a tent as well as food and water. The tent was for David and Helen, who planned to camp overnight on the shore of the lake.

Our trek began with a gradual up-hill climb lead by Slava and the rest of us followed in Indian file. After an hour or so we arrived at Slava's normal lunch place in the forest as the young couple appeared to be struggling, and I was the least out of breath. After a moment of feeling rather smug, I had to remember it was not only humid but they were carrying heavy rucksacks! There, we discovered the whole area a mess, with fires still burning. On investigation, it seems someone had set fire to an anthill and it in turn had spread the fire around the whole area with whole trees burning. Slava expressed his disquiet about the wanton damage and destruction but more importantly, the humble little ant is superior to the tick. It seems that where ants live the tick will not be found, and there must be a moral in this story.

Slava, explained that the number of fires has greatly increased and the culprit is nearly always man and told us that a recent annual statistic of 30,000 forest fires were recorded across the country, almost all in the taiga. This is poor gratitude considering that the forest has always yielded most of man's needs: animals and birds for the pot, bark for shoes, wax for candles, hides for leather and honey for consumption.

Despite this mini inferno and its gnawing pong, we stopped here and Slava prepared an impromptu lunch from food that he brought along. He quickly lit a small well controlled fire and filled his pot from the nearby stream to make some tea. Whilst sipping my tea, I raised my head and could only see a scrap of sky between the tops of the giant trees. The impression is that one is at the bottom of a woody canyon, separated from the outer world by endless high trees. Other than the cracking of burning trees, the solemn silence was only occasionally interrupted by the shrill cries of nutcrackers and the hollow drumming knocks of woodpeckers, Though it is quiet and silent, the dense *taiga* was full of life.

We all enjoyed his lunch, checked our bodies for any tick bites and set off again. At a cross road of paths, one heading up, the other heading down, Slava enquired again if I would like to take the easy option, but in good boy scout's tradition, I declined. In view of my difficulties later, this was the worst decision I'd made in the entire trip … so far! We climbed higher and as we neared the highest point, it started to rain. From here it was now downhill all the way to the lake's shore where David and Helen planned to camp for the night. It was easy going up, but what goes up must come down. This was the most difficult part! Downhill, and down a very sharp gradient was where I tweaked a ligament in my left knee.

We carried on, but I had difficulty keeping up with the others as my knee became very painful. Wondering what would have happened had I done something more serious and had been unable to walk at all. How to get out of here? Air ambulance was very unlikely in this remote area, and I imagine rather pricey. At least I did have an insurance policy but doubted it would stretch to a spin in a chopper. These thoughts were rather alarming and luckily I wasn't in too bad a way, and anyway, didn't want to dwell on them, but perhaps I should have considered this possibility before starting out.

After about an hour walking slowly downhill, we finally reached the waters edge. Slava proceeded to pitch his tent on the shale by the waters edge and what a relief it must have been for him - having carried it since the start of the day. When the tent was up, it was time to say goodbye to my new English friends who were now going to camp here overnight. As I watched them organise themselves I was reminded of Yeats' famous poem. *The Lake Isle of Innisfree* and a few of its lines came to mind, "I will arise and go now, for always night and day, I hear lake water lapping with low sounds by the shore".

I asked Slava how much further we had to go to the village and was unpleasantly surprised by his reply. "About one and a half hours, except only this time, it would be up and down over four different mountains", he said. Not really mountains but sizeable hills. This was not what I, nor my painful knee wanted to hear, and as we prepared to set off, I listened to his "if only" story. This referred to travel in the old days before Mr Khruschev decided to build a dam on the nearby Angara River. Back then, there used to be a road from here all along the lake to Listvyanka, but the dam meant raising the water level in Lake Baikal - and the road is now history. There was no alternative but to set off on our perilous journey where one slip meant certain death, falling 600 metres to the lake below. Wondering, why on earth had I volunteered for this trekking when the alternative was a leisurely boat trip on the lake?

We started back, rather slowly, and especially slowly, on the dangerous parts, which resulted in a terrifying, slithering, two-hour odyssey on ground, which was still damp from the recent rain. At times there were small trees which I clung to for support, but my slip-slide-sore-knee advance took all my concentration - not helped by occasionally looking down over my left shoulder and the sheer drop down to eternity. Finally, we left the forest and arrived on a concrete road close to an electricity pylon and safety.

Shortly afterwards, Slava said goodbye having established I could find my way back to the village from here. He told me he was returning to David and Helen by the same route I'd just managed. "What on earth for", I asked. "To cook dinner for them, of course", he replied. Is there no end to Russian hospitality?

I hobbled to the village without further incident and passed its little market, which had just opened. There were many stalls selling anything from fish to souvenirs, and I noticed one stall in particular – not only because of its lovely onyx *objects d'art*, but also the lovely girl running it. She was very pretty and went over for a chat. In her beautiful, gravely Russian accent she told me she was of Cossack extraction and explained how life was very tough for people living here. Having endured the long dreary Siberian winter, she has to make enough money to survive by selling goods to tourists from now until September, when the season will finish again.

She was lithe and tall, held her head aloft, and looked at me so innocently from her lovely grey-blue eyes. Her clear gipsy complexion was illuminated by the strings of many coloured beads, worn round her neck. Amongst them was a handsome amber necklace hanging down which added even more to her beauty. She had a mass of rich golden hair tied loosely in two plaits at the back of her neck. My only regret was not being able to buy any of her souvenirs, because they were all heavy and I did not want to burden myself with more weight. But I will long remember her beauty and that enchanting voice.

Walking slightly better now – obviously a few minutes with a pretty girl does wonders for forgetting one's pain – I continued through the village and down Sudzeilovoskogo Road where I met Zoya coming in the opposite direction. She had been out looking for me because that little trek in the forest of only twelve kilometres had in fact taken eight hours! I was now two hours late for dinner and the delightful Zoya had been genuinely worried about me. We went to her house and whilst doing a thorough *tick* check, Zoya set up the *banja* for me and afterwards cooked an excellent dinner. I was tired and sore but my knee had survived the day.

Feeling well restored, later in the evening and just before darkness, I strolled down to the lake. There was a full moon with just one star nearby for company and both were reflected in the lake's water. There was little traffic around but the young of the village were getting ready for their Friday night out. Apart from the odd car, the only noise I could hear came from dogs barking as I wandered along the shore road in search of a bar I'd noticed earlier. It was a noisy establishment and was crowded mostly with young locals, but in one corner I spotted some of the Germans from the Moscow train, and having recognised me, they invited me to join their table.

In their company was their Buryat guide, Julya and we chatted about her Asiatic ancestors who have lived in Siberia long before the Russian settlers arrived from the west, and who were a nomadic Buddhist people with strong trends in *shamanism*. I had heard about this phenomenon but did not know much about it. Julya explained that this whole area of Siberia and Mongolia is native for *shamanism*. The *shaman* is the chosen one, chosen by the spirit, the go-between who journeys from our world into the spirit world, who asks for help from their spirit world, for ours. Their principle is a simple one: everything, and everyone, has a guardian spirit. In times of difficulty, the shaman can be asked to go to those spirits and plead with them on our behalf. No one can choose to be a *shaman*, it is the spirit who chooses them to become an emissary of the spirit, but having decided to accept, they become outsiders in their community and suffer emotional strain. Females are called *shamanka* in Russian and have different powers to male *shamans,* as you would expect.

I found it all very confusing, but I suppose it's a bit like Catholicism: you don't fully understand it, but you just want to believe in it.

Stalin, it seems, inflicted great pain and suffering on the *shamans* during his purges of the 1930's, liquidating them, whilst also destroying the Buryat and Mongolian Buddhist monasteries. I thanked Julya for her spiritual lesson and wandered home under the moonlight, with the noise of dogs still barking in the distance.

Saturday 21st May

As usual, Zoya had my breakfast ready and waiting, and as usual – it was delicious. I packed up all my belongings, and as my transport would not arrive for half an hour, had one last walk around the village, and on towards Baikal. This word is not native to the Russian language and the most popular theory is that it is derived from the Buryat word "baigal" meaning "pillar of fire". This was a beautiful windless morning with clear blue skies, but other times the lake is frequently whipped up by great storms. The northeast wind blows along its entire length, whilst the *sarma*, the northwest wind, whips the waves up to a considerable height. Walking back, I noticed the war memorial with nearly a hundred names inscribed on it, all casualties from the Great Patriotic War and buried somewhere between here and Berlin. This was an incredible number for such a small village and seems totally out of proportion to its size. In 1945 - what a devastating effect this must have had on the families living here!

When my transport finally arrived, I said farewell to Zoya and took some photographs of her in front of the house, and what now felt like, my home! On the journey to Irkutsk, on that highway ostensibly built for Dwight D. Eisenhower, we passed some traditional wooden stockade villages on the fringe of the *taiga*. This time I was sharing the bus with a Canadian couple from Vancouver whom we dropped off in a downtown hotel. For this one night in Irkutsk, I was staying at number 17 Chekhov Street a residential area just off the main thoroughfare called Karl Marx Avenue. Opposite number seventeen was a shop called "Sex Supermarket", all lit-up with flashing neon lights – now that I decided, could be useful … should I need to give directions to a taxi driver to get me home!

Olga was due to be my host but instead Kathya, her twenty-two year old daughter, and a student of English and German, greeted me. My bedroom in their apartment was comfortable and perfectly adequate, dumping my luggage and set off to see the city, which used to be known as the Paris of eastern Siberia.

I needed to buy some postcards, and with difficulty, eventually found some in a small bookshop. For some strange reason, the kiosks around the place do not sell them! I then found the post office, and for a few roubles, was able to telephone Kate in London to check her arrangements were on track and that everything was in order for our 'meet up' at Beijing Railway Station, next Friday. I advised her to look out for the greeting board with my name - as the guide book warns that train arrivals from Mongolia can be chaotic, with lots of pushing and shoving. Plans confirmed I set off to discover Irkutsk, which was just like any other city on a hot Saturday afternoon - crowded with shoppers.

I consulted the map and headed north towards the Polish Catholic Church. Of Gothic design, it was built by Polish exiles in the 19th century, and in a good state of repair. The front door was closed but at the side entrance a bell was there to ring for assistance. I wasn't too hopeful, but gave it a quick burst and after quite an interval, an elderly lady appeared at the window and opened it just enough to announce in broken English, "no open today". So I set off to see its next-door neighbour, the Church of the Saviour, which, like the Polish Church, miraculously survived the great fire of Irkutsk of 1879. Apart from its golden domes and icons inside, the outside was decorated with frescos covering every square inch.

By Train to Shanghai

What a splendid building, whilst nearby, stands the impressive war memorial, with its eternal flame, dedicated to the citizens of Irkutsk who died in World War II.

Returning to the city centre along Karl Marx Avenue, I noticed, a man dressed in a full *lederhosen* outfit standing outside what looked like a bar. Initially perplexed, soon discovered there was a perfectly reasonable explanation – advertising! His task was to attract business for the nearby "beer keller", and being both curious, and in need of a drink, went down its basement stairs, past a cloakroom with a female attendant, and into a very modern bar. There were very few customers to be served by the two attractive blond waitresses all dressed up in *dirndl* skirts, but who were indeed Russian.

There was German beer and draught Guinness for sale, but at Bavarian prices. I ordered a Guinness and wondered, with beer on sale in the local kiosks for a few roubles, who, in Irkutsk, a city with twelve universities could afford to drink here, in this over-priced theme bar? Perhaps the answer lies with the Trans-Siberian Railway. A large number of Germans, and most travellers, break their journey in Irkutsk, so perhaps this was a good customer base. In any event maybe the Germans can now be happy that they have a "base" - in Karl Marx Avenue - in Irkutsk - capital of eastern Siberia - having cost the lives of countless millions of Russian lives in Hitler's war of aggression.

This city is famous for its exiles, so it was important to see the two homes of Prince Sergey Trubetskoy and Count Sergey Volkonsky, which are known as the Decembrist Houses and are now museums. Back in 1825, in St Petersburg, these two aristocratic army officers had called on Tsar Nicholas to implement reform and abolish serfdom. On 26th December, the day of the coronation, the "Decembrists" as they became known, occupied Senate Square but were quickly overpowered by loyal troops. The rebels were poorly organised and in some cases misguided, and after a stand off lasting less than a day in which many people were killed, the rebels dispersed. Afterwards, five of the rebels were executed and the remaining one hundred odd were sentenced to hard labour, in exile, in Siberia.

Thus the "Decembrists" became romantic heroes. Having served their sentences they settled in Irkutsk in 1844, and were joined by their wives who had followed their men into exile. These aristocrats played an important part in the city's cultural development, opening schools and establishing newspapers. One of the wives, Maria Volkonskaya, who was known as the Princess of Siberia, established a hospital and theatre here. Sergey Volkonsky, who was a decorated hero from the 1812 victory over Napoleon, is the romantic hero from *War and Peace,* but Tolstoy renamed him Bolkonsky to avoid any problem with the censor of the day. It was a rather touching experience to visit these simple houses, complete with family memorabilia and furnished with pictures of family and friends and numerous exhibits about the lives of their two loyal and loving wives.

Tatyana had recommended a visit to the city market, which I found in full swing when arriving. The idea was to buy some fruit for the next stage of the train journey, and I was spoilt for choice as it was well-stocked with an abundance of fresh produce including lots of horseradish, meats and cheeses, fish

By Train to Shanghai

from the barrel, berries by the bucket - and wild garlic – like the ones I'd seen in the forest yesterday. As I wandered round I felt a bump on my backside and saw a young man, dressed all in black, walk quickly away. He was out of luck if he expected to find my wallet – I'm a cannier traveller than that, but this experience rang a bell with me. Tatyana had warned that pickpockets operate in this crowded market area, so decided to buy my fruit and make a quick exit. I bought a large quantity of apples, oranges and pears from the female stallholder whilst she was being 'watched over' by three men. She weighed the items with care, seemed happy with my business, and smiled as I left. I've no idea who the men were, but wasn't about to hang around and find out!

From here it was only a short walk to my host's house on Chekhov Street where dinner would be ready at 7 o'clock and already knew we would be eating the local dish –*pel'meni* – tortelloni shaped pasta, containing spiced lamb, because Kathya had briefed me this morning. Trotsky said: "Any society is only three square meals away from a revolution". No culinary revolution has yet reached Siberia, where the main criterion of a good meal is that it should have sufficient bulk that you need a nice nap to recover!

During dinner I talked to Kathya about her student career and discovered she had completed two years of a six-year course in architecture, and hoped to start her own practice. I found this surprising, as she had mentioned her English and German studies earlier in the day. Then I noticed her hair was darker than before, and while I was having second thoughts she became aware of my confusion. To avoid any further embarrassment, explained to me that she was not Kathya, but her sister, Maria.

I had rightly been confused - they were identical twins. So, over coffee, the subject changed to architecture and Maria asked me what I thought of the buildings in Moscow, and in particular, the seven bizarre Gothic skyscrapers, built immediately after the war as Stalin's landmark.

Yes, I had seen the 260 metre high one on the Moscow River at Kievskaya, which is used by the Foreign Ministry, but its status as a tall building has long since been overtaken by the newer skyscrapers in the Middle and Far East. Russians, she said always insist that things have to be big in a country so vast, and to a Russian, big is beautiful and larger than anything conceived elsewhere. The Rossiya hotel opposite the Kremlin is another case in point. In building it, to outdo the Americans, sadly dozens of historic little streets were razed to the ground to make way for what was then, the biggest hotel in the world with 3,150 rooms. In parts of it, one has to walk for half a mile down carpeted corridors to find your room in a hotel now scheduled for demolition.

Wide roads also impress the Russians as I noticed in Moscow with its three concentric circles, facilitating the marching army divisions in Soviet times, and accommodating the mass of vehicular traffic of today. Maria also wanted to know if I had been to the Kremlin and, if so, did I see the two monsters which hold the world record for size? The Tsar's Bell, so big that it could not be rung and now sits on the ground because at 200 tons was too heavy for the existing bell-tower. Whilst nearby, sits the Tsar's Cannon, the largest calibre of any gun ever made, so cumbersome in fact, that it could not be fired. Yes, I had seen them!

By Train to Shanghai

Maria joked about how Russians write books and operas, so long, that you need Russian - sized backsides to sit comfortably through them. During all this time, Kathya had been sitting quietly reading at the other end of the living room, but obviously listening to our conversation. She now joined in and told her joke about how back in Soviet times, President Reagan had tried to deny advanced computer technology to the Russians - so they came up with a clever satire on the basis that everything in the Soviet Union is the biggest and the best. To out-do the Americans, the Kremlin decided to develop a native computer industry and published a suitable slogan "The Soviet micro-chip, the biggest micro-chip in the world".

In view of my early start next morning, I suggested to the sisters that perhaps it was time to retire to bed, but not before Kathya mentioned that time for Russians also arrives in large units. If you drop in on friends, you stay for hours, even days. If you go ice-fishing in winter, you remain immobile beside the hole in the ice almost until you have frostbite. If you go mushrooming, you tramp through the woods from dawn till dusk. No one thinks twice about waiting three hours in a queue, travelling four days on a train or letting their mothers spend five hours at a Russian Orthodox Easter service!

Chapter Five
Mongolia

Sunday – 22nd May

I was awoken at 5 a.m. with a cup of tea from Kathya or was it Maria; it was difficult to tell at the best of times, let alone this ungodly hour. It was cold and dawn was breaking as my taxi sped through the deserted streets on its way to the railway station. It was Sunday morning and the only activity was the arrival of people at the station. Along the way, we passed through old neighbourhoods and I noticed row after row of traditional Siberian wooden buildings with wood-carved decorations on their walls. The taxi crossed a bridge over the mighty Angara River, which is the only outlet from Lake Baikal. As the taxi reached its destination, the Trans-Mongolian No. TR 6, Irkutsk to Ulaan Baatar, was slowly pulling into the station. The platform indicator was showing a departure time of 01.06a.m. This was confusing in the early morning haze until I remembered it was set on Moscow time, whereas it was 6.06 a.m. here in Irkutsk.

This train had left Moscow the previous Wednesday and the crew and passengers were mainly Mongolian, other than the usual assortment of tourists. A pretty Mongolian *provodnitsa* in a light blue uniform showed me to carriage number 5 and my soft-sleeper number 9, but the compartment was locked from the inside. It took some persuasion from her and banging on the door to finally allow me to enter after a young bleary-eyed Mongolian girl slowly opened the door. She did not expect an interruption to her sleep, nor want any company, and I felt sorry for her, as it was so early in the morning. I had heard about these Mongolian trains, which are affectionately called supermarkets on wheels. Surveying the disorder around me with boxes and goods all over the place, I thought my compartment must be part of this supermarket!

I had been told that the next stage to Ulan Ude was going to be the most spectacular of the trip so far, so I eagerly anticipated travelling the 200 kilometres along the edge of the cold blue waters of Lake Baikal. When the train set off, and to secure the best viewpoint, I went to the restaurant car where they were serving breakfast, and found a good seat by the window. After two hour's travel, I spotted over the horizon, the southernmost edge of the lake. My fellow passengers rushed to the left hand windows with their videos and cameras in hand. (Thank goodness this wasn't a ship – without a doubt we'd have capsized!) It wasn't long before we were running alongside the shore, and continuing round a huge bend, before arriving at a small station called Slyudyanka. It was here that passengers used to disembark and run down to the lake to wash their hands in its supposedly healing waters.

That was a long time ago, this time our stop was only five minutes, before the train continued along the lake whilst out of the right hand windows were views of the snow-capped Khamar Daban Mountains. In the stillness of the morning the only sound was the rhythmic clackety-clack, as we entered tunnels and crossed elegant bridges over some of the three hundred and thirty-six rivers which feed into the lake. There was little sign of human habitation except the occasional small wooden stockade settlement and the odd boatman out fishing.

Mysovaya at 5,477 kilometres from Moscow was the next stop. We had travelled for five hours since departing Irkutsk, mostly along the southernmost shore of the lake. This great lake is so narrow and shaped like a banana, that only 60 kilometres across as the crow flies on the western bank, is Port Baikal and the village of Listvyanka where I had spent those few pleasant days. Mysovaya operated as the ferry port for trains and passengers on the Baikal and Angara ferries, which used to transport them across the lake before the railway line - on which we have just travelled was completed in 1904.

Back then, the train terminated at Port Baikal and the icebreaker *M.V. Baikal* transported the passengers and carriages from the train on her deck. Built in the United Kingdom, it was delivered by train in kit-form and put together on the shore of the lake in a construction job that presented great difficulties due to the rocky shore and frequent storms on the lake. Sadly, the 1919 revolution resulted in it being sunk. However, the smaller *M.V. Angara* still survives to this day. She was also sent from the United Kingdom in kit-form, and is now moored on the Angara River in Irkutsk and used as an office by a local newspaper. Travelling in early May of 1902, the American writer, Michael Myers Shoemaker described his journey across the lake, on the *M.V. Angara*, in his book –*The Great Siberian Railway-St. Petersburg to Pekin.*

By Train to Shanghai

The ice-breaker *M.V. Baikal* was already ahead clearing a pass through the ice but had only reached half-way, about 30 kilometres. Shoemaker describes the *Angara* having reached that point when the gangplank was let down, and all the passengers disembarked in the middle of the lake frozen to a metre, and described it as a "singular experience", to which it is difficult to disagree with. Waiting to take them the remainder of the journey were one hundred sleighs, some with one, some with two, and others with three horses. The sleighs were crude, wooden structures filled with loose straw and each covered with a robe of fur. The driver mounted his post and to the jingle of bells, they set off. Shoemaker described the animated scene; "the big puffing steamer apparently frozen in solid, the pushing passengers descending from her, the crowd of men, horses and sleighs all around with the babble of voices, the whole surrounded by the glistening white surface of the lake".

Continuing the journey, he passed the *M.V. Baikal,* hard at work, at a speed of 800 yards per hour, crushing the ice in front of it and Shoemaker described "the crack and roar, with muttered thundering - far down beneath and around as the ice gives way and great blocks turn their glistening edges upward, and, piling for a moment on either side, close again behind the ship, which finally seems to mount for a third of her length upon the ice, but settles back again, her great weight of 4,200 tons not having broken through".

The American was the first passenger to reach the shore in his *troika* drawn by three sturdy horses travelling silently except for the bells hung on an arch over the middle horse, describing the ride as delightful in the wonderfully clear air although it was necessary to keep bundled up in furs.

Every now and then with an extra flourish and shout, the horses were sent forward at greater speed, and passed with a jump one of the many crevasses, sometimes a foot wide. Looking downward it was possible to see the black waters and he rejoiced when safely over. The last mile was very slow as the snow became slushy, the ice became mud and with a final sturdy haul he was landed at the railway station. He gazed backwards over the great Baikal Lake and remarked that the passage of which, "he shall always remember as one of the most interesting in all his years of travel". Two years later in 1904, the Circumbaikal loop line around Lake Baikal was completed and the two ships became redundant.

When the Meakins reached Mysovaya, the train director announced that the train waiting for them in the station contained only 4th class carriages, as there were "no others available on the line". He told them the sad news that for the next four days and three nights, they would be in close proximity to filthy emigrants as the train would be crowded. Annette happened to meet a Dutchman in the post office and hearing the plight of the Meakins offered to help with the comment, "This is not a fit place for ladies and English ladies at that. This will never do. I will arrange something better for you".

So the kind Dutchman arranged for them to share the luggage van with a captain and six soldiers for the duration of the journey. They took their travelling rugs and food hamper to the luggage van, and instead, spent the next four days in close proximity to the soldiers. But, of course, they did not complain - true British stoicism!

Today, after leaving Mysovaya our journey was taking us in a north-easterly direction and I noticed white objects floating and glistening in the mid-day sun. They then became more frequent the further we travelled, and eventually realised they were lumps of melting ice until they became solid ice. So, George, the bore from Manchester, whom I had met in Moscow, had in fact, been correct!

The lake was still frozen solid the further north we travelled. This was a unique experience and only possible in late May as the temperature rises and melts the ice gradually from the south. Then dramatically and suddenly, cliffs appear on the west side of the lake, revealing a seemingly endless vista and far away on the horizon, snowy peaks rise mistily. This 200 kilometres of railway must indeed be one of the most scenic train journeys in the world, when viewed in a panorama of sheer cliffs, a frozen lake, snow capped mountains on both sides – and all enjoyed from the pleasure of riding on the unique Trains-Siberian Railway.

Meanwhile back in carriage number 5, our young Mongolian lady showed no interest whatsoever in the scenery as she had probably seen it many times before. She was much more concerned with her bartering and smuggling business. As she had been alone in the compartment when I'd arrived, she had taken full advantage of the situation and had been using my bunk, and the storage area underneath it, to house her bags and numerous boxes of black boots - which seemed to be her speciality. There were also children's shoes, clothes, hats, jackets, large tins of coffee and many, many more items. No wonder the door was locked from the inside!

At this stage the train turns east, which means it is farewell to Lake Baikal in all its glory and for the next two hours there was great deal of business activity. Back in the compartment I noticed the lady spending a great deal of time climbing to the upper bunks and re-adjusting what she had stored up there, including in the large overhead bay. Boxes came down and the contents were emptied into smaller bags and put back up again. Leaving the compartment with various goods, she always arrived back with something different. It was a hive of activity. Some of her compatriots also walked up and down the corridor carrying bags and boxes, some even visited our compartment. This would all appear to be barter Mongolian style and my companion's speciality was most definitely black boots – a much prized possession when worn on the Mongolian *steppe!*

They were everywhere. I had heard Mongolia had a shortage of most things, and I'm pleased to report that my fellow travellers were certainly doing their best to alleviate the situation, one way or the other and as we approached the Mongolian border, there appeared to be some urgency in proceedings.

The train was about to cross the mighty Selenga River, and followed it, through a beautiful valley, right into Mongolia. But before we reached the Selenga, the train stopped at Ulan Ude, capital of Buryatia where a few local Buryats get off carrying large boxes all stuffed with goods - and no doubt part of the barter operation. Ulan Ude was founded in 1666 as the winter quarters for Cossacks and has the atmosphere of a remote frontier town, which is 5,640 kilometres from Moscow. Today its proud boast is having the world's largest head of Lenin.

By Train to Shanghai

With a fifteen-minute stop, this was a good opportunity to buy water from a *babushka* and stretch my legs, as I watched the departing passengers load their goods into waiting vans, with the border conveniently close by.

Returning to my compartment, there was no sign of my travelling companion. Eventually she did return, this time smiling. Perhaps because everything had been sold and her business transactions were complete, therefore all her goods, and or, dodgy dealings were well out of sight of the impending customs inspection? Her smile, though rather unattractive with its numerous gaps in her teeth, at least looked much better than the grumpy person I'd met at 6 a.m. this morning when her sleep was interrupted by my arrival. Just outside Ulan Ude is Zaudinsky and it is here that our train leaves the main Trans-Siberian route to Vladivostok.

The Meakins, in their epic journey carried on from here to Vladivostok, tucked up in the luggage van, with Russian soldiers for company, but not complaining. From the ruler of the East they took a ship to Japan and another one to Vancouver. It was thence by train across the Rockies and from New York yet another ship to Liverpool, finally arriving back in London on 31st August 1900 from a journey which started back in March.

For me, it was also goodbye to Siberia, I shall always remember it as vast stretches of a sadly silent country, limitless *steppes*, silent forests, snow-capped mountains, all leading up to one great point of interest, that sea of ice, frozen Lake Baikal. From here, we were now heading south through the semi-autonomous Republic of Buryatia. Having left the mountains behind, we now had the beautiful wide Selenga River for company. Its river valley is lush, with herds grazing as we passed village after village with the window shutters of their little houses, painted in colourful fashion and all against a backdrop of green hills and a wide, lazy river.

Mirjam and Raoul invited me to join them at their table in the restaurant car for lunch. They were a Dutch couple in their early thirties, travelling independently and whom I had met on the train from Moscow. They planned to take a year away, travelling throughout Asia, before finishing in India. They had made all arrangements for their trip and with modern communications will still be able to conduct their business affairs even when travelling through inaccessible places and countries.

At 6 p.m., we arrived at Nauski a small town that acts as the Russian border post. When I returned to the compartment could not believe my eyes - it had been transformed. It had been cleaned up and instead of boxes and boxes of black boots; there were just a few jars of coffee and pickles plus a handful of clothes lying around. There was an eerie silence as the first uniformed official arrived at our door. I was asked to produce my passport and in order to satisfy the official, I had to remove my glasses, look him straight in the eye whilst he checked the eight-year-old passport photo against my current likeness. After that he took my passport away. Meantime, my travelling companion, having prepared for this visit by styling her hair, applying some much needed dollops of make-up, smiled as innocently as she could and went though the same procedure with her documentation. After it was over and the official had departed ... she was gone in a flash! But, I wonder - where to?

Another official in a blue uniform gave me a customs declaration form, which asked if I was exporting any of the following: Radioactive Materials, Weapons, Ammunition or Explosives. This was just the beginning and it would take another four hours to complete formalities. After two hours my passport was returned and this time the compartment was inspected by a female customs official. She checked the upper bunks and the large overhead bay and then declared it free of whatever it was she had been looking for, but to all intents and purposes I felt this was just a cursory inspection. Lastly, there was a final visit by yet another official, this time returning to stamp my passport – which, at last, meant I was finally free to get out and go for a walk along the platform.

Whilst having a beer with Raoul, a shifty looking character approached me and offered to change my remaining roubles into Mongolian currency. He offered thirty-five togrogs to the rouble, which gave me 48,000 togrogs for my remaining roubles, and with all those noughts, I now felt rich! At 10 p.m. it was dark outside, and the train slowly pulled into the Mongolian border town called Sukhbaatar. After a distance of 5,900 kilometres from leaving Moscow was finally was out of Russia. A pretty customs lady arrived and gave me a customs form in Mongolian. This was easy to complete as the reply was negative but with her experience was not completely satisfied that my travelling companion was declaring all the goods in her possession. The customs lady had a good look around including the upper storage area, but still did not seem convinced. She returned ten minutes later to ask more questions which I could not understand, but I kept a very discreet silence whilst her eyes glanced around the place. Then an attractive border policewoman dressed in a smart, dark blue uniform, arrived. She completed yet more passport formalities, before finally a middle-aged man came to take away the Mongolian entry forms.

That was the end of formal paperwork procedures, which had taken six hours on both sides of the border. Just after mid-night the train moved on towards the Mongolian capital, Ulaan Baatar and in normal circumstances the passengers would have retired for the night.

As soon as we left the station the frantic activity began again in earnest as I tried to get some sleep. My companion started moving about our compartment again, pulling boxes from here, there and everywhere, which had been successfully hidden from the eyes of the customs officials. The same black boots reappeared and the same movement of goods between carriages resumed with a vengeance. This became very irritating as I was trying to sleep and with the constant opening and closing of the door became infuriating. The *provodnitsa's* compartment down the corridor was where I went - announcing to her that if these activities did not stop immediately, that I would summon the travelling policeman. This threat seemed to work as the smuggling activities ceased forthwith, and I finally got some sleep.

Monday 23rd May

After a very short night's sleep I awoke at dawn and by 7 a.m. the train was approaching Ulaan Baatar. The landscape had turned green and grassy, covered with wildflowers and grazing animals. In the distance it was possible to see clusters of birch and pine trees as the train descended into the valley of the Mongolian capital. On the table the jars of coffee and pickle

By Train to Shanghai

had gone and been replaced with six large cartons of what looked like powdered milk. Obviously, 'someone' had declared these to customs because nearby I saw a customs receipt for 400 togrogs, about twenty pence. It had been a very interesting day yesterday, if a little tedious, with having to suffer the long border crossing and the annoying fact that someone had decided to detach the restaurant car at the Russian border - as I discovered when I set-off to enjoy some breakfast. I had seen the great Mongolian smuggling at first hand and had travelled with a young, but very experienced practitioner. Although, throughout the entire twenty-four hours, we had not exchanged a single word!

It was a chilly morning as the train pulled into Ulaan Baatar Station and I suppose this shouldn't have been too much of a surprise considering the altitude was 1,350 metres above sea level. Four adults arrived to greet my travelling companion as she gathered up what remained of her goods including a supply of black boots. They could have been her family or perhaps part of the smuggling gang – whatever – I was pleased to see the back of her. I gathered up my belongings and said goodbye to the *provodnitsa*. Walking down the platform towards the exit I was greeted by Oki, my guide for the next three days. She was standing with three other people, a couple from Essex called Steve and Karin, and a red haired Yorkshire girl called Stephanie whom I had befriended earlier on the train. She was on her way to China then on to Australia to work, another one opting out.

Oki said she planned to take us to our *ger* camp later in the day and meantime had arranged for us to use a local hotel for a much-needed shower. As we entered the hotel, an elderly

American couple were checking in. I spoke briefly to the man and he told me he had just arrived from his evangelical mission station in eastern Mongolia close to the Chinese border. This puzzled me and I wondered in a country like Mongolia which had a devout Buddhist population of 90 per cent and where there is now a huge resurgence in the cult of Genghis Khan, how, and from where, would he get his flock? Outside in the hotel car park was a large four-wheel vehicle with diplomatic plates, and marked in large red letters on the sides "U.S. AID - A GIFT FROM THE AMERICAN PEOPLE". Perhaps that gave me the answer!

With a welcome shower enjoyed and a decent breakfast our small party of four was ready to explore Ulaan Baatar and Oki suggested that we start with a walk down the main thoroughfare called Peace Avenue. It was Monday morning and just as in any other city the rush hour had started. The traffic was heavy with everything from small vans to big trucks, and modern cars to battered, old bangers. Crossing the road was a dangerous experience - Mongolian drivers seem to think that pedestrians do not exist or, if they do, they shouldn't! Even pedestrian crossing-points, controlled by lights including the obligatory green man, meant nothing – we all had to run for our lives when a lorry hurtled towards us – on the wrong side of the road!

This day, 23rd May, was also a major religious, but not a state holiday, as it was the official birthday of Buddha. It was obvious from the large crowd of people heading for the Gandan Monastery that something special was about to occur. This was the only monastery, whose name is Tibetan, to survive the anti-religious purges of the 1930's and now totally restored.

It houses a ninety-ton Buddhist statue built of copper, silver and gold, and decorated with precious stones. Back then in the 1930's, when the Red army arrived and wreaked havoc, they closed all monasteries in the country except Gandan, forcing the monks to flee or be killed. This policy left approximately 10,000 dead. Stalin's idea was to stamp out religion altogether, but looking around today he, was plainly unsuccessful.

Outside the Great Temple which houses the Great Buddha Statue a group of monks were chanting prayers, which from a distance sounded like Gregorian chanting. A parade of children all carrying colourful lanterns, with the Buddha's life inscribed on them, arrived and lined up to join the ceremony. Then I noticed that no one was smoking and Oki told me that on this holy day, the following were forbidden - smoking, drinking, fighting or swearing, but luckily, this only applied to Mongolians! There was a holiday atmosphere with grandparents escorting their grandchildren and all were dressed in their very best clothes. Some wore their traditional Mongolian costumes and many wore brand new black boots, perhaps some of these had arrived earlier in the day by train!

Yesterday had presidential elections, which had been won by a politician called Enkhbayar who had secured more than fifty per cent of the vote. As if to celebrate, and perhaps give thanks to Buddha, he was here on a podium, erected outside the Great Temple, with no great security around him. He made a short speech and the whole ceremony was beamed live on TV. Leaving this unique occasion we walked back down Peace Avenue noticing something new. In this poor country without many mobile phones, it was still possible however to make a call. All along the pavement and sitting on little boxes or chairs were hawkers offering use of satellite phones for a few togrogs. Essentially, forming a series of mobile telephone boxes!

Soon after lunch we were in our bus and on our way to the *ger* camp, which was to be our home for the next two days. Oki was also coming and would stay even though she had two young children at home – being looked after by her husband. The route took us south east and for a time parallel with the main railway line to China. A very long goods train carrying coal passed in the opposite direction, travelling effortlessly towards the capital. With the Mongolian *steppe* in the background it made a very pretty picture. On the way we passed yaks, sheep and horses grazing, whilst a lone female hitchhiker tried her luck by the side of the road. We turned right and then left and there in front of us in the valley below our *ger* camp appeared.

A *ger* is the traditional style of accommodation, used in Mongolia for centuries - right back to the time of Genghis Khan. It is a framed tent in two parts. The lower is of interlocking fencing type wood with the upper resting on it and consisting of radial roof-supports reaching towards a central strut. In the centre, a stove and the door always faces south.

The final kilometre was on a dirt track, and avoiding the potholes was our driver's main preoccupation. On arrival we were subjected to the normal Mongolian welcoming ritual which entailed all the local staff lining up to greet us after emerging off the bus. They smiled and bowed their heads as the luggage was carried to our allotted *ger*. In the heat of the afternoon sun directly above, this camp had a distinctly peaceful feel about it with the sheer silence. Here we were on top of the world, surrounded by the wide rolling Mongolian *steppe* and not a sound to be heard. The camp consisted of twenty individual *gers* as well as a large communal building with adjoining toilets and shower rooms, so not as primitive as expected. I was allocated number seven and, after checking it out, watched some other people who were already in residence, playing archery - a sport that Mongolians seem to excel at. A nearby pen held some thirty horses and foals. The horse is also synonymous with Mongolia since the time of the Mongol Empire and most Mongolian males are excellent horsemen.

For dinner, special arrangements were made for Steve and Karin, who announced that they were vegetarians – in fact, there were so keen on the policy, admitted they'd tried a vegetarian diet on their cats at home – alas their experiment failed! After dinner, there was not very much to do in this isolated place so Oki suggested watching a promotional video showing the delights of Mongolia including their famous Naadam festival.

This takes place in July and includes three male sports; horse racing, archery and the most important of the three, wrestling. Archery is now a little out of fashion, but horse racing is an obsession with the most popular race being the final one with riders as young as seven year old. Earlier in the evening, Oyunaa the housekeeper had come to light the stove as the evening light faded and the temperature dropped to freezing or below. The full moon was still directly above but probably for the last night. Oyunaa said she expected it to be a very cold night and would return early next morning to light the fire again.

Tuesday — 24th May

Indeed, as promised, the *ger* door opened at dawn with Oyunaa clutching a bundle of wood for the fire - which was badly needed after a very cold night. Her country Mongolia, is the 9th largest land mass in the world but only has a population of two and a half million, and which in the 12th century, had been the biggest empire in the history of the world. It ran from China to Hungary under the leadership of Genghis Khan, or Chinggis Khan, as he was known. And just to prove his legacy a recent study by geneticists of 2,000 men across Eurasia from the Caspian Sea to the Pacific, found that sixteen million men from the entire population of this region, including Mongolia, are in effect part of his vast family. The extraordinary inference of this study concluded that a man living in Mongolia in the 12th century had sewn his reproductive seeds across the region to the extent that this genetic DNA is now shared by one in two hundred of all men living today!

Therefore it is possible that Genghis and his immediate family and forbearers were responsible for scattering their genes right across their vast empire. Women were part of the booty of warfare and handed around as gifts. With access to an unlimited supply of beautiful women, over his forty years of empire, it is possible to grant him at least twenty male surviving children, which a few hundred years later, multiplies into millions. Genghis Khan has been proclaimed the "most important man of the last thousand years". One thousand years ago in the year 1,000 AD, the population of the entire world was only something between fifty and three hundred million. This represents, at a maximum, around five per cent of the current population of six billion.

By Train to Shanghai

Never before in our history has a single species exerted such an important impact on humanity. And, this is without taking into account what might have happened if the expedition of his grandson, Khubilai Khan, to Japan, had succeeded in its objective. In the year 1281 his 4,400 strong fleet set sail for Japan from China then under Mongol control. It simply disappeared off the mainland of Japan with the loss of 70,000 Mongols, mainly because they did not have a maritime history and more importantly they had used the wrong flat-bottomed ships, which simply sank, when hit by a typhoon. It was not until the recent D-Day landings in 1944 that an equivalent size fleet was ever assembled again. This disaster off the Japanese coast was the beginning of the end of the Mongol Empire.

To this day, Mongolia still remains a nation of horsemen and today was an opportunity to experience some horse-riding myself and watch the Mongols in action on their horses. Over breakfast Oki explained that experienced horses had been selected for our party to ride. Karin expressed some disquiet about her lack of experience, whilst Stephanie admitted to some previous riding, back in Yorkshire, but that was some time ago. Steve and I had no such qualms, and it was a case of, bring on the horses, with Steve making a quotation attributed to Winston Churchill – 'there is something about the outside of a horse, that is good for the inside of a man'. Oki then produced a disclaimer to sign. This was a long list of dos and don'ts, so it seems bureaucracy has finally reached, even these remote parts.

Outside, we were each given a saddle, helmet, plus leggings and walked to the pen holding the horses - all of which are related, as they do not take kindly to outsiders. The horses became quite excited as the horsemen entered the pen and approached the chosen nags. I was allocated a ten-year-old, that looked reasonably relaxed, and was assured he would be happy to carry my weight for the next few hours! The horsemen were very patient with us, checking saddles and making sure everything was in order before we set off, accompanied by Oki, and the lead Mongolian horseman. Under a clear blue sky we cantered along on the grasslands of the *steppe*, past low hills, another *ger,* and a herd of sheep. There are no roads or boundary fences here and herds can wander freely over the *steppe* whilst we carried on until we reached the banks of a shallow river.

Here the horses took some water and we all relaxed before starting the journey back. The two girls seemed to have survived the ride so far. But then it was at a gentle pace, and mostly in Indian file, because these horses are experienced and have some sort of hierarchy where they are content to follow one another. Occasionally our leader would increase the pace, which was automatically matched by the other horses without a hint of command. On the way back, by a different route, we encountered thousands more sheep and goats spread out over the *steppe.* We arrived back at the camp without incidence, and overall, this had been a wonderful experience. Although not riding at any great speed, it gave me some idea of the life of a Mongolian horseman. It also reminded me of Yeats, self-written epitaph – Cast a cold Eye – On life, on Death – Horseman, pass by!

On the way home the clear blue sky had suddenly vanished, only to be replaced by heavy cloud and a wind, which was light in the early morning, but which gained in strength and by the time we were dismounting, it started raining. We were indeed lucky as we had been out on the *steppe* for nearly three hours and now it looked as if a nasty storm was brewing. As we left the horses, a minibus was arriving with some new arrivals. Again, the same ritual was performed with the staff out, greeting, bowing and smiling to all, and I instantly recognised the Dutch party from the Moscow train. Of all places to meet again – right in the heart of Mongolia!

First off the bus, the trio of heavyweights, plastic bags in hand, no doubt full of vodka. We greeted one another like long lost brothers and went for lunch in the communal building, well out of the rain. The wind had switched direction to northerly, gained in strength and it had suddenly become very cold. It was now late May and I tried to picture what it must be like in winter for these nomadic people, living in *gers* when the temperature plunges to minus 40' centigrade as it frequently does. Other than the Eskimos, in Alaska, these must be the toughest and hardiest people on earth with their weather-beaten, but always smiling faces.

That afternoon, Oki had arranged a visit to a nearby *ger* used by a family as their home, with two adults and three children living there. The idea was to see something of the real life of an ordinary Mongolian family. This whole countryside was a vista of *gers,* horses and other animals, just as it had been in Genghis' day. Although it wasn't raining, walking against the strong wind was a struggle on the sandy grassland.

For security, most *ger* families keep a household dog around the place so Oki checked that there was not one on the loose when we arrived, because some of these dogs are ferocious.

Once that hound-check was completed, our host appeared and invited us inside his *ger*. There, in the space of just five square metres, we saw how a typical family live. Their children were away at school in Ulaan Baatar, and his wife was out visiting relatives. Inside, it contained, as usual, a necessary stove, three beds, a TV set, radio and other normal household items. Our host was a tall, weather-beaten, but good-looking man who was about forty years old and dressed in national costume with (new!) black boots, and could easily have been a descendent of Genghis Khan. His *ger* had been pitched on this spot for four months. When it was erected, the grass had been lush and green, but now, the blades had all but gone and the floor had become just brown sand. The only green I could see now was under the beds where no one had walked!

We exchanged pleasantries as he lit his stove to make tea for us. This was most definitely not normal tea. It was ghastly! As far as I could tell it was no more than a concoction of boiled milk, to which boiled water had been added, plus a pinch of salt for flavour. Later, Oki told me it is fermented mare's milk and is called *airag*. I think I'll just call it 'an acquired taste'! With Oki acting as interpreter, the Mongolian man discussed his life on the grasslands and how his livelihood entirely depends on his animals, which are constantly under attack from wolves. To protect them, he is forever setting wolf-traps, and sometimes has to shoot the beasts. He then promptly pulled out from under the bed, an old .22 rifle, complete with a hoard of bullets, all handed down by his father. The gun must have been over eighty years old and was literally held together with sticking plaster – but he assured us it still worked well – confirmed by his recent slaying of particularly nasty wolf that had been attacking his animals.

By Train to Shanghai

We thanked him for his hospitality, handed over the usual gifts and said goodbye. The next day he was going to be on the move again - to better pastures for the summer, as is the way of life for these nomadic people. They can go anywhere they fancy for the best grassland because there are no boundaries, but they must leave their children behind in the city, as education from the age of seven is compulsory.

During the course of the evening, the wind abated but the temperature again dropped to zero. Back came Oyunna to light the fire, which was most definitely needed and made my *ger* warm and cosy. Everyone, including the Dutch party, was in the communal building for dinner, and my choice was a local speciality called *buuz*. Afterwards, whilst sipping a coffee with Oki we talked about her country, Mongolia which effectively is a new country taking its place amongst the nations of the earth as it has only enjoyed true independence since 1990 without interference from outsiders.

Their history is one of subjugation, first by the Chinese until 1924 when they were thrown out by a Russian sponsored Socialist Revolution, which then became a satellite state of the USSR. The memory of the Chinese occupation has left a bitter taste after three centuries of domination. During that time the Mongolian population were severely repressed with their language and alphabet banned and deliberately kept poor in order to prevent any possible uprising. With arrival of the Russians they at least built some infrastructure, but only in a way that benefited them. Railway lines were built which enabled Russia to repatriate Mongolia's mineral wealth for little or no money. This continues because Mongolia lacks the smelting plants and refineries and is forced to sell its raw materials because of its landlocked position. This leaves the country very poor, but it should not be, because of the abundance of natural resources.

Outside, in the fading light I watched the vapour trails of the planes passing overhead, travelling in a southeast direction. Kate was due to leave London about now and I wondered as these planes were heading for China, could she possibly be on board one and directly overhead? For the last two days I had watched plane after plane go in the same direction - to China. Something must be going on there with all that traffic! The ancient tea caravans travelling between Beijing and Moscow in the 18th and 19th centuries travelled along this route through Ulaan Baatar and they took about 40 days. The railway now takes 6 days, but the aeroplanes overhead a mere 10 hours, with the passengers travelling in luxury. How times have changed!

Wednesday 25th May

Outside, it had been a cold freezing night, which did not affect me, as I was warm and comfortable and was awakened at 6 a.m. by Oyunaa arriving to light the stove. At 9 o'clock after breakfast of a typical Mongolian dish called *poozy*, I went for a final walk around the camp as the sun rose in the east, rising over the mountaintop. In the stillness of the morning the only noise came from the camp staff going about their business whilst a couple of Dutch men were heading for the washroom looking the worst for wear after their party last night. In the distance I saw two horses tethered together, one standing and the other lying down on the ground. This was strange and went to investigate. The older one was lying down with blood streaming from his nostrils and appeared to have been kicked

By Train to Shanghai

by the other one. I went back to the camp to raise the alarm and get help. One of the horsemen arrived quickly on the scene, cut the tether and freed the animals. He was aware that the older animal had been ill for some time and was tethered for security against wandering off and being attacked by wolves during the night.

Soon it was time to say goodbye and for that, the entire staff again lined up to bade farewell as we climbed aboard our bus. Driving away up the hill on the dirt track the leading horseman escorted our vehicle on his horse, keeping pace with us until the bus reached the road. Looking back down the valley it was possible to see the camp in the distance through the dust whilst the horseman stood on his stirrups and waved his hat at us in true Mongolian style. Re-joining the main road and whilst avoiding the potholes the bus passed a large military camp. Oki told me that military conscription was still in force and compulsory for young males for one year. Entering the city the driver had to pay 500 togrogs, about twenty pence to enter, which seemed to emulate the money raising idea of the London mayor, but at a fraction of his charge. High above in the Asralt Mountains, Oki pointed out a large observatory building, funded by the Americans where for twenty-four hours of the day is used to gaze up to the stars.

Our hotel was in the city centre close to Sukhbaatar Square and having checked in, walked over for a final look around. This square is called after the founder of modern Mongolia in 1921, Damdin Sukhbaatar. With help from Bolshevik Russia he kicked out the Chinese and declared the People's Government of Mongolia. Shortly afterwards in 1924 the city was re-named Ulaan Baatar (red hero) and made capital. Sadly,

Sukhbaatar did not survive very long and shortly afterwards was found dead in mysterious circumstances, leaving Stalin free to appoint a puppet leader.

This square, which has a distinct Stalinist feel about it, is the geographical and cultural centre and a large statue of Sukhbaatar sits in the middle. This is a ten-metre statue of Sukhbaatar on his horse, whilst opposite it, is his closed mausoleum, modelled on Lenin's in Moscow. Dominating the square on the northern side is the Parliament Building, whilst the east side contains the Soviet-built Opera and Ballet Building which was used for cultural exchanges in Communist times. The west side has the National Museum of Mongolian History and various cultural institutions in a square, which seemed to be a place of relaxation as well as a meeting spot for locals.

Walking down Peace Avenue I heard my name being shouted from the open-air café across the road. It was Mirjam and Raoul again, who were sitting outside in the sun sipping a beer and they invited me over. They had stayed at a *ger* camp as well, but a different one to ours, so it seems that everyone arriving here visits one. Stephanie, the redhead, walked by and Raoul invited her to join us as we discussed our various exploits of the last few days.

The cafe notice board had a warning about the dangers of life in Ulaan Baatar after nightfall and recommended avoiding dark places. The problem appears to be the large number of urchins that roam the city at night. They are homeless children who have migrated to the city during the harsh winters. Sometimes because their parents cannot cope with them so they deliver the children to the city and leave them, where at least they can get some warmth and food. Even as we sat here it was noticeable how many of these children were out and about with their begging bowls and oblivious to any discouragement we addressed at them.

For evening entertainment, Oki recommended the "Song and Dance Show" at the small theatre near the hotel. Performed in front of an audience of tourists by a group of twenty artists, including children, all dressed in national costume and with a background of Mongolian music. Well received by the audience it was a perfect end to my short visit. Walking back towards my hotel I reflected on their country and their capital city which is often described as the world's coldest capital, when the temperature plunges to minus 40 C sometimes, but rises to 38 C in summer. This is a very poor country but the people are charming and cheerful and always smiling as I experienced first hand, with all of them I met.

After centuries of being dominated, firstly by the Chinese and then by the Russians where even mention of the Genghis Khan name was illegal, but this has all changed and he has now become an obsession again. The Russians did at least re-build the capital, Ulaan Baatar but in the mould of another Soviet-style city. Mongolia was only recognised as an independent country in 1961 when it joined the United Nations, but it took until 1990 to become truly independent when the Russians finally left and the people were free to choose their own government as they had done last Sunday, but there are still problems with their neighbour China, who attempted to prevent a visit by the Dalai Lama a few years ago,

The Dalai Lama, who won the Nobel Peace Prize in 1989, is regarded as a god-king by Tibetans, but has long been a thorn in the side of the Chinese. He fled the capital Lhasa in 1959 after a failed uprising against Chinese rule - nine years after Communist troops entered Tibet. The Chinese government has long proclaimed the Dalai Lama as a dangerous separatist, who wants to declare independence for 2.7 million Tibetans. He lives in Dharamsala, in the Himalayas, heading his government in exile and hoping, one day to return to his remote, mountainous homeland, he has not seen for nearly 50 years.

On leaving, the Russians had the temerity to present an invoice to the new Mongolian Government. The invoice was for work done on buildings and infrastructure since 1924. The quantum was twenty four billion dollars. It was ignored and to this day remains unpaid. Had the Mongolians not ignored it, this new country would be bankrupt!

Thursday 26th May

I took the advice seriously, stayed indoors during darkness and prepared for the next stage of my journey, which would be through the Gobi Desert. At the buffet breakfast, the other English travellers joined me as we were all catching the same train. Oki had arrived which was surprising, as we had said goodbye yesterday, and this was her day off work. When the bus came, we headed off for the station, passing on the way a collection of old steam engines, a relic from the past.

Ulaan Baatar Railway Station was a hive of activity as our driver delivered us outside on the concourse. Our train number TR 24 was due to leave at 8.05 a.m. which would be heading

By Train to Shanghai

for Beijing on a single-track line. The morning was cold with a chill northerly wind blowing, which looked if it could be the start of a sand storm. This was the weekly service so I expected to see some acquaintances among the passengers as missing this train could have serious consequences and mean an extra week awaiting the next one. On the platform I recognised some familiar faces amongst the waiting crowd with the Dutch and German groups already there and sipping coffee. I was greeted as a long lost friend and were now on Christian name terms, perhaps not surprising since we have been travelling together all the way from Moscow.

Oki, who had come along with us to say a final farewell, remained on the platform right up until our train pulled out. She had given our group the most attentive attention and no task was too small for her to attend to. After exchanging e-mail addresses she said goodbye and said she hoped to see us back in Mongolia sometime in the future. The *provodnitsa* closed the door, when this train of twenty carriages, the pride of the Mongolian fleet, slowly pulled out of the station as the wind increased in strength. The sand storm became more intense and obliterated the view of the passing suburbs, which in an event looked drab and grey, so perhaps it was just as well. Having been together for the past three days, I was finally parted from my English friends. This time my companions were two male Koreans and a Chinese man who spoke little English.

As the train left the station, the Koreans got on bended knee and said their traditional, prayer of the traveller. I had been allocated this time, a soft-seat berth in compartment number seven of carriage number one. The benefit of being in the first carriage was the unique view when gazing out of the window, watching the remainder of the train following behind, as we slowly rounded bend after bend. Then snaking its way round the bottom of the mountain in a series of spectacular switchbacks through valleys and making the familiar rhythmic clackety-clack noise.

One thing you have to control whilst travelling on long train journeys is your bladder. To answer the call of nature I walked along the corridor to the WC and to my extreme disappointment its door showed a schedule of opening and closing times. This was the latter and as the train was still leaving the outskirts of the city I would have to wait another thirty minutes, so I returned to the compartment … and crossed my legs! After one hour the line ran parallel to the main highway south, which only had the odd car or truck on it. We passed a small rural station where standing outside, a uniformed attendant stood to attention as if in homage to the mighty train, with a red and green flag in each hand facing downwards, presumably this was the all clear signal.

I could see a lone horseman in the distance riding down from the hilltop: his herd of sheep and goats were already at the bottom. Then the train driver made a warning noise, like a ships foghorn and the reason was a group of motor bikers, who had dismounted and stood close to the rail line with only a light fence for protection. This was the driver's warning to stay away. By now the trees had disappeared and the landscape had become a panorama of *steppe*. We passed more small villages on the way with grazing horses and the odd *ger* camp. My travelling companions did not appear interested in the scenery and had retired to their upper bunks as I went in search of the restaurant car which was further away this time at the usual number six. .

By Train to Shanghai

Just like the Russian train this restaurant car was being used more as a social centre except that it was beautifully decorated in Mongolian style ornate wooden panelling and was by far the most attractive thus far. It was crowded and I recognised acquaintances from previous journeys and over a few beers, exchanged details of our respective experiences. The time went quickly and after four and a half hours the train pulled into the dusty little town of Choir made worse by the howling wind. This town sits on the edge of the Gobi Desert and when the Soviet military were here they built a large military air base. Today, the Russians have long gone leaving many buildings empty and the place has an air of a ghost town. However standing proudly in front of the railway station is a statue of the first Mongolia cosmonaut named Ertvuntz.

To my delight, on the platform I had met up again with Bridgette and Sidonie. They related to me their experiences of the past few days, which was similar to mine. They had stayed at a different *ger* camp and survived a horse-ride on the grasslands. By now, all greenery had disappeared as we sped through the desert. At a small station further on we stopped for what seemed an eternity. It was a necessary stop. Because up ahead and travelling towards us were sixty-odd wagons of a long goods train. On this single track, this is what happens and must be a headache for the railway management as the goods train duly arrived and we were on our way again.

By now, Mirjam and Raoul had become friends and we managed to get a table in the crowded restaurant for lunch. The waitress recommended *buuz*, which is the national staple food of Mongolia, and consists of boiled meat-filled dumplings. As we enjoyed our food and beer, we talked about their country,

Holland and the consequences of their involvement in the affairs of my own country, reverberations of which are all too evident today, not least the affect on my own genealogy.

When William of Orange came to Ireland, he brought along with him his good friend Godert de Ginkel. After success at the Battle of the Boyne in 1690, William returned to Holland and left Godert, by now a general in charge of the victorious protestant army and whose new title was 1st Earl of Athlone. The story goes that he went to live at Kilwaughter Castle in County Antrim and fathered a child whilst there. The child was called "Ginkel's" as a surname but was soon changed to Gingles by the locals and the male line has retained this name till now. My great grandfather; was born in Kilwaughter, so perhaps am a direct descended of the 1st Earl of Athlone but sadly Irish genealogy suffered a massive loss when the old IRA decided to burn down the Customs House in Dublin during the civil war. Up in smoke went hundreds of years of irreplaceable parish records kept there, including mine

Mirjam also reminded me of the Dutch connection to Peter the Great who went to Holland as an ordinary worker to learn the principles of shipbuilding and navigation before eventually establishing the Russian navy. In 1698 he came to England and befriended the English King, William of Orange. William it is said enjoyed Peter's company and presented him with his best yacht, the Royal Standard, which he sailed back to Russia with a British crew. In his autobiography, the late English actor, Oliver Reed, makes the astonishing claim that Peter the Great was his great-great grandfather as a result of a liaison with a local girl from Kent during his visit to England!

By Train to Shanghai

Raoul outlined the couple's proposed itinerary for the next year, which would take them through south-east Asia, eventually ending in India. We exchanged e-mails and he promised to send periodic messages as to their progress as they travel from one exotic location to another. By now the whole restaurant car was in high spirits, perhaps as a result of the wine and beer as well as the excellent choice of food, newly stocked-up in Ulaan Baatar and served by engagingly cheerful Mongolian staff.

The train was now well and truly in the Gobi Desert, as out of the window I pondered its barren landscape which brought back memories of the time ten years ago when I lived in Saudia Arabia. Whilst there, I went to visit what remained of the old Hejaz railway, which was built in 1904 along the old Haj route from Damascus to Medina. They never completed the section to Mecca. It probably would have been - had a certain Englishman called T. E. Lawrence - also known as Lawrence of Arabia, not intervened. During the Arab revolt of 1916 the line was used to reinforce the Turkish garrisons in Arabia. Lawrence and the forces of the Sherif of Mecca attacked and destroyed much of it in 1917. After that, the line never fully recovered and the section south of Ma'an in Jordan was closed in 1924.

I went to see what remained of it, to the Nabatean town of Medain Saleh north of Medina. This is a sister city of Petra in Jordan which flourished with the passing trade some two thousand years ago. After it was abandoned the central area of houses and shops disappeared and all that now remains are tombs cut into the sandstone rocks. Slightly more remains of the rolling stock but almost none of the original rails. It is still possible to follow the rail track on a beautiful route between purple jagged mountains making it a memorable experience. Some of the stock remains beside and on the railway to this day and has hardly rusted. An engine with wagons can be seen lying on its side at Hadiya and a well-preserved engine stands in a restored shed. Visitors to this area are usually expatriates living in Saudi Arabia. This country is one of the few in the world that does not facilitate or encourage tourism other than religious, and even then, the pilgrims are confined to the cities, thus making these historical sites isolated and very inaccessible to many.

We had one last stop before the Chinese border at Sainshand by which time we had covered 876 kilometres. Here, there was time for a walk along the platform and to meet some of my newfound friends. Two young girls were selling bottled water and when I offered one dollar for one they were more than pleased with their transaction. Soon it was time to continue the journey through the vast wilderness of the Gobi Desert or at least this part of its grassy *steppe* which is rich in wildlife but sadly now endangered due to poaching and changes in the environment. Underneath, it houses billions of tons of coal and extracting it could have a serious affect on the environmental balance. Threatened with extinction are animals like the Gobi bear and the wild Bactrian camel. Back in the 1930's an American lead expedition into the Gobi Desert, found large numbers of dinosaur remains. The Mongolian Government of the time took cash from the Americans and allowed them to be exported back to America, thus leaving this poor country bereft of some of its heritage.

After leaving Sainshand, there were no more stations in this vast desert but signalmen are still required to monitor the line. To fulfil this job, the Mongolians devised a novel way of dealing with this requirement by utilising their oldest friend, the horse. At periodic intervals we passed a signalman standing by the perimeter fence along the line. In his right hand he held a yellow flag - whilst in his left hand was a red flag facing downwards. By his side was his horse, tied to the fence and on which he used as transport. A very important man guarding this piece of single track and to whom I would bestow the title of mobile signalman.

Just before the Chinese border as I walked in the direction of the bar I met the Dutch guys coming back who announced that the bar had run dry. Perhaps this was not surprising since we were ten hours into our journey and had some very thirsty passengers on board and all in high spirits. Perhaps also, it was a blessing in disguise as the approaching border formalities can take up to six hours, including the time taken for bogie changing, and all this time the toilets are locked!

The Mongolian customs procedure was quick and smooth. A uniformed official stamped my passport, collected the completed customs form, and we were on our way into China or rather the Chinese Province of Inner Mongolia, whose capital is Hohhot. Also known as Huhehaote, its Mongolian name means "green city", which houses a number of Buddhist temples and although an ancient frontier trading town, it only became capital of Inner Mongolia in 1952. This was shortly after the carve-up of territory following the Second World War. Outer Mongolia became a Soviet satellite calling itself the Mongolian People's Republic, whilst Inner Mongolia was designated the first of the five Autonomous Regions of the People's Republic of China.

Physically similar to Outer Mongolia from where we have just come, as the Chinese prefer to call it nowadays, it has a majority Chinese population and a fifteen per cent Mongolian minority. Lying within a few hundred-kilometre radius of Hohhot, is some of the famous Mongolian grasslands but little remains of the Great Palace of Xanadu. This was where Khubilai Khan kept his legendary summer residence, which was abandoned as his empire crumbled. At its peak, this grandson of Ghengis Khan, who befriended the Venetian traveller and writer Marco Polo, commanded an empire that was the largest area of land than perhaps anyone in history has ruled over, before or since. It encompassed China, central Asia, parts of Russia and Persia – modern Iran.

The Chinese border post was situated at Erlian a further five kilometres down the line where we waited outside the station for a huge goods train to pass by. Then we moved slowly into a station manned by Chinese border military police, all looking smart in their light green uniforms. We were now officially in China and as daylight was fading fast the flashing neon lights around the station lit up the sky as the Chinese station staff shouted instructions to one another. Since leaving Ulaan Baatar my journey had advanced another 1,113 kilometres.

The first official to enter our compartment took away the customs declaration then the second delivered a Chinese entry form and health questionnaire. This was followed by a pretty young lady in a white coat who took away the health and quarantine questionnaire. Finally a man in uniform with three stars in his lapel stamped my passport. So far so good and quick but there was however one other major operation to take place, that of bogie changing.

By Train to Shanghai

The Chinese railway system operates on the same standard gauge as the rest of the world. The Russian and Mongolian gauge is five feet and so wider by 3.5 inches, hence the necessity to change bogies here. After half an hour of formalities in the station, our train reversed out and proceeded, ever so slowly to the nearby bogie-changing shed. There, under military supervision each carriage was detached and hydraulically lifted upwards whilst all passengers were locked inside. After the lifting, the Chinese gauge bogie was then rolled out to replace the original Mongolian one. Dedicated staff wearing smart round bamboo hats, rather than the usual hard ones, carried this out and the whole operation was completed in about three hours. As we were in carriage number one, our changeover was first to be completed and then shunted out of the shed with our new bogie. Thereafter, all other carriages would follow a similar pattern until there was a complete train again. It was now past midnight, and I called it a day, and went to sleep without witnessing its completion.

Chapter Six
Beijing
Friday, 27th May

Dawn was breaking when out of the window I glimpsed the first sight of the Chinese countryside. The train had slowed down to a speed of only a few kilometres an hour due to railway works and by the track were groups of workers in bright orange uniforms, huddled around a small fire trying to keep warm in the chill early morning mist. The train stopped and one Chinese worker made eye contact with me as if exchanging greetings, like, - welcome to China through the window. At long last the day had arrived and was eagerly anticipating my arrival in Beijing later in the day when hopefully, Kate will be waiting at the station. I had advised her to expect chaotic scenes as the arrival of the weekly Trans-Mongolian Train causes great excitement with lots of pushing and shoving. Before that and on the way, there was to be my first sight of The Great Wall of China, one of the Seven Wonders of the World.

From the Chinese border to Beijing the distance is 842 kilometres and the first scheduled stop was at Jining. At this station in the early morning mist there was little activity, nor was there any at smaller stations subsequently, except for the

By Train to Shanghai

uniformed officials, standing to attention, on the platforms and holding their downward facing flags in either hand. By now the train had left the province of Inner Mongolia behind and arrived in Shanxi province, one of the earliest centres of Chinese civilisation.

As well as coupling Chinese bogies to our train at the border, a Chinese restaurant car was also attached. This is normal procedure for cross border trains as it is customary to attach a restaurant car from the host country whose territory it is traversing. My travelling companions were still asleep when I walked down the corridors in search of breakfast. The smoke filled restaurant car was already crowded and noisy with mainly Chinese passengers, most of who appeared to be smoking as I managed to get a seat sharing with two others. The menu was in Chinese only which seemed to bring out some stares from the others as I glanced at it. After a few minutes the waitress without waiting for my order brought me two fried eggs, some bread with jam on it and chopsticks to eat it with. This caused more amusement with the others when I requested different utensils, explaining that chopsticks were not ideal for a fry! Eventually, I was given a spoon and fork.

To-day, modern China is divided into thirty-one provinces and has 600 cities with a population in excess of one million people. One of these is the city of Datong our next stop, which used to be the ancient capital of the region, but is now sadly polluted. Here the local locomotive factory used to manufacture 250 steam engine locomotives per annum until recently but now it maintains only a museum of old steam engines in memory. Departing Datong and whilst crossing the Sangan River, there appeared a spectacular view of the river against a mountainous background. The landscape had also become much greener as we headed for Zhangjiakou. It was here that the ancient tea caravans crossed the Great Wall through its ancient gate. According to the guide book we should by now have a sighting of the Great Wall but because of the morning mist this was not possible, but to ease the disappointment we could admire the nearby mountains as the train headed for Kanzuang.

At this station a banking engine is attached to the train. This is needed because of the steep ascent up towards the Great Wall, whilst on the descent to Beijing it will be used for braking. By now most of the passengers were out in the corridors on the right hand side by the windows, waiting with videos and cameras for their first glimpse of this truly wonder of the world. Then the train entered a 2 kilometre long tunnel and as we slowly exited the tunnel, there it was. Through the mist I could see this mighty structure or at least a very small segment of its ramparts, which originally stretched 6,000 kilometres from the Bohai Sea in the east to the Gobi Desert in the west. I marvelled at how could they have built such a structure over two thousand years ago and on top of the mountain?

It was built to keep out the marauding barbarians from the north and hundreds of thousands of workers utilised in the construction - whose remains it is said form part of the infrastructure! On both sides, more and more of the structure came into view as the train slowly pulled into the long platform at Badaling, which acts as the railway station for the Great Wall. After a short delay which allowed time to take some spectacular photos the train now does a slow reversal downhill, ever so slowly, because of the steep descent round tortuous

By Train to Shanghai

wide bends. The continuous braking of the two engines made for a loud screeching noise as the train driver slowly inched us down the mountain. With the train reversal at Badaling, our number one carriage was now at the rear, which was much better, offering good views of the Wall and the spectacular mountainside as we slowly continued our descent.

Finally, after about 20 kilometres, we arrived at Nankou and here the extra engine was detached, to be used for the next ascent. The terrain here is flat so we sped off across the fertile plains to the Chinese capital now only 50 kilometres away. As we reached the uninspiring Beijing suburbs, it was time to reflect on my long journey of nearly 8,000 kilometres so far. No doubt, this recent stage was one of the highlights, along with the section around the southern shore of Lake Baikal, whilst not forgetting the single track journey through the Gobi Desert.

Now it was time to pack our bags and get ready for our arrival. I said goodbye to my Korean travelling companions. We had not conversed very much but in broken English they told me that on arrival they were going to take an aeroplane to fly to Western China. From there they intended continuing their journey by train to Lhasa, capital of Tibet. Apparently, this is the highest railway in the world at over 5,000 metres, which gave me an idea for some future travel. However, I subsequently found out that this newly constructed line would not open to the public until the middle of 2006, and hope that the Koreans were not too disappointed.

As we approached the railway station I could not but notice the large number of new high-rise buildings, either completed or in the course of construction. But then, in three years time this city will be at the centre of world attention. Beijing is scheduled to play host to the 2008 Olympic Games and it was obvious that preparations to cater for the expected influx of people are well in place. Finally our train pulled into a new modern station only five minutes late at 3.35p.m. then glanced at my watch. The platform was wide and spacious and not very crowded as I was told to expect - because those awaiting arrivals are kept outside the barriers. On the platform it was time to say goodbye. Firstly, to the two French girls but we hoped to meet up later in Xi'an. Secondly, to my friends from Holland and this time it was farewell as they were heading for Kunming in the south of China so our paths would not cross again. The English couple, Steve and Karin were staying in the same hotel as mine, whilst Mirjam and Raoul were also heading for Xi'an.

As everyone departed and went their separate ways I was left alone on the platform except for a few railway employees and stragglers. But where was Kate? Had something happened to her? I had telephoned her a few days ago to confirm my arrival time 3.30p.m. and now it was nearly 4 p.m. So, I rang her mobile, again nothing, it was switched off. Then I glanced at the huge station clock nearby which was showing 3 o'clock. It then dawned on me there may be a time difference between Mongolia and China although no one had told me so. I checked with a railway official who confirmed that Mongolian time is in fact one hour ahead of the Chinese and that the correct time was 3 o'clock. This was the reason for her non-arrival, so I waited on the platform as planned. Then at precisely 3.15 this bubbly attractive Irishwoman in a splendid pink dress came running down the platform along with her

Chinese friend Tina. I knew she would not let me down and after nearly three weeks I was very pleased to see a familiar, friendly face again!

It was outside the station's main entrance where all the chaos was happening. This was supposed to be on the platform but the general public is kept outside as we joined the queue for a taxi. Easier said than done as it was Friday afternoon and the concourse was crowded with locals preparing to exit the city for the weekend. Large swathes of China's countryside may be as they were decades ago, but in the cities nothing stands still. Everyone seemed to have a mobile telephone and most people seemed to be using them most of the time. Eventually we were successful and went in search of the Chuming Zhuang Hotel close to the Forbidden City where I was staying.

On the way there I noticed how construction is becoming feverish, In a city which always prides itself on being a city of mandarins traditional one-storey *hutong* houses are being torn down to make way for tower blocks and wide highways and all in preparation for the 2008 Olympic Games. It seems China has joined the rest of the world largely on its own terms but with a big bang and seems to be racing to make up for lost time.

Kate's Chinese friend, Psyche runs a medical clinic nearby and after checking into my hotel, we went over to see her. There I was invited to take a badly needed Chinese body massage by David, a medical doctor now specialising in traditional massage which was just ideal for my aches and pains. David told me that an extract from his curriculum vitae, included a commission to treat a former prime minister of China and on this information felt I was receiving the best treatment. Later, we all went out to dinner and enjoyed my first taste of the famous Beijing duck in a crowded restaurant and in the taxi back, marvelled at the night skyline of the new Beijing.

When the explorer Marco Polo reported on his adventures after returning home from Beijing, few believed his tales. It was no reflection on the way they were told, it was just that it was impossible for people in 14th century Europe to comprehend that such a "city of marvels", could exist on the other side of the world. Marco Polo spoke of an ancient city of great size and splendour that boasted magnificent palaces and broad avenues. At the time most people believed that China was a wilderness. The Venetian was fortunate to see the city during its first golden age when it was the showcase capital of Khubilai Khan, the Mongol, who established it.

Saturday - 28th May

In the early morning, the hotel had delivered to my room the local English language newspaper called *The China News*. The great pleasure of the past three weeks has been the lack of news – good or bad - usually bad - that has been happening in the outside world. However, a small item about an English footballer caught my eye. This particular footballer was holding out on his employers about renewing his employment contract and was demanding a salary of 125,000 pounds. Not, per annum as most people's salaries are accounted for, but per week and all he had to do was to kick a football? And then I thought, wait a minute, what about the important people who had ensured that I reached my destination safe and in one piece? What about Oleg, the train driver who had the

By Train to Shanghai

responsibility of taking his mighty train across the Urals to arrive in Irkutsk on time after four days travelling? His salary is very low when considering that the average national Russian wage is 40 pounds per week and the average weekly wage for Moscow is only 80 pounds. In our western world, it seems that kicking a football has become so important that it commands a salary of 125,000 pounds per week? Difficult to justify!

After breakfast, I went to explore the area around my hotel which was close to Tiananmen Square. It was already hot and humid as I walked past the Dang Lai Shan Muslim restaurant with its logo of sheep, towards Chang An Avenue one of the main thoroughfares in Beijing. At the end of this avenue was the vast expanse of Tiananmen Square, the world's largest enclosed space. This is the square that is best remembered throughout the world for the 1989 massacre of demonstrators and the lone student protestor who stood and faced the tanks of the Chinese army. Although it was only eight o'clock in the morning, the place was humming with people. Cyclists in their own wide lane, expensive cars and the odd stretch limo went by. The kiosks were already open and doing a brisk business selling badges of Mao Tse-tung, whose face gazes down from the wall by the main entrance to the Forbidden City. Mao proclaimed the establishment of the People's Republic of China in 1949 and when he died in 1976 over one million people attended his funeral here in the square but since that date the spirit of China has shifted hugely. The Cultural Revolution, which was Mao's ill-fated attempt to revive their revolutionary spirit, is now held up as a terrible mistake.

From here I walked through Zhongshan Park, which is close to the main entrance, and again all the little shops were open.

On the right hand side was a barracks for the military where they hold their morning parades and finishing with gymnastic exercises, a good healthy start to the day. Another group of soldiers marched off towards the main entrance before going on guard duty. In fact everyone seemed to be pre-occupied with exercise and to be the main order of the day. Walking through the park I spotted a group of elderly people partaking in exercises complete with swords whilst in the background others played badminton.

After avoiding the endless, aggressive, souvenir sellers I arrived back at my hotel and noticed a plaque on the wall near the front door. It read "Brief introduction of Chuming Manor - Built in 1930. Between 1946 – 47, it was used as the office of the Chinese Communist Party. It was an important transit post for the Communist Party of China and transported and conveyed a great number of cadres and batches of goods to the liberated areas, greatly contributing to the liberation of the Chinese people. Many well-known personages once stayed here. Chuming Manor was designated a protected site of historical interest of Beijing at the city level in 1995 and the part where the Chinese Communist Party delegation once lived was restored to its old looks in 1998".

So that was it, I was staying in a very important place close to Tiananmen Square. I could even have been using the same room as these famous cadres or maybe even Chairman Mao, who helped found the modern Peoples Republic of China!

Later in the morning, I met up with Kate and we headed off to see inside the magnificent Forbidden City, the largest and best-preserved group of ancient buildings in China. With its great marble courtyards, richly decorated halls and mazes of passageways, it is certainly an enduring monument to the longest-lived imperial system on earth. Behind the four-kilometre red ramparts, an extraordinary 500-year saga took place in the Forbidden City - variously known as the 'graveyard of souls', or 'the gilded prison'. To help explain its history and obtain maximum benefit from our visit, we hired a young Chinese teacher called Sue. She explained how it has been the centre of Chinese civilisation from 1406 and is known to thousands of tourists as the jewel of Beijing, with its four grand entrance gates, temples, pagodas, deep red walls, white marble platforms and roofs topped with brilliant yellow tiles.

We entered through Tiananmen Gate under a large portrait of Mao Tse-tung gazing down into an expanse spread over 200 acres and containing 1,000 different buildings. Inside 'The Great Within', life was exceedingly formal. Rank dictated everything from dress, to the shade of ink for your pen or colour of the crockery you could use to sip tea. The Emperor's wives were not allowed to leave the 9,000-room enclosure and common people were forbidden entrance. Instead, they lived outside, in low grey houses around its walls in 'The Great Without'-the city beyond the palace walls. Reigning supreme over this closed society was the mother of the emperor and beneath her, existed a strict female hierarchy, down to the kitchen maid. The wheels of this great machine were tended by an army of eunuchs - males as young as ten, who were rendered sexually impotent by the complete removal of their genitals.

Every culture based on the harem has used eunuchs, but in China, they achieved more power than anywhere else in the world. They were trusted by the emperors above other men for the one very obvious reason - that there was no danger of them siring a rival dynasty. Non-eunuch males were barred from the concubine quarters on pain of death. So these emasculated men became a sort of dedicated civil service within the Forbidden City, untroubled by human ties, the demands of children or the lure of the flesh. However, the rewards of such a sacrifice were immense and there was no shortage of willing candidates, partly because of the chasm between the poverty outside the palace walls with the wealth and opportunity within, ensured a steady stream of young men. At one time in the 17th century there were up to 50,000 eunuchs within the palace walls, whose primary purpose was to guard the Emperor's concubines. In all, there were 14 ranks of concubine and these women of whom there were at times thousands, slept with the Emperor, as was his whim.

After dinner, the eunuch in charge of the imperial bedchamber would present the emperor with a silver salver bearing the names of his favourite concubines. Then the eunuch would then cross the courtyard to notify and escort the chosen one. She would wash and undress and always arrive naked for security reasons of not being able to conceal a weapon beneath her clothing. Then, wrapped in a feathered quilt, she would be carried into the royal chamber on the eunuch's back.

Sue went on to explain how the Forbidden City remained an extraordinary dark recess of wealth and privilege, cut-off from the outside world until the early 20th century, when the infant king, Pu-yi came to the throne at the age of two in 1908. Henry Pu-yi was the hand-chosen successor of the Empress whose grand- nephew he happened to be, but his reign only lasted for three years. The republican revolution of 1911 ended 267 years of Manchu rule and his life story was immortalised in the Oscar-winning film called *The Last Emperor*. He was allowed to continue living in the Royal Palace but eventually realised he was both ruler and prisoner. Forced to remain inside the palace walls until 1924 when his English tutor helped him escape into the hands of Japanese diplomats as they had use for him. During the 1930's, the Japanese took control of Manchuria, renaming it Manchukuo. Pu-yi saw his chance of former glory and co-operated with the Japanese. Made Emperor, he assumed the title Kang Te, ruling Manchuria until the Japanese defeat in 1945. At the time of his death in 1967, Pu-yi was working as a park attendant in Beijing. His ashes now lie in a commercial cemetery near to the tombs where four of the nine Qing Emperors, who had preceded him, are buried, as well as princes, princesses and concubines.

As we walked along, Sue explained that today, many of the buildings on view are restored and date from post 18th century, mainly because of arson and accidental fires damaging the original infrastructure. In the extreme heat, we were walking along the main north-south access route, past various courtyards, pagodas and buildings, up and down well-worn steps, which for centuries would have been used to carry the sedan of the emperors around the city, before arriving at two temples.

One was called 'Hall of Union and Peace' and the other 'Hall of Earthly Tranquillity'. Both had information boards by their doors in English and Chinese explaining their history. At the bottom of each, it proclaimed, 'Made possible by the American Express Co' and the American Express logo attached. So I enquired of Sue, as to what on earth did the Americans make possible? And why was this advertising inside the Forbidden City the best-preserved cluster of ancient halls and buildings in the whole of China and advertising an American company at that? Sue explained that as there are over 9,000 chambers in the city, there is constant renovation work going on, all year long. It seems that the President of American Express came here a few years ago and in a fit of generosity, offered to finance the renovation work on these two temples, which was readily accepted by the Chinese authorities. But, I asked her, is it really necessary for them to show their logo inside this historic old city? The Chinese Government is not exactly short of money now and has enormous economic leverage over America through its purchase of 260 billion dollars of U.S. government debt. As well as investing so heavily in new infrastructure for the next Olympic Games and three new metro lines.

Further on, we passed three main ceremonial halls with the exotic sounding names like, Hall of Supreme Harmony, Hall of Middle Harmony and Preserving Harmony Hall, before reaching the northern gate. We entered a marble courtyard which contained some very ancient buildings, and there in a corner, was a tree, said to be over 400 years old, and just about standing with the aid of some props. Continuing along a maze of passageways and down a corridor nearly one kilometre in length, we arrived at a building known as the Clock House.

We paid our few yuan extra in order to see this vast collection of clocks of varying size, shape and design from the 17th and 18th century and all laid out in their glass cases. Some were Chinese in origin but a large proportion came from Europe, in particular, England and France, mainly the result of a Qing Emperor's passion for collecting clocks, the highlight of which is the rhino-sized Chinese water clock. The collection also includes clocks manufactured by two Englishmen named Cox and Harrison. Cox had the foresight to establish a clock factory in Canton, now re-named Guangzhou in the 19th century. His plan was to establish a lucrative business of selling English clocks to the emperor and obviously succeeded, as some of his ornate works are on display here today. Before the European influence reached these parts, the Chinese used sun dials as a means of telling the time, some of which are still in evidence around the Forbidden City.

So this ended our visit and we said goodbye to Sue. On departing we now encountered a different problem, this time from aggressive souvenir sellers, all lined up outside the exit. They just would not take no for an answer and were a complete menace. We finally made it to the refuge of a nearby restaurant for a well earned beer and a chance to sample some more Beijing duck, a northern Chinese culinary specialty, crisp and juicy and eaten in a pancake. Then it was an early night in preparation of a dawn start tomorrow morning for the trek to the Great Wall of China.

Sunday - 29th May

Richard Milhous Nixon became the first American President to visit the Great Wall of China in 1972 and is reputed to have said, "This is a Great Wall and only a great people with a great past could have a great wall and such a great people with such a great wall will surely have a great future". It is the only structure visible from outer space and if the bricks used to build it were made into a single wall six meters high and one meter thick, it would encircle the earth. This was the day when Kate and I would finally achieve a long held ambition and walk on its ramparts.

One of the Seven Wonders of the World and a world heritage site, the Wall itself was not built in one very large contiguous construction project. Around two thousand years ago under Emperor Qin Shi Huang, more famous for his terra-cotta army individual walls were simply joined together to make one continuous defensive wall. It had a dual use in that the wall also served as an elevated highway for the transportation of men and equipment across mountainous terrain, as there was room for five horses, abreast most of the way. Thereafter, the wall suffered neglect for hundreds of years until it was re-vamped under the Ming dynasty (1368-1644). This is what remains from the Ming dynasty that visitors from around the world come to see today.

Kate was staying in a hotel on the Workers Stadium Road in the north of the city and our coach trip started from there. Because of the notorious Beijing traffic we were going to Badaling at seventy kilometres the nearest point of the Wall to the city. Badaling Station through which I had arrived on Friday receives the majority of visitors and was the first section to be restored in 1957 for the benefit of tourists. Other less-visited sites at Simatai and Mutianyu are less developed and available to see but are further away. Setting off our party comprised fourteen tourists of various nationalities collected from city hotels.

Our guide for the day was a young Chinese female who introduced herself as what sounded like Linda, but who spoke so fast from a well rehearsed script it was difficult to interpret. It was just 7 o'clock on a Sunday morning but already traffic jams were forming as people went about their daily business, either by car but also on bicycles or on foot. Along the way, Linda pointed out a half finished stadium which would feature in the next Olympic Games in 2008. After 20 kilometres we stopped at a government controlled jade shop. Even at this early hour I counted fifty coaches - large and small, already parked up. Linda recommended a stop of thirty minutes to peruse the place but to please note the registration number of our vehicle in order to avoid any confusion later. Inside this vast expanse of a shopping mall, there were willing bi-lingual staff at your elbow, calculator in hand ready to assist.

The next stop was not scheduled and came as a complete surprise. We stopped at a large building, which was called "China Academy of Traditional Chinese Medicine". On going inside we were shown wall photos of various important dignitaries, like politicians visiting this academy, supposedly to impress us. Then it was upstairs to a room with sketches on the wall of the human anatomy. The door opened and in stepped a middle-aged rather ugly female with glasses in a white coat. She addressed our party on the Chinese approach to the human body and the six important arteries or channels as she described them, in our bodies - similar to a professor lecturing medical students.

Then the door opened suddenly and in walked three middle-aged doctors in white coats who seated themselves at the table in front of us. Each one was accompanied by a young female interpreter in pink coats who stood by their side. The nurse then introduced the males in white coats and indicated they would perform free of charge a medical examination for each willing participant. All that was required was to merely step forward and allow a pulse check and a view of ones tongues, just by opening your mouth. I stepped forward as first volunteer and expected a good report and two others followed, one an elderly Estonian male. My diagnosis was far from what I'd expected. In the space of one minute the doctor speaking through the interpreter, announced a kidney mal-function and some arterial problems. A prepared list of medicine was then produced and numbers eleven and thirteen recommended for my ailment.

The suggested cure was a two-week supply of Chinese herbal medicines, costing 1,000 Yuan or 120 dollars. The doctor recommended the treatment as urgent, but politely declined his offer. Afterwards all the party volunteered and everyone, young and old, had something wrong that needed Chinese herbal medicine and which, for a fee, could be supplied instantly. Kate's prognosis seemed equally grim. Give up drink, take these recommended medicines, pay us money, but otherwise she was in good shape for her age. Then I wondered - could a doctor tell a medical condition just by looking into your mouth, feeling your pulse, and all in a matter of one minute?

One thing for sure, this is a great money making place. Ten of our party were persuaded to buy some medicine and we were just a small party from all the coaches heading for the Great Wall. You do not need to be a great mathematician to work out the potential sales revenue - just for one day. Who was it that decided to bring us here, as I did not see it in any tourist literature?

By Train to Shanghai

There was one further stop conveniently placed on the way to Badaling and that was to view the Ming Tombs. Like the Pharaohs, the Chinese Emperors were also very fond of building magnificent tombs for their heavenly life thereafter. Thirteen emperors from the Ming dynasty are buried here, in ornate surroundings, in a tranquil valley at the foot of the mountain, chosen for its landscape, which is undeniably one of the loveliest around. At the end of the visit it was time for lunch nearby. Sue directed us into a vast dining hall capable of seating 2,000 diners and should the need arise, there is additional seating for 1,000 in an adjoining area.

Fortunately, we were one of the first to arrive, which was just as well as coming in last might result in a long wait for food. Our party of fourteen divided into two groups and formally introduced ourselves for the first time as we ate a typical Chinese buffet lunch whilst the dining hall started to fill up. Apart from ourselves, our table consisted of a Hungarian lady here to organise a cultural week on behalf of her government later in the year, and a Finnish lady working in Beijing for Nokia. There was the elderly gentleman from Tallin who refused to buy the Chinese medicine recommended for him and a Swedish man with his Chinese wife working for the U.N. in Afghanistan. We all had one thing in common: we eagerly anticipated first sight of the towers and battlements of the Great Wall of China.

Back in the coach and as we got nearer, it sadly started to rain. Visibility was poor with the mist, which was very disappointing and it was no consolation to hear Linda say that 'it rarely rains up here'! Kate and I did manage to buy waterproofs as we surveyed the scene on arrival, being greeted by a giant tourist circus at the entrance, with rank after rank of souvenir stalls. This is a seriously busy place, daily besieged by masses of Chinese and foreign tourists. Looking upwards and through the mist and rain, it was possible to see the first watch-tower and people walking along the battlement walls. Linda explained that to reach the top, it was necessary to take the slide as she called it on payment of a small fee. This slide is best described as the Beijing Badaling Biconvex Pulley. Sitting on a plastic seat, the attendant strapped us in and when a dozen seats were filled, the biconvex moved upwards on a single track, until reaching the top station at about 250 metres.

From the first watchtower, we started our walk along the four-metre wide battlement walls, being careful on the slippery surface and wet steps. Walking this wall is no easy stroll. The gradients can be tough, and the steps uneven. In the distance it was possible to see the highest watchtower, which was our ultimate goal. These watchtowers rise at frequent but irregular intervals, sometimes a few hundred metres apart but where the wall ascends the steep sides of the mountains, the distances between them is much greater. But it was a difficult walk in the rain and having to contend with a large number of fellow walkers, mainly Chinese who were out in force on this wet Sunday afternoon.

Peering over the parapet on the north side, there was a sheer drop down to eternity. Beyond, are the endless, yellow and barren grasslands of Mongolia from where Genghis Khan and his successors rode. No one could have scaled the parapet at this point, which was the original purpose anyway. Behind, to the south, lies the civilization that gave us silk and invented paper and gunpowder. Today, obscured by mist, lay a green and fertile valley and beyond it were more steep hills as we continued slowly with our walk, going uphill on more steep gradients, until reaching our destination.

Standing on the upper watchtower, the mind is confused, dumbfounded by the prospect. These are no mere hills over which the wall winds its way, but very sizeable mountains. Up and down, firstly in the deepest valley and then upon the highest peaks and so placed that it is never at any point commanded by the surrounding hills. There is no position at which its defenders could be taken at a disadvantage. The wall wanders on and on, until the mountains sink into hills, which in turn vanish into endless plains and on into the Bohai Sea to the east and the Gobi Desert in the west.

Then it was time to retrace our steps and return back down the battlement walls, until arriving safely at the lower watchtower, From here the journey down to the car park was in the same biconvex, and this time the young driver liked to scare his passengers by going as fast as he possibly could on a sharp bumpy downhill track, round many curving bends. We could see a cable-car in the distance and at the bottom we again had to negotiate past the ranks of souvenir stalls. After our exploits of the previous few hours and to pacify them, we bought a couple of pullovers, inscribed, 'I climbed the great wall'.

Back on the bus and drying out, Linda explained that what we had seen today - was a modern restored reconstruction set on the ancient foundations. To truly appreciate the magnificence of this ancient structure, Linda recommended exploring the untouched, crumbling ruins at a less-visited site like Simatai, northeast of Beijing. This site has 135 watchtowers along the way as well as obstacle walls, used as defences against enemies who had already scaled the Great Wall. She also did warn that this was not a trip for the faint-hearted. "It is very steep and has many treacherous passes" she said as our bus headed back down the highway, joining the returning traffic going to Beijing.

Later, Kate left for a business meeting and I headed back towards Tiananmen Square to see it whilst floodlight. Walking towards it an attractive young Chinese girl approached me to enquire my reason for being in Beijing. She introduced herself as Lisa, a twenty two year old student of English. As we walked along the middle of the square, Lisa pointed out the names of all the famous buildings we passed by, including the Great Hall of the People, which is the Chinese Parliament. Lisa, who spoke very good English explained that Tiananmen Square is physically at the city's centre and symbolically the heart of China and events it has witnessed have shaped the history of her country. It may have been designed as a space for mass declarations of loyalty but in the last century was often used as a venue for expressions of popular dissent. Lisa did not know anything about the events of 1989 when nearly one million protesters demonstrated against lack of freedom and Martial Law was imposed when the army moved in. No one knows how many died in the subsequent massacre of the demonstrators.

On the southern end is one of the remaining inner city gates, which once formed part of the original city wall, itself demolished after the 1949 revolution for unexplained reasons. We continued walking south to an area far removed from the opulence of the city I had just left. Life here was different.

This was old Beijing with its narrow streets of hutongs and souks bustling with activity. Lisa now turned the subject on to tea and asked if I liked tea and so on! At this stage I remembered from my morning conversation with Steve and Karin about their story from the night before. It seems they were also approached by a Chinese lady, who asked permission to practise her English conversation with them. Their walk also ended in some back street and up some stairs to a dingy room for the sole purpose to sample and drink the best tea. Having agreed to everything - their visit ended with a bill for 900 yuan or about 100 dollars, which shocked the English couple. After some haggling it was subsequently reduced - so the tea warning flashed when Lisa mentioned tea again and wondered whether I was outside the same teahouse, then decided quickly that I had had enough tea for one day, thanked her and said goodbye.

Walking back down the narrow streets towards Tiananmen Square, and avoiding the numerous rickshaw men who would rather I utilised their vehicles, than walk. Reaching its centre, there were police vans with loudspeakers blaring something in Chinese. Not another protest perhaps? No – it was just the police clearing the square of people. It was ten o'clock and it seems this square is declared people free during the night. It is obviously of huge symbolic importance with soldiers standing to attention at each entry point as if in homage to the square itself.

Passing the Chinese Revolution History Museum, I noticed a large digital clock showing in red letters, 1166 days, 22 hours, 10 minutes, and 20 seconds. When this period has elapsed the 2008 Olympic Games will have started here in Beijing, and confirmed by Omega, official timekeepers to the games,

Monday - 30th May

This morning I telephoned Chris in Shanghai who confirmed that he would meet me at the railway station on Friday morning and that a game of golf was arranged for Saturday at the Shanghai Links. This was my last day here in Beijing and had wanted to see the inside of some of the important buildings nearby as well as the Summer Palace, if there was time. Mao Tse-tung is reposing in his mausoleum on the south side of Tiananmen Square, named in his honour and is a place of pilgrimage for Chinese tourists. On this Monday morning as the temperature rose and the tourists started to arrive, I walked across to the entrance, past a group of adults flying kites, but sadly was about to be disappointed.

Outside the mausoleum a notice said, "opening days were Tuesday-Sunday". Therefore my viewing of the Chairman Mao's remains would have to wait for another day but by way of compensation a man offered to sell me a book called the "*little red book*", which was a collection of Mao's political writings, and in English.

Then, I reflected on what is it about countries like Russia and China who like to keep their dead leaders embalmed and on public display? Is it - to remind their peoples of the past? At least the Russian Orthodox Church is now in favour of holding a referendum to decide the fate of Lenin's body, but worried it could "inflame passions". No doubt, Lenin and Mao were monumental figures in their countries history and both changed the course of it by overthrowing existing unpopular regimes. Subsequently these changes cost millions and millions of lives, so that today their Communist ideology is discredited and has

By Train to Shanghai

largely disappeared, but not their embalmed bodies. Today, Mao's portrait and his corpse still dominate Tiananmen Square in the heart of the Chinese capital. The current Communist regime declares itself to be Mao's heir and fiercely perpetuates the myth of Mao. The reality is somewhat different.

Mao Tse-tung was born in 1893 in Hunan province the son of a peasant farmer who after leaving college, borrowed some money and set out to try his luck in the capital, then called Peking in 1918. Peking then was one of the most beautiful cities in the world where camels strolled in the streets, but here as in much of China was still very poor so that the freedom and opportunities of modernisation had brought no real advantage. Mao stayed with seven other friends in three small rooms. Four of them slept in a heated brick bed, under a single quilt, packed so tight that when one of them needed to turn, he had to tell the man on either side. Between the eight men, they only had two coats and as it was winter time, they had to take turns going out. Mao worked as a junior librarian earning a few yuan a month, one of his jobs was to record the names of people who came to read the newspapers. After six months, he returned home disillusioned with life in the capital and got a job as a teacher in a primary school.

By 1920, the Bolsheviks had taken Central Siberia and established an overland link with China and shortly afterwards, Mao helped to establish the Chinese Communist Party in 1921, although not one of the original eight founders. His first public expression of Communist belief was when in a letter to friends, "declared that he agreed to using the Russian model to reform China and the world". In the 1930s, Mao with his guerrilla army of peasants, and with Soviet backing, attacked the Guomindang Nationalist forces under Chiang Kai-shek, but were forced to retreat, which became known as the "Long March", a 10,000 kilometre journey on foot, across snow capped mountains and many rivers. It took one year for the retreat and by the time they reached the safety of the province of Shaanxi, of all that remained of the original 80,000 men that started the march - fewer than 4,000 survived.

However, the Communists had turned a humiliating defeat into a potential victory and Mao was undisputed leader and not feeling at all defeated as he felt the Party was now to all intents and purposes - his. Mao had created the most enduring myth in modern Chinese history, his "Long March".

Following the defeat of Japan in the Sino-Japanese War of 1937-45 in which the Communists and Guomindang joined forces, civil war resumed, ending in Communist victory. In 1949, Mao proclaimed the establishment of the Peoples Republic of China, whilst Chiang Kai-shek got into a plane, headed for Taiwan with the country's entire gold reserves to form the Republic of China. Massive problems faced the Chinese mainland with the Americans predictably refusing to recognise Mao's Government, maintaining that Chiang Kai-shek and the Guomindang alone represented the Chinese people.

Mao's political writings formed the theoretical basis of the new government one of which was the "Hundred Flower" campaign in 1957 under the slogan "Let a hundred flowers bloom, and a hundred schools of thought contend". This was misread by the intellectuals who openly criticized the Communist system and totally backfired on Mao. The following year the slogan was the "Great Leap Forward", in which in return for hard work,

China would eventually overtake the Western economies. Not learning from the disastrous policies of Stalin in the 1930's, Mao also changed the agricultural system.

Mao decreed, that all land held privately by peasant farmers, had to be pooled into collective farms, linked together as self-governing communes. Five hundred million peasants were to be spread over 24,000 communes and the aim was to turn them into super-efficient agricultural areas. Having fought to get their land, the peasants now were losing it again and collective farming does not suit the Chinese. The result was a disaster, resulting in an immediate slump in agriculture and in the years 1959 and 1960 both harvests failed and millions starved. At this time, Mao stepped down as chairman, purportedly due to ill health but re-appeared with greater standing during the "Cultural Revolution". This occurred in 1966 when a group of Beijing students denounced their university administration and supported the revolution. Under Mao's guidance they organised themselves into a political militia called "Red Guards". Anything attached to capitalism or the West, or even the Soviets, was attacked. They burned books; temples and ancient monuments were desecrated, and they became a law unto themselves because the police and army were forbidden to intervene. Tens of thousands were killed or imprisoned or paraded through the streets wearing placards carrying humiliating slogans.

By 1967 the international standing of China was at an all time low, and Mao was forced to intervene and arrested the most fanatical Red Guards, but they did not go quietly and it needed the army to storm the guard's university stronghold. In 1972 the bamboo curtain had finally parted when following

American negotiations known as ping-pong diplomacy - President Nixon walked on the Great Wall and commerce with the West began.

China suffered a disastrous earthquake in July 1976 in Hebei province, killing half a million people, and Mao died in September aged 83 years. By 1980 with memories of his Cultural Revolution still fresh in the mind, condemnation of his actions became official policy and his portraits and statues began to fall, but his body remains in Tiananmen Square where his portrait still gazes down from the wall of the Forbidden City.

In all, well over 70 million Chinese had perished under Mao's rule, and that, largely in peacetime. His ultimate ambition was to dominate the world, arguing that the world needed to be united where other empires had failed in the past and who was implicit in starting the Korean war by encouraging the North to invade the South and volunteering Chinese manpower in that war. Perhaps, his most callous act was to deny medical treatment: to Chou En-lai who was suffering from cancer. Chou was prime minister under Mao for a quarter of a century and the executor of his foreign policy.

Under Mao, even a cancer illness was not just a medical matter and he controlled when and how his Politburo members could receive treatment. Doctors reported first to Mao requesting immediate action to cure it. Mao decreed, first, keep it a secret and do not tell the prime minister. Secondly - no examination. Thirdly - no surgery, on the pretext that Chou was too old at - 74 years! What a miserable reward for decades of loyal service!

By Train to Shanghai

The nearby Museum of the Revolution covers the period from the first republic in 1919 up to 1949 and I was anxious to see inside. Again, there was to be disappointment as without a proper explanation, a notice said, "closed until further notice." An elderly weather-beaten souvenir seller approached me and we struck up a conversation. I wanted to know if he was around during the Cultural Revolution, and what was it like if so. "I lived in a village near Beijing. I wasn't a Red Guard and I didn't know any. I was just a farmer, but China's very different now", he said.

The Cultural Revolution was one of the darkest, periods of recent Chinese history. Forty years ago, Chairman Mao Tse-tung's Communist Party, ordered a return to their ideological roots, prompting a frenzy that led to hundreds of thousands of deaths and many more lives destroyed, over 10 years. "There is a Chinese proverb which says you should use history as a mirror" the souvenir man said, "and with history as a mirror, under no circumstances must we allow the tragedy of the Cultural Revolution to be repeated".

The Communist Party still does not accept responsibility for what happened and it remains a deeply divisive issue in China. The official party line is that history has judged the Cultural Revolution as a mistake by the Leaders and that - Mao was seventy per cent good, and thirty per cent bad. This makes for a busy time for the revisionist historians who constantly have to re-write the period after 1949, depending on which Party line is being adopted.

By way of compensation for the disappointment of the Revolution Museum, they offered the Museum of History instead. Although small, it contained artefacts and pottery sentinels from as far back as 2,000 BC up to 1919. But in relation to its long history, this museum was rather small and limited, when compared to the massive museums in St. Petersburg and Moscow. So, where were the rest of their artefacts and why were they not on display? There is probably a simple answer!

Back in the 1930s when the Japanese invaded and occupied parts of China a lot of their priceless art was shipped to the island of Formosa for safe keeping. When the Guomindang under Chiang Kai-shek were defeated by the Communists in 1949, they also fled there and took with them all the treasures they could lay their hands on. Since that date the Government of the People's Republic of China has been trying to recover the island - now re-named Taiwan as well as its treasures reported still kept there. China has viewed Taiwan as a renegade province since 1949 and recently Congress passed a law, which it said gave it a legal basis to invade Taiwan, if it ever declared independence.

Most of the west side of the square is taken up by the very imposing building with its twelve large pillars, called the Great Hall of the People, which was built in 1959. It is here that the Chinese Parliament sits as the National People's Congress. Today, Congress was not in session, so it was possible to visit. I joined the rest of the mainly Chinese tourists queue to pay my few yuan and enter this Great Hall, which I have seen many times before on TV. In order to protect the marble floors and the near one-inch thick carpet, the attendants offered plastic covers for our shoes. Inside, it has a main assembly hall for 10,000 and a banquet hall with seats for 5,000. The main reception rooms are all called after cities or regions and sumptuously decorated.

The visit took less than thirty minutes, as there was little activity other than the groups of visitors listening intently to their guides. Yet inside this building, legislators of the National People's Congress take the task seriously of monitoring government and drafting laws which affect one point three billion people or nearly one quarter of the world's population. For administrative purposes the country is divided into provinces, autonomous regions and municipalities directly under the Central Government. In turn these are sub-divided into autonomous prefectures, counties, autonomous counties or cities, in turn, sub-divided further into townships and towns and so on. Marxism may be dead, but democracy has not quite replaced it yet!

Outside, descending the steps it was noticeable that the car park had row after row of black limousines with tinted windows, all lined up and parked almost by number plate. So, there must have been legislators around, but in a different part of the Great Hall and out of view. It was now time to travel the Beijing metro where its map looked fairly simple, with a main line running east to west, interconnected to a circle line and a further one on the north side. The plan was to meet Kate in her office and the journey started at Tiananmen East station with the purchase of a single ticket for three yuan, about 25 pence.

At the barrier an attendant checked the ticket before boarding the train. The station and train were air-conditioned making it comfortable for travel and cooler than the extreme heat outside. On the train, the passengers were well dressed in summer clothes and generally in happy spirits travelling in a new train - contrasting this with Moscow and their old trains, morose faces and shabby clothes, but their stations had wonderful architecture as a consolation.

A Chinese man who was a double amputee above the knee came shuffling into our carriage on what remained of his thighs, without prosthesis, accompanied by a young boy, probably his son holding a begging bowl for money. I had heard about the problem with industrial accidents and the poor record in health and safety when workers like farmers are becoming miners to earn more money with little or no training. 6,000 miners died in 2004 in floods and explosions that made China's mining industry the world's deadliest. Last year, China produced about one-third of the world's coal but accounted for eighty per cent of mining deaths. Every million tonnes of coal produced here cost the lives of five Chinese workers. This amputee was a very sad sight, but just one of the statistics.

With a little help from a friendly newsagent I did manage to locate Kate and along with her friend we went for lunch in a nearby restaurant. Afterwards, it was time to say goodbye for the present as we planned to meet up again in Shanghai later in the week. In spite of the heat I decided to walk back to the metro. This way it was possible to at least witness the skyline emerging whilst Beijing grapples with modernity and where a lot of the city seems to be ripped up and rebuilt at a furious pace.

Walking down the main avenue, Jianguomenwai Dajie where traffic was almost stationary and so slow moving that

I almost kept pace with the vehicles. Along the way were more souvenir sellers and more disabled beggars, whilst passing modern department stores stocked with the latest designer clothes.

China has changed so much since I was last here in 1987 in Guangzhou, when known as Canton. Back then it was very much old China. My memories are of the streets full of bicycles and few cars creating their own humming noise. Now, here in Beijing it is few bicycles and many cars both big and small, creating their own pollution problem, accentuated greatly during the hot summer months, with choking smog as well as polluted rivers.

There was still time for the last visit of the day before leaving and that was to see the Summer Palace a short distance away in the northern suburbs. Taking the metro to Xizhimen, a taxi took me the remainder of the way to this lovely spot. Built around a vast public park, the centrepiece is a huge lake, called Kunming Lake, which forms the majority of the space. Here, boating is a popular pursuit in summer whilst in winter it is used as a giant skating rink. The palaces are situated to the north along the lakeside and the key character associated with them is Empress Dowager Cixi, who ruled over the fast disintegrating Manchu dynasty until her death in 1908 and who schemed to have her grandnephew Pu Yi become the last emperor when only two years old in the same year. Although this site has had summer palaces for centuries, it was Cixi who rebuilt and restored the palaces in the 19th century, including her passion for building a magnificent marble boat. One can understand why the imperial court would decamp here during the hot summer months as it is surrounded by hills, and cooled by the lake in beautiful landscape surroundings.

Chinese taxis are unique in that the driver sits protected by a Perspex contraption around him. His vehicle is fully computerised and gives instant receipts, showing time of entering and departing as well as total distance travelled, with price. There was no arguing therefore when he dropped me outside the station concourse of what looked like a new modern railway station. The tickets had already been delivered to the hotel so it was just a case of finding the correct platform, but for the first time, all baggage had to be passed through an x-ray machine. Then it was into a waiting area the size of a football pitch with scarcely an empty seat, but this was evening rush hour and trains were departing for towns and cities to the west of Beijing.

Eventually the electronic departure board announced that train TR 141 to Xi'an was ready for boarding which resulted in a mini stampede when the gate opened. I had heard good reports about Chinese trains and this one did not disappoint. It was a new, twenty-carriage monster complete with air conditioning, good wide berths, and individual TV monitors.

A smiling Chinese providnitsa greeted me at the door and showed me to my soft-seat compartment and handed me clean sheets. It was good to be back on a train again and for this overnight trip my fellow travellers were a Turkish lady and two Chinese, one male and one female. The evening light was fast fading as the train slowly pulled out of the

By Train to Shanghai

station at precisely 8.28 p.m. on a journey that would take twelve hours. Because the total size of the Beijing Municipality is 16,800 square kilometres, which is roughly the size of Belgium - it had taken a long time before we finally departed the sprawling capital city of 14 million. Before retiring for the night, I went to say goodnight to the English couple over a few Chinese beers in the restaurant car and later fell asleep watching the TV in my compartment as this new Chinese train made a different clickity-clack noise, or so it sounded.

Chapter Seven
Xi'an

Tuesday 31ˢᵗ May

Dawn revealed a totally different landscape. During the night we had crossed the Yellow River and were now in the central province of Shaanxi. This mighty river flows for 4,350 kilometres through nine provinces from the Tibetan plateau through Inner Mongolia before it meanders through the central China flood plains and enters the sea at Bohai Gulf. The river is often likened to a dragon, a reference to its uncontrolled nature. It causes problems because of the vast quantity of yellow silt that it carries along on its journey, which results in massive floods in the lower reaches. Chinese civilisation started here and neolithic habitation has been unearthed along the riverbank and for long periods, every Chinese dynasty had its capital somewhere in the area.

Glancing out of the window it was noticeable that the landscape was much greener with lots of trees. This was an agricultural region where all available space was neatly cultivated in contrast to the industrial area north of Beijing. The dawn sun reflected on the rocks as we sped through tunnel after tunnel

By Train to Shanghai

and village after village. Here we were in a large plateau area covered with a thick layer of wind blown soil covering the original landform.

Throughout time, this landscape of deep ravines and almost vertical cliffs has been deeply eroded. The nearby city of Yan'an was where Mao ended his famous "long march" so the whole region gave strong support to the Communists, when Mao created the myth of victory from a humiliating defeat, winning many recruits to the Communists.

I shared an early morning coffee with Serpil, the lady from Ankara in Turkey. She was on a flying visit to Xi'an and planned to return to Beijing on the train tonight. Serpil told me she was a lecturer in Islamic Art at the University of Ankara and wanted to visit Xi'an, which has its large Mosque, and Islamic past with Persian and Syrian influences on its history. We reflected on the *"No"* vote in the recent French referendum. She was philosophical about it all and believes that the Europeans are not yet ready to admit Turkey into the European Union.

After twelve hours and nearly 900 kilometres the train pulled into Xi'an Station. This is a city of six million people that once vied with Rome and later Constantinople for the title of the greatest city in the world, when it was the starting point of the main silk route to Europe. Over a period of 2,000 years, Xi'an has seen the rise and fall of numerous Chinese dynasties and the monuments and archaeological sites in the city and surrounding area are a reminder that in the past, Xi'an was at the centre of the Chinese world. Its Islamic element gives the city a touch of the exotic rarely found in Chinese cities.

At the railway station there was the usual activity with hawkers lined up by the entrance selling their goods. They were also there to greet the visitors at the north gate and the old Xi'an Wall. The Chinese have walled their cities since earliest times, and Xi'an is no exception except this one survives largely intact and these walls are the most distinct feature of the modern city. Totalling twelve kilometres in length, forming a twelve metre high rectangle, it had a major restoration job implemented a few years ago.

There was an orderly queue for taxis whose livery colour was a pale shade of green as I shared one with Steve and Karin to the Jianguo Hotel. In the early morning rush hour traffic, our driver used his local knowledge of the back streets but had pedestrians jumping for their lives as he seemed in one big rush to deliver us to our destination as we watched in trepidation. The hotel was very busy with the reception desk manned by twelve attendants in front of a dozen clocks showing the time in every part of the world. Again, my lucky number seven came up as I was allocated, room 27 on the 7th floor, which overlooked a small lake.

My visit to the terra-cotta army was planned for tomorrow, and instead went to view the capital of Shaanxi province, the most cosmopolitan and prosperous city, in inland China, whose centre is dominated by the twin structures of the Drum Tower and the Bell Tower. The former was built way back in 1380, signifying the importance that drums have with their long history in China. First used to boost the morale of their soldiers and entering the tower, I found drums of all shapes and sizes called, Flower Pot Drums, Mud Drums, Stone Drums, Fighting Drums, Bronze Drums, Gold Drums, and Elephant

Feet Drums. In all, quite a selection! On a small stage nearby and at the appointed hour a small troupe arrived to entertain the audience with some Chinese traditional music played on drums only. This was followed by a solo act, when an attractive young lady decked out in a dress full of drums arrived and danced around the stage to the sound of drum music!

That was enough of drums for one morning so I went in search of some lunch to the nearby Muslim quarter. I knew I was in the correct area when a couple passed-by. The man, who looked to be Chinese was wearing a *tope,* whilst the woman wore a *hijab.* The English translation of the lunch menu was a few hand-written lines on the back of a soiled greasy menu as I ordered the local dish of lamb and watched the local community go about their daily lives. A rather sharp young man sat down beside me and offered to help with the menu. After the usual explanation that he would like to practice his English, he told me a story about some antiques he had managed to get out of a provincial collection and could even sell them to me at a very reasonable price. I declined, making the excuse that I did not have space in my luggage.

After lunch it was time to pay a visit to the other ancient structure, the Bell Tower. This round building acts as a giant roundabout, which stands at the centre of a crossroads where the four main streets meet, north, south, east, and west. The original building was built in 1384 when the function of the bell was basically to help the peasants working in the fields. It was rung at dusk, presumably signalling the end of the working day. This present one is a monster of six tons, cast in bronze, and two and a half metres high. For a few yuan you are allowed to ring it and feel important, which I did but did anyone hear it? It was doubtful - because of the heavy loud noise of traffic below. As in the Drum Tower, this place also had its own stage and again at the appointed hour another troupe of musicians arrived to play more Chinese music, this time with a heavy emphasis on bells.

So, after the bells and drums it was a good time to look around the Xian Kaiyuan shopping mall and just as in Beijing business appeared good. Busiest of all was the section selling mobile telephones. Here the fifty or so young female assistants in their smart blue uniforms were kept busy serving an endless number of equally youthful customers. Just as in the capital Beijing, everyone seems to have a mobile phone. The rest of the mall, which had six floors round an atrium, was flooded with consumer goods.

As I walked back to my hotel along the main thoroughfare it was noticeable the streets were clogged with new cars, whilst the pavements crowded with locals many wearing white face masks. Shop after shop was full of customers and it seems the Chinese have embarked on a giant shopping spree - but how are they paying for it? Salaries are relatively low where a factory worker earns 30 dollars per week. However, the one exception that was not doing very well happened to be the *sushi* bar. Inside it was empty of clients and the staff stood looking outwards with glum faces. Perhaps the recent Sino-Japanese confrontation had something to do with it. It seems the Japanese school curriculum has been re-written to delete any reference to the Japanese occupation much to the annoyance of the Chinese, who suffered greatly under occupation. My walk finished just outside the west gate where I watched a group sitting outside a café as they played the favourite Chinese game of mah-jong.

By Train to Shanghai

It had been a long day from the dawn breaking in the fertile plains of Shaanxi and as fatigue had set in, a quiet dinner, I decided in a nearby restaurant, was best. It was crowded as I tried to make my way through its Chinese menu when I was joined by an attractive young Chinese girl. She introduced herself and grabbed hold of the menu, offering her assistance as she had obviously observed my difficulties. Her name was Ski and a twenty-two year old student out celebrating her graduation from university. She had been sitting at a nearby table with three other university friends but had left them and now sat at my table instead, as if asserting her maturity and sophistication. Ski spoke good English and was very interested in talking about my train journey.

Like all young educated Chinese she wanted to travel outside her country to gain more education and experience, but costs a lot of money, which only those with wealthy parents can achieve. The subject then changed to the Chinese Zodiac and she enquired the year of my birth. Replying to her, she confirmed this was the year of the dragon and a lucky one and then went on to explain all twelve animals of the Chinese Zodiac and named them as: rat, ox, tiger, rabbit, dragon, snake, horse, goat, monkey, rooster, dog, pig, and how some are unlucky as well and how Chinese people are very superstitious.

Ski went on to explain that these have existed in folk tradition for over two thousand years and that each lunar year is represented by one of the twelve animal signs. Why animals emerged as the focus is unclear. One popular story relates that an emperor held a race to determine the fastest animals. The first twelve to cross a chosen river would be picked to represent the twelve earthly branches in the lunar calendar. By now her other friends had departed leaving us alone but I knew I was safe when she enquired if I had any children or grandchildren. But she had already ascertained that as her own animal sign was the dog and most definitely not compatible with the dragon.

Ski went on to explain how she had already auditioned in a preliminary round of a reality TV show called *Super Girls,* just one of the 120,000 women hopefuls hoping to be voted the one Super Girl. This programme is merely the latest show in a frenzy of mass-entertainment, western-style TV to hit China's screens, prompted by the strong growth of a new rich middle class. TV is a serious business in China—state broadcaster CCTV claims to have one billion viewers. The old days of endless programmes showing the achievements of the air force, or military marches or programmes on farming are giving way to reality TV shows and chat shows and of course, Super Girl.

A recent survey in - major cities showed that 40 per cent of city dwellers under 45 watch the show and while you can't elect the government, you certainly can vote for Super Girl. Across the country fingers are twitching furiously as fans vote by mobile phone SMS message making it a very lucrative business because in one city the best three candidates received over 300,000 message votes, each costing up to 20 pence. Ski told me that packs of girls patrol the shopping precincts of China's cities, urging people to send text messages, avowing their support for a particular candidate. Right now there are just three teenage wannabe starlets left in this hugely popular show and nerves all over the country are jangling because the stakes are high - the chance to be a celebrity, to stand out from the crowd in a country of 1.3 billion, and to make big money in a society where cash is king.

But it was not always like that. For decades it was a crime punishable by imprisonment or death. Then it became a mere social taboo to be furtively practised away from disapproving eyes. But now, being wealthy is a cause for celebration, prompting thousands of Chinese millionaires to come out of the closet and flaunt their wealth.

More than twenty years after Deng Xiao-ping pronounced the end of Communism with the phrase 'to get rich is glorious', a new generation of self-made tycoons is starting to have the money and confidence to flaunt their wealth - in public! In Shanghai this was evident at the "Best of the Best" gala dinner, where twenty of the wealthiest entrepreneurs joined hundreds of luxury goods providers at an awards ceremony for those judged best able to satisfy the country's most expensive tastes.

600 Chinese with an annual income in excess of 10 million yuan (£700,000) voted for their favourite brands. And the results were, favourite sports car; Ferrari: favourite yacht: Princess; best fashion label: Giorgio Armani; best cigar; Davidoff; favourite auction house; Christie's.

Yet this is a country which is still ruled by a nominally Communist government and where 800 million people live in the countryside and where tens of millions are still living on less than a dollar a day. With income disparities widening, some question whether having award ceremonies or the publication of rich lists is good for social stability. Amnesty International believes there were 10,000 judicial executions last year, which if true, means that China executes more people than all other governments put together. There are 68 capital offences, ranging from murder and rape to smuggling, tax evasion, corruption and anti-government acts. Even the Communist Party members are not immune, as 115,000 *cadres* were also punished for corruption and other offences last year.

Wednesday, 1st June

The month of June had finally arrived when I would be able to see the terra-cotta army, artefacts from a period in history over two thousand years ago. On a more topical subject and having watched the morning news on TV, it included an item about Shanghai property prices. These have been rising at a very fast pace lately, but economists are sceptical it can continue as the Chinese government are implementing measures, like higher deposits, to slow it down. This might happen in the short term but what will be the situation in the future, with the projection of 400 million Chinese moving from rural areas to the cities? All of these people will need housing, so that will surely put pressure on property prices!

Our tour guide for the day introduced herself as Jesie as she arrived with the bus to collect Steve and Karin as well as myself and another English couple staying in our hotel. On the way we stopped at the Shrangli-La Golden Flower Hotel to pick up two couples, one from Hawaii and one from Greece. Just outside the city we made the first stop at a large garden site incorporating a temple and pagoda. This was the Da Cien Temple and the Dayan Pagoda also known as the big wild goose pagoda. The temple was built in the year 648 in honour of Empress Wen by the Tang dynasty Crown Prince Li Zhi. On the other hand, the pagoda was built for an entirely different reason.

By Train to Shanghai

A local monk named Xuan Zang, travelled to India to study and it is said to have walked all the way back home to Xi'an carrying Sanskrit sutras or Buddhism scriptures with him. He then translated the scriptures into Chinese and at his request the Big Goose Pagoda was built at the centre of the temple as a store for his precious sutras.

This open society was reflected in its religious tolerance and was a greatest period for Buddhism. Sadly, a subsequent fire destroyed the lot and now only replicas remains. This pagoda is sixty-five metres high and spread over seven floors. Jesie invited us to pay another twenty-five yuan for the privilege of walking to the top and anxious to prove to the Beijing doctor that not only did I not require his medicine, the top floor was achieved in less than ten minutes. From there the vast expanse of the city of Xi'an could be seen from every angle.

Within half an hour our party was back on board the bus and on to the Huaqing Hot Spring also known as Huaqing Palace. This rather heavenly place at the foot of the Lishan Mountains boasts 3,000 years of history as a royal garden - and 6,000 years as a source of hot springs. In generations gone by, it was the favourite visiting place of emperors from the nearby ancient capital of Xi'an. This tradition is still maintained by the present Chinese leaders as well as world statesmen like - Chirac, Hussein and Kissinger from abroad. Its centrepiece is the so-called nine-dragon lake, which has by its edge a large marble statue of the Empress Yang. The lake is surrounded by five ancient royal bathing sites and various buildings and pavilions with exotic sounding names such as Flying-Frost Palace, Stone Dragon House, Nine Curve Winding Corridor, Spelling Dragon Pavilion and the Fragrance Palace. One can only imagine what it was like when the Empress Yang lived here, but today, one hour was not nearly enough to inhale the tranquillity of this exotic location.

Since the terra-cotta discovery in 1974, it has spawned a huge replica industry as the site now attracts more visitors than the Great Wall, with an estimate of 3,000 every day according to Jesie. So on the way we paid a visit to a factory and watched craftsmen making their replicas in all shapes and sizes. The salesman offered any one item for sale and when considering his offer, replied there might be a problem with the weight, he promptly included in his cost the shipping price as well!

From here it was a short drive towards Mount Li, past some vineyards until our bus arrived by some green fields, where on March 29th, 1974 local farmers from Xi Yang village were drilling a series of wells in search of water. They accidentally discovered pottery fragments and ancient bronze weapons. This news aroused attention and the government arranged for an archaeological team to visit the following July. As a result - the Qin Shi Huangdi terra-cotta museum opened in 1979. Today, it is described by the Chinese as the 8th Wonder of the World and listed as a Unesco world-class heritage site, which is the greatest archaeological find of the 20th century.

To trace its origin we have to go back to Qin Shi Huangdi, the first Emperor of China and the founder of the Qin dynasty which reigned from 221 BC - 206 BC. Qin led vast battalions of Chin warriors into battle against equally vast hordes of enemies from the neighbouring states. He proved victorious and united the warring states, which made up ancient China, into one united country - China. Declaring himself - emperor,

By Train to Shanghai

he established a centralised state with the abolition of the old feudal system and standardised the weights and measures. He destroyed many ancient records and burned Confucian writings, but his most lasting legacy is for building the Great Wall and establishing the political principles that still hold in China today.

Qin had an obsession and fear of death and employed great energies and resources in his search for the elixir of immortality. Ironically, it was his search for immortality - through a regular diet of mercury pills - that first destroyed his mind, and all too soon proved that he was as mortal as anyone else. But before that, he had already started the construction of his own tomb and a massive palace building programme had been embarked on.

The Chinese population was around twenty million at the time and it is estimated that ten percent was used in its construction. Qin died suddenly at the age of fifty years in 210 BC before his tomb was completed. His son, Hu Hai, succeeded to the throne as second emperor and under his supervision, completed the mausoleum - two years after his death in 208 BC. Qin had believed in the after life underground and in its continuation there, which is the reason for the construction of his giant necropolis. Now 2,200 years later and thanks to the local farmers, it is now possible to view this legend based on reality.

Qin's underground tomb was constructed as a subterranean palace having a protective outer perimeter wall 6,200 metres in length. The burial ground itself was surrounded by an inner wall and the whole area had the trappings of existing life as if the emperor was still alive. Divided into three underground pits housing an estimated 8,000 life size pottery warriors and horses, the main army was housed in the first one. Pit number two had charioteers, archers, cavalrymen and many infantrymen, whilst army headquarters was situated in number three. All were located to the east of the emperor's mausoleum determining that his army was facing with its back to the tomb, serving as guardians to protect the entrance to the emperor's burial ground. The pits were constructed seven metres beneath the existing ground level with the terra-cotta figures placed in corridors. The roof was then covered by strong rafters and covered with layers of fibre mats and then earth-filled to totally conceal the army.

The weight of these warriors varied between 110 to 300 kilos, with an average height of 1.8 metres. Using local clay, they were probably constructed from a number of separate moulds. The legs were solid and the remainder hollow, then glued together before entering the kiln for baking. Of all the figures unearthed so far, none have the same features or expression, leaving experts with the conclusion that real soldiers served as the models. Also, on the back of some, the names of the craftsmen are inscribed or printed. Divided into seven main categories as high ranking officer, officer, armed and unarmed soldier, charioteer, cavalryman, kneeling archer, and standing archer, the officer class is identified by his greater size and more ornate armour. The cavalryman is identified by his tight fitting helmet tied under his chin, whilst the charioteer by armoured sleeves and hands firmly held out as if to hold the reins.

Originally, all would have been painted and indeed during discovery, many have been unearthed, still with their original paint. However, once exposed to the light after so long buried away, the colour started to fade and the paint flaked away. This problem has tormented archaeological experts for years but recently with the help of German experts, new inventions have been discovered, enabling the warriors to keep their original paint from fading and flaking.

This is how the tomb was in 208 BC, but just four years after Qin's death and two years after completion of the mausoleum, a major catastrophe occurred. According to the records in the historians book *Shiji*, a rebel and arsonist from the Qin dynasty named Xiang Yu, started a fire, which burned the emperors palace and mausoleum. The fire damaged the pits and collapsing roofs smashed the terra-cotta warriors and horses into fragments.

Not one complete figure survived the fire intact. Today, mending these broken figures has become a painstaking exercise for the dedicated archaeological workers. It is indeed a lucky day if they find two pieces that fit together - in any day - in the ongoing excavation of the site. What items that have been excavated so far are now on display in the three original pits - the largest of which is number one with a total area of 15,000 square metres and five metres deep. At the outer edge is what remains of the well, which started this all off back in 1974.

Laid out in front of us were warriors and horses arrayed in battle formation. There were rows and rows of soldiers and in between them twelve chariots, each drawn by four horses. In total an estimated 2,000 pieces on display, all facing towards you in eerie silence as if staring one in the face. When the excavation is finally completed in this pit - the assumption is that 6,000 warriors and horses will have been unearthed. Entering this pit, is surely one of the most memorable sights in China today?

In 1976, pit number two was discovered and which is much smaller at 6,000 square metres. Originally, this housed the archers, both kneeling and standing as well as sixty-four chariots arrayed in columns with the war chariot in front. The north area was devoted to the cavalry. Each of the one hundred cavalrymen stands in front of his saddled warhorse, holding the reins in one hand and a bow in the other. That was how it was, but today only a small number are on display, and excavation work continues. At the same time, pit number three, which is the smallest, was unearthed. This was the command centre for the entire army and well protected by the armies of the two larger pits. Originally, this housed sixty-eight figures and one chariot drawn by four horses.

Nearby, is the multiple exhibition hall which houses two restored bronze chariots and horses. Discovered in 1980, they had been crushed into thousands of pieces that it took all of eight years of painstaking restoration work by archaeologists to restore both to the condition they are in today, inside their glass cases. Called deluxe sedans, the emperor was to use them as he went on inspection tours in his afterlife or so he envisaged. These were modelled on real chariots, horses and driver but only half in size. Re-named "high chariot and comfortable chariot", each has a single shaft, two wheels and drawn by four horses. They are the biggest, most deluxe and best-preserved bronze chariots and horses so far unearthed.

By Train to Shanghai

Emperor Qin Shi Huangdi's actual burial mound is two kilometres west of his terra-cotta army - but has yet to be excavated. This is a mound of earth the size of the pyramids and is said to contain the largest mausoleum on earth. Sealed within, is the vast tomb of one of the most powerful men who ever lived. Said to surround this necropolis is a gigantic bronze replica of the world he conquered and ruled, complete with rivers and seas of flowing mercury. That's the story, anyway. Given the nearby pits containing the kind of artefacts that a man who believed in himself - to be divine and immortal would need to keep his wits about him in the afterlife - experts have every reason to believe this is a legend based on reality. Other pits, one hundred and eighty of them, have been found to contain yet more wondrous objects. Amongst them are figures, also terra-cotta, and also life-sized, of dancers, musicians, acrobats, beautifully crafted birds, as a result of the continuing archaeological digging which will continue into the foreseeable future.

The farmer, Yang Zhifa, who started it all when he discovered pottery fragments whilst looking for water back in 1974, now spends most days of his twilight years in his souvenir shop here. This is his reward from the government and I met him signing copies of the latest book called *Qin's Terra-Cotta Army*, sitting under a notice "no photography".

Jesie told me to be cautious of the local farmers who have a reputation of aggressive selling, and to expect hassle at every step when exiting. Indeed, I had underestimated their aggression, as I was manhandled by them in selling me their replica warriors. In the end, it worked out well having obtained a few bargains and we were soon back on the highway, heading towards Xi'an. That was until a car driver decided to stop his vehicle in the fast lane causing our bus driver to swerve violently to avoid an accident.

The driver apparently had missed his exit and was in the course of reversing back to avoid the tollbooth ahead. Due to the quick thinking of our driver a nasty incident was avoided, which could otherwise have marred what was thus far, a memorable day.

When we arrived back in Xi'an - Jesie recommended an evening at the Chinese opera and she duly arranged a ticket whilst both the English couples declined her offer, blaming tiredness. It was to see the authentic tang dynasty cultural presentation, a spectacular performance by over 100 performing artists. It combined authentic music and dance with magnificent costumes and choreography in a theatre that can accommodate 650 people in its auditorium. Since 1988, they have performed nightly, now over 7,000 times and the cast includes some of China's most gifted artists. Some of the audience had arrived earlier for dinner in the auditorium - and departed afterwards in large coaches parked outside. Empty taxis were non-existent for some unknown reason and required the best endeavours of the manager, his assistant and another employee on the road outside the theatre to obtain the elusive taxi to take me back to my hotel.

Thursday - 2nd June

In the evening I was due to depart Xi'an for Shanghai but before that - a visit to the Great Mosque of Xi'an having been highly recommended. This morning after breakfast a smiling female taxi driver drove me to the Bell Tower from where I walked down a narrow street leading to the Muslim quarter. Here, the width of the street constricts to a narrow un-surfaced alley, which is the middle of the quarter, for centuries the home of the Hui minority - now numbering about forty thousand - and whom are said to be descended from eight-century Arab soldiers. A street sign on the left hand side read, "important historical site," which lead down an even narrower alley with little shops, and rows of street stalls in front and their owners trying to entice me inside. Until finally - down one more winding alley, I arrived at the largest and most famous mosque in China. Behind an enclosed wall, ten metres high, with an inside area totalling - 13,000 square metres of which 6,000 relates to floor space.

According to historical records carved in stone tablets and preserved inside, this mosque was established in 742 AD during the Tang dynasty and restored and expanded during the Ming and Qing dynasties from 1368 to 1911. Because of its historical importance - the present Chinese government allocates special funds for its annual upkeep. Nevertheless, I did have to pay an entrance fee just as in any other tourist site whilst worshippers were arriving for their mid-day prayers and entering the rectangular complex built east to west and divided into four courtyards.

In the first courtyard I walked through a wooden archway of upturned eaves and glazed roof tiles. This archway - built in the 17th century has several houses on both sides having displays of Ming and Qing furniture. The second courtyard has three connected stone memorial gateways and the main gate is inscribed in Chinese calligraphy "The Court of the Heaven". Behind, are stone tablets having decorations of carved dragons

- both carrying inscriptions about repairing of the mosque on the imperial orders of Ming and Qing dynasties. Some of these are also inscribed with Chinese characters written by famous calligraphers and regarded as some of the best works of art in China.

The imperial hall in the third courtyard is the oldest building in the mosque. In the middle is the introspection tower, which serves as the minaret for calling Muslims to prayer, and is the tallest building. On the northern side is the lecture hall, which houses a hand written copy of the Koran from the Ming dynasty, and a well preserved map of Mecca from the Qing dynasty. Walking into the fourth courtyard the first building in front of me was called "the one god pavilion", whose inscription "one god" was written by a high ranking official - also from the Ming period. Both sides of the pavilion, houses many historical and cultural relics - one has an old stone sundial and stone tablets with important inscriptions about the mosque from the Tang dynasty, 618-907 AD.

Finally there was the magnificent hall of worship which has the capacity for a thousand worshippers under its huge eaves and brackets and a roof covered with blue glazed roof tiles. Its ceilings are carved with classical scriptures while inside - all pages of the Koran are carved in six hundred pieces of wooden boards - some in Chinese - and the rest Arabic. These carvings are rarely seen in any other mosques - anywhere and this is the reason Muslims arrive here from all over the world, and why, in 1988, it was designated a key national historical site under special protection.

On the way out it was noticeable how the bath-house was crowded with worshippers - washing before prayer, and again avoiding the souvenir sellers walked back down the same narrow alley. At the end, I was approached by a soft spoken educated Chinese man who introduced himself as Peter. He was curator of the ancient house of Gao Yue which dates from the Ming period and where he was standing outside. After paying a small entrance fee, Peter showed me around the complex, which includes antique furniture, pottery, and porcelain from this period. It won a Unesco prize for cultural heritage a few years ago and the government of Norway have decided to offer their financial assistance.

At the end of Bei-Yuan-Men street and while searching for a restaurant for lunch I was pleasantly surprised to meet again Mirjam and Raoul, the young Dutch couple I befriended on the train in Mongolia. This was a real chance meeting so we decided to have lunch together. Raoul suggested the restaurant with the strange name - little potato-chicken, which was nearby up a side street. We ate some chicken chilli whilst discussing our experiences of the past few days and talked about the history of Xi'an. One thing we both agreed - was that Xi'an must have been a city of great tolerance – with the two great religions of Buddhism and Islam – flourishing side by side as far back as their first existence. Then we talked about the Silk Road, whilst eating in the middle of the Muslim quarter.

From this city the Silk Road curved northwest past the Great Wall to Kasgar in central Asia. Here the merchants traded their goods with middlemen who carried them beyond the frontiers of China, either north to Samarkland and beyond to Persia or even the Mediterranean or south to Afghanistan and India. These caravans would carry jade, porcelain amongst others and of course silk, which had a fascination with the

Romans. The Chinese were determined to keep their secret and the silkworm which had been domesticated for hundreds of years was forbidden to be exported under pain of death.

Then laden with western goods like figs, dates, grapes, ivory, linen and wool, the caravans would return to China by an arduous, slow and dangerous journey - avoiding marauding bandits on the way home which could take up to six months. In the 2nd century BC, nothing was known in China of the existence of people beyond its border except by rumour, until they sent an emissary to investigate.

Afterwards the foundations for this famous road to the west, which was to become one of the most important arteries of trade and culture in world history, were laid. Then the caravans started to roll, reaching its zenith under the Tang dynasty, and religion also arrived. Buddhism became an influential force gaining rapid acceptance in northern China where Buddhism became the official religion. By the 13th century, the Silk Road came under Mongol control and flourished, but this was its peak. Shortly afterwards, this overland route went out of favour with the opening up of the sea routes between China and the West.

Soon it was time to say a final goodbye to my new Dutch friends, but we promised to keep in contact whilst they travelled in Asia. Walking back down the narrow street was like an obstacle course in avoiding the taxis, motorised rickshaws and bicycles as I admired an attractive lady wearing a hat and holding an umbrella in one hand to avoid the hot sun, as she went past me on her bicycle.

From here it was a short distance to the giant Drum Tower and under its marble floored circular subway housing a shopping mall - whilst at ground level it acts as a large roundabout for the heavy traffic converging from six lanes. Another female taxi driver took me back to my hotel to collect my luggage for the last leg of my rail journey. The English couple from Warrington were waiting in the foyer and offered to share their taxi with me to the railway station. It was evening rush hour this time and we were both anxious not to miss the last scheduled train to Shanghai by getting caught up in heavy Xi'an traffic jams.

At the station there was the usual check-in queue past x-ray security into a large waiting area before the electronic departure announced departure of T140 for Shanghai. Again, the attendant checked my ticket in exchange for clean sheets and at 18.44 p.m. - right on schedule - the train departed. I was in carriage number twelve and my lucky number seven berth had come up again. This time I was sharing with the same Warrington couple and a female Chinese university student. The English girl was called Ming, who was of Chinese origin with a Chinese name but did not speak the language. The man's name was Nathan and they both worked in psychology. The Chinese girl had an English name called Irene and was on her way to take English examinations in Shanghai and spoke good English.

There was still daylight to admire the landscape as I noticed the same Lishan Mountains where yesterday we had been to Mount Li to see the terra-cotta army. This was an agricultural area with men and women working in fields but these days, some Chinese head for the city, with the lure of the bright lights and the 21st century and of course where there are jobs. Looking out the train window with Irene, she surprised me with her comments about this being where the real China is - not in the heavily polluted cities with their tower blocks and shopping malls - but here amongst the small villages.

She explained that there are 800 million rural residents, mostly living on a dollar a day, and roughly one third of what city dwellers earn - which is why there is this exodus from the land. The Communist Party recently admitted that the countryside was "still arduously crawling uphill", and are anxious to improve the lot of poor farmers and want to address the rural-urban divide. As the fires of burning chaff from the corn lit up the horizon, my fellow passengers prepared for bed and the train continued its smooth journey.

Chapter Eight
Shanghai

Friday – 3rd June

The restaurant car had closed early last night - an ideal opportunity for an early night ahead of the weekend in Shanghai. At six o'clock it was possible to view the sunrise, whilst my fellow passengers were still asleep. Since leaving St. Petersburg on 12th May, I have followed the sun and seen many sunrises from the train window - but this one was a different - in advance of the upcoming polluted cities, when the sun will disappear behind a cloud of smog. Outside, in the fields, the farmers were already working with their wheat, while the landscape looked more like England in August. Then we passed some rice fields and as the train slowed down - saw an elderly woman, stooped from years of rice-picking go by, a stick in her right hand and an umbrella in the other. Further on, more farmers were beating rice straw whilst another one herded, what looked like a flock of brown ducks down a country lane.

As we continued towards Shanghai, the queue for the washroom got longer. It seemed that third class passengers found our water more enticing as I went in search of some food. As usual the restaurant car was a crowded smoke-filled place as I ordered two fried eggs from the waitress. Enjoying my Chinese breakfast it was time to reflect on my mammoth journey, now nearing its end, after nearly 10,000 kilometres. Was the long journey up to expectation? It was better and more comfortable than anticipated! It had taken me through three large countries - seen some of the greatest historical sites in the world, as well as ancient artefacts and priceless works of art. It had been possible to retrace some of the route of those early travellers like the Meakins and Shoemaker in the last century, about which they elegantly wrote.

Whilst still in the restaurant car - at 8.30 a.m. the train crossed the mighty Yangtze River. This is the third longest river in the world at 6,400 kilometres. It rises 18,000 feet above sea level in Tibet and before reaching the sea, cuts its way through a land of mountain and plain, of snow and desert. It tumbles and foams downward in a gigantic funnel through the deep gorges of Sichuan, twisting past the rocky promontory of Chongqing, until its last giant waterfall spills into a sudden stillness, with all the magic of a lake, where the lowlands begin. From there the Yangtze flows majestically, the king of rivers, across one thousand, five hundred kilometres of rich, fertile plains dotted with farms, villages, towns and cities, until finally, coffee-coloured and turbid, it reaches the open sea, just north of Shanghai.

Its most dangerous stretch is the 200 kilometre of rapids and sharp hairpin bends around the area known as the Three Gorges, in Hubei Province. Although difficult to navigate in this area, nevertheless it flows through some spectacular scenery. When passing the east edge of the Sichuan Basin, it cleaved a path through the mountains and formed these uniquely beautiful, magnificent and wonderful gorges, named Qutang, Wu and Xiling - the Three Gorges. However, after a century of planning and in order to control the Yangtze's tendency to flood as well as to generate hydro-electric potential, a giant dam called the Three Gorges Project is currently under construction. This is the largest water conservancy project ever built, anywhere in the world and will eventually be the world's biggest hydro power station. When finished in 2008, it will play an important function in flood control - of the middle and lower reaches of the Yangtze River. However, one of the downsides is the fact this will raise the water level 100 metres and sadly mean submerging whole communities and cost over 200 billion yuan – about 25 billion dollars.

The large iron bridge over the Yangtze is called the Yangtze River Bridge, which was built in the 1960's and carried us into Nanjing station where all along one side, workers toiled away at what looked like a new station complex in this important rail junction. Just as Beijing changed its name from Peking - Nanjing used to be known as Nanking, which means southern capital as distinct from the northern capital – Beijing. Some people still consider it to be the rightful capital with its gateway position to the Yangtze. In 1937 the name Nanking became synonymous with one of worst atrocities of World War 11, after the so-called Rape of Nanking, in which an estimated 300,000 civilians were butchered and tens of thousands of women were raped by invading Japanese soldiers. It was the recent publication of a revisionist history text-book that prompted widespread anti-Japanese protests. The text-book which was adopted by the Tokyo Board of Education, glosses over the Nanking massacre. Following the Japanese surrender in 1945, Nanking briefly resumed its status as the official capital of China, but just four years later in 1949, the victorious Communists choose instead to return to Beijing. When the Opium Wars ended by the signing of the Treaty of Nanking - Hong Kong was ceded to Britain in 1841.

The train had stopped for twenty minutes with the usual change over of passengers and visibility was now poor, with a thick vapour of smog, probably coming from the large petrochemical complex nearby. The smog persisted and at Chang-Zhou the visibility was so bad it was not possible to see the top of the nearby high-rise buildings. An attendant walked along the corridor selling maps of Shanghai in Chinese, which was of no use to me as an announcement confirmed our train was running late. This was disappointing as I knew that Chris would be waiting on the platform and could only hope that this message was relayed back to Shanghai Station.

At least my wait was nothing compared to the unfortunate crew of the British warship –*Amethyst,* who spent the whole hot summer of 1949 stranded on a mud-bank in the Yangtze estuary. Their bad luck was to be in the wrong place at the wrong time - whilst attempting to deliver supplies to the British Embassy, then in Nanjing - and got caught up in the Chinese Civil War.

It so happened, that as the *Amethyst* moved upriver towards Nanjing the Communist forces of Mao Tse-tung were poised in force on the north banks of the Yangtze, ready to mount their first waterborne assault against the Nationalist forces on the south bank - but unknown to the British crew. Suddenly,

By Train to Shanghai

and without warning the Communist guns opened up, hitting the *Amethyst*, knocking out its engine and killing seventeen crew members, whilst forcing the vessel on to a mud-bank.

Shortly afterwards, the Communists prevailed in the civil war, but as the British government did not initially recognise Mao's regime the poor old *Amethyst* and its crew remained in the middle of the Yangtze throughout that hot and very humid summer. While negotiations dragged on and on, suddenly, out of the blue relief came in the shape of the weather. Luck was finally at hand, in the shape of a huge monsoon during November. This raised the river level - sufficient for the captain to make a quick dash for the open sea. He succeeded, with the Chinese in hot pursuit, firing their guns at the *Amethyst*, as the captain went full steam ahead!

There were further stops at Wu Zi an industrial city where a lot of passengers got off and Shoo Fang with its many new factories under construction. A large power station appeared on the horizon with barges full of coal heading up a canal towards it. Further on there were row after row of new apartment blocks, ready for the factory workers. Then these buildings disappeared behind some tall poplar trees which someone had the wisdom to plant along the line and obliterate the ugly concrete skyline.

Whilst waiting at the aptly named Weiting station, I had a brief conversation with Irene about the present education system. She confirmed that basic education is free - but that books, uniforms and school food, all have to be paid by the parents plus any kindergarten costs. Parents are fully aware that the quickest route to riches and a good job for their children is through education and a heavy emphasis is made on this. When examination time arrives, parents will accompany their children to the exam centres and will sit outside all day and remain to offer their support. This is education in modern China, where great sacrifices are made. Whilst talking to Irene, the young English couple were busy packing their luggage. Ming had bought so many items and souvenirs that she had difficulty closing her bags.

For what seemed like eternity but was only twenty minutes and without explanation we finally departed Weiting Station. Visibility was still poor as we passed old dilapidated factories with their chimneys belching out black smoke. We passed a new motor plant and more new apartments whilst under a canal bridge, a barge passed beneath it with minimum clearance. Suddenly, the skyline of the great metropolis of Shanghai started to appear on the horizon. It was obvious, that this great city is currently undergoing a fast economic expansion - from its skyline, now filled with new skyscrapers. It seems to be well on the way to re-capture its old, pre-eminent position as east-Asia's leading business city.

Then we finally pulled slowly into Shanghai Train Station and for the first time on my journey of nearly 10,000 kilometres, I was running late - by about one hour. In spite of this delay, Chris had remained on the platform and was there to greet me when I struggled down the train steps with my luggage. With him were David Gu and Mr Wu, two business colleagues who had come along as well. For whatever reason, the railway authorities had not even bothered to make an announcement about the train's late arrival, and were left to wait, in something of a quandary.

By Train to Shanghai

All's well that ends well and as it was now mid-day and time for lunch, we all set off in one of the half a million taxis that ply their trade here - to an open-air restaurant by the Huangpu River. Because the estuary of the Yangtze was wide and unprotected Shanghai itself grew fifteen kilometres inland on the banks of the Huangpu, which flows into the Yangtze near its mouth. There, under a very hot sun we ate lunch whilst watching the ships and barges go by on the crowded river, whilst admiring the Oriental Pearl Tower, the highest TV tower in Asia at, 468 metres, on the opposite bank at Pudong.

Located on the confluence of the Yangtze River, the Pacific Ocean and the Grand Canal - Shanghai has been a major port, from as far back as the Song dynasty. The British moved in here in 1842 under the Treaty of Nanking, which granted the right to trade in several ports, including the swamp and mud between the Sozhou Creek and the walled Chinese city. Soon afterwards the French came in 1847 setting up the first concessions. After that, the Americans came in 1863 - followed by the Japanese in 1895. So, having divided the city up into their own concessions - they lived indefinitely under their own national laws - policed by their own police force - their own customs authorities and own municipal councils. The original tract of land became the unique International Settlement - a Western oasis in China.

Before the Second World War, Shanghai had become a unique International City which continued to function under its foreign rulers even after the Japanese invaded China. After Pearl Harbour, the Japanese occupied Shanghai until VJ-Day in 1945, by which time - Shanghai had changed its status and became a Chinese city again. A few years earlier in 1943, the British, Americans and the French had abrogated their extraterritorial rights to the Nationalist leader, Chiang Kai-shek, whose troops and politicians took control following the Japanese defeat in 1945.

It sprang to life again and despite the struggle for power in the ensuing Chinese Civil War - Shanghai, with its foreign residents continued to prosper, until 1949, when the Communists crossed the Yangtze and Shanghai fell to Mao Tse-tung. Before that, Asia's greatest city - one of the largest ports in the world - had stood alone, in a strange way aloof. Without any concern for the future, it appeared as though its six million inhabitants had closed a collective eye to the civil war around them. They were determined that - until the enemy reached the gates - the city would remain in all its glory - a last oasis of yesterday - in the China of tomorrow.

When the Communists arrived they took control of the most important business and trading centres and life changed dramatically for the worse, as the Communists put their own brand on the city and dimmed the bright lights of the previous era. They inherited a city that was broke because the Nationalist leader, Chiang Kai-shek, had managed to rob the Bank of China of all the gold reserves and flee to Taiwan.

This was Chiang's most daring coup and the culmination point of his treachery, nothing less than a plan to rob the Bank of China of its stocks of bullion - of all the gold reserves in the country. There had always been large reserves of gold and silver in the vaults, so plans were laid with the utmost care. A freighter was tied up opposite the Peace hotel, then called the

By Train to Shanghai

Cathay and its hand-picked naval crew dressed down so as not to attract undue attention. Several senior executives of the Bank of China had been admitted into the plot as they were needed to open the vaults and in return were offered passage on the freighter along with the gold.

The robbery had to be kept secret, as long as possible as time was needed for the vessel to reach the open sea. By pure chance, an English Journalist, named George Vine, was working late in his office when suddenly he heard a sound not normally heard in downtown Shanghai after dark—the peculiar chant of coolies carrying heavy loads and the soft pad sound of their feet. Gazing down from his fifth-floor office, he could hardly believe his eyes. In Indian file, the coolies padded out of the bank. Each coolie carried two pans or parcels, and attached by a rope to one end of the bending bamboo pole, arched across his shoulders. They loped up the gangplank of the freighter, which was drenched in light and handed over their cargo, then to return for more.

Realising immediately what was happening; Vine cabled the news to his London office. He had witnessed Chiang's latest master-stroke leaving China broke and felt there was something pleasantly ironic about the fact that all the gold in China was being carried away in the traditional manner - by coolies.

That was just over fifty years ago. Since then, and in spite of the suicidal policies inflicted on the people by Mao, nevertheless by 2005 - China did indeed pass the U.K. and France to become the world's fourth-largest economy. On present trends, China will pass Germany in about 2008 and Japan around 2015, to become second only to the USA in terms of size. What is astounding is how recent the progress has been, for 20 years ago, its GDP was a few hundred dollars a head. So the renaissance is on the one hand very new, but, on the other, merely a re-establishment of an ancient relationship, where the global pecking order before the Industrial Revolution had taken off, - was a world dominated by China!

Construction here is also becoming feverish, as I noticed on the way back to the Tao Lin Road in Pudong where Chris lives and where a whole new city is being built on virgin land on the east bank of the Huangpu River. From his apartment window, it was possible to get a panoramic view of the city, with the busy Huangpu River in the foreground.

Kate had arrived earlier in the day by plane from Beijing, so a social evening - planned some months earlier - had been arranged in a city with a legendary reputation for the expatriate social life. Long gone is the pre-Communist, all-male Shanghai Club with its famous Long Bar at No. 1, The Bund, so instead on the agenda will be the recent arrivals in Shanghai, the Irish theme bars, carrying the names, Blarney Stone, Dublin Exchange and O'Malleys, which keep respectable opening times - unlike the old Roxy's club which had a sign, "This nightclub will close at 6 a.m. unless requested to remain open longer by our patrons".

The Shanghai Club was very much a "British" club, which boasted a billiards room, its tables covered with brushed green baize. Unlike normal tables, each was supported by short stubby legs resting on wooden platforms. Some members were puzzled until it was explained to them - 'These tables used to be the finest until those bloody little Japanese took over the club during the war and cut down the legs because of their short legs - they could not reach the tables to play'!

Saturday - 4th June

And what a night it was amongst the expatriate community of Shanghai, which included Irish, Australian, New Zealand, South African, English and the odd American. Maybe it's not like the chic café society before the Communists changed it all in 1949, but with its cosmopolitan air and easy communication with the locals - which has allowed a greater interest in leisure activities and nightlife and a wide variety of public entertainment on offer - it is certainly a lively place!

As well as the nightlife, golf is also available. Chris had booked a starting time of noon at the Shanghai Golf and Country Club, about 50 kilometres up the coast. The temperature was over thirty degrees, as we arrived by taxi, passing the new airport on the way. On arrival, the smiling cheerful staff handed me a leather wallet, which included a locker key, scorecard and a blank invoice on which to include all purchases - as the bar staff do not accept cash! Then on leaving the smiling girl will take my money, which seems all very simple and straightforward and Chinese fashion! Our playing partner was a Norwegian named Kjetil, who happened to live in a house on the course, which made him very popular and useful, as his cold beers are very welcome during the round. We also had the assistance of three caddies, two boys and one girl as we set off under the hot mid-day sun.

The course itself sits alongside the East China Sea in an extremely busy shipping lane at the mouth of the Yangtze

River. It was one month since putting my toe in the cold waters of the Gulf of Finland and this was my first sight of the muddy waters here. In spite of lack of practise and a strong wind off the sea with hired clubs but with a little help from Chen my caddie - I scored brilliantly on the par threes. My score went 2,3,2,3 which is two under par gross and something I had not managed to do for some considerable time, even if the water was a magnet for my golf balls at the long holes.

Afterwards, as we sipped a few beers with Kjetil on the terrace outside, we discussed how China, as in most countries in the world has experienced a boom in new golf course construction. Golf, unheard of in China 20 years ago, now has over 200 courses, but in reality, only caters for the very wealthy Chinese or expatriates. Corporate membership of the very top and exclusive clubs in both Beijing and Shanghai cost in excess of 25,000 dollars per annum. And this, in a country where the average salary of a manual worker is 1,500 dollars per annum, whilst in rural areas tens of millions are still living on less than one dollar a day!

The Chinese government have a thin line to follow. On the plus side, their economists have identified that golfers spend ten times more than the average non-golfing tourist. On the negative side is the scarcity of land to build more new courses and the social imbalance, where caddies, usually female, in rural areas can earn in one month, what it takes three years for their farmer parents to accrue. There is also the exclusiveness, where ordinary Chinese can not get near a golf course, other than to work or caddy, unlike the recent lifestyle survey of the very wealthy Chinese, who voted the game of golf as third choice on the list after foreign travel. Multi-nationals desperately want to get their brand name across to the huge potential market place and from time to time stage their own golf tournaments here and pay huge appearance money to the top professionals to play. What is very embarrassing for them is the sparse attendance, with sometimes only a few hundred spectators standing around the fairways.

On returning to London, I was astounded by a headline in the Daily Mail. It read, "Scots bunkered as Chinese say: We invented golf". According to one of their leading academics, the game was played in China in 945 A.D. – some 500 years before the Scots traditionally first struck a ball with a club.

Professor Ling Hongling, a physical education expert, confirms there are literary references to a pastime called – *chuiwan-chui*, meaning "to hit a ball" and it is believed – Genghis Khan's Mongol hordes took golf to Europe centuries later. The professor backed his claims with two paintings from the late 13th century, showing noblemen hitting balls into holes with sticks that look remarkable like to-days golf clubs. He maintains there is strong evidence the "we - the Chinese, invented the game".

After the golf, Chris and I were due to have dinner with his neighbour Mr Wu who lives in the same apartment block and who was at the station yesterday. We were due to meet a lady called Zuan Liguan, a friend of Mr Wu who had travelled down from Wenzhou by bus just to meet and thank me. This was a journey of 700 kilometres, which was surprising, and a long way to come just to say thanks and deliver a present. It was the result of a small favour I did for her daughter Lisa a few months before. All I did was to meet her at Heathrow Airport and put her on the correct bus to Cheltenham. Lisa was going to spend one year there studying English and is just another statistic. Lisa, is just one of the thousands of young Chinese who leave their country every year to improve their education - outside China at great expense and sacrifice by their parents. We eat dinner in the old French Concession area from a menu of Shanghainese fare and afterwards thanked Zuan for her present and said goodbye.

Afterwards, Chris and I went across the city by taxi to meet up with Kate who was waiting in the Dublin Exchange. This is the best time to enjoy the Shanghai night skyline, a city of thirteen million people, which reminds me of Manhattan Island but much more glamorous as no two buildings have the same design and dominating the whole horizon is the vaguely futuristic - Oriental Pearl Tower at 468 metres.

Sunday 5th June

After a late Saturday night, which should have been an opportunity for a lie-in this morning, but it was not to be. Chris was travelling to London at mid-day and he normally takes the new fast train to the international airport. It was an opportunity therefore, to accompany him and experience the Chinese equivalent to the Japanese bullet train. Called the Shanghai Maglev Train and built a couple of years ago by Siemens the German company. In test runs it reached speeds of 500 kilometres per hour and it runs from Longyang Road district in Pudong, directly into the new airport on a system called, magnetic levitation.

Longyang Road was a short taxi ride away as we boarded this new wonder train which just two minutes later reached the maximum permitted speed of 430 KPH, over two hundred and fifty miles per hour as we sped past the cars and trucks on the parallel motorway. In air-conditioned comfort, we reached the airport in seven minutes, having covered a distance of 50 kilometres for the cost of 50 Yuan, which is equivalent to six dollars. There to greet us on the platform were smiling uniformed female staff, assisting with any luggage as we entered this newly constructed airport, which was clean, bright and spacious. Having checked in, I said goodbye to Chris, until meeting up again in London in a few days time. I had just witnessed and experienced modern Shanghai, now it was time to look at its glorious past and its fusty colonial architecture, of a city described as queen of the East.

In the afternoon I met up with Kate at her hotel as we planned to walk around the old city as well as the Bund, on this sunny warm Sunday afternoon. The most impressive street in Shanghai has always been the Bund, whose official name since 1949 is Zhongshan Lu. In its heyday, this was the city's financial district, alongside a busy working harbour, with the river alive with every type of ship, from cruisers anchored in midstream, to tiny sailing junks and small steamers.

Before 1949, the Bund was the heart of Shanghai, perhaps the single most famous street in the East, in those days. It curved along the riverbank for nearly a mile, from the old Shanghai Club at No. 1, to the British Consulate by the Sozhou Creek, with its manicured lawns, high walls and gates guarded by turbaned Sikhs, recruited by the British as police and guards. Between these points stood the offices of the great "trading" houses which had helped establish the city in the early settler days, names like — Jardine Matheson, Sassoon, Butterfield

& Swire and the Chartered Bank. With its kaleidoscope of movement, the Bund was unique in those early days, for it was the waterfront as well as Shanghai's main street, noisy, with a phalanx of motor cars, wheelbarrows, pedicabs and rickshaws.

Today, we started our walk down the old city's main avenue called Nanjing Lu, often described as a cross between Oxford Street and Broadway because of its neon lights and cavernous department stores. It used to be one huge traffic jam from dawn to dusk, but today it was crowded only with pedestrians as we reached the Peace Hotel on the Bund. This grand old hotel has a north and a south building on both sides of Nanjing Lu - The oldest was built in 1906 and called - Sassoon House after its owner. The north one was built in the 1920's and was the former Cathy Hotel, which was renamed, Peace Hotel in 1956.

During the Japanese occupation it was badly damaged, when its finest suites boasted marble baths with silver taps and vitreous china lavatories, all imported from England with the water specially piped from the nearby Bubbling Wells springs. Every visitor of note stayed here - having a guest list including past Presidents of America, Brazil, Mexico and Portugal as well as Queen Elizabeth 11. If a visitor was really famous then their stay was recorded with a suite named after them. Noel Coward had his name so enshrined whilst writing *Private Lives* here in four days. Boasting eighteen restaurants, Kate and I admired its Art Deco elegance but the famous jazz band was not on hand as they only play during the evening, so we would have to return later.

Walking north, we passed a succession of grandiose Neo-classical edifices, which were owned by the foreign enterprises

By Train to Shanghai

that opened up Shanghai to foreign trade. Entrepreneurs like William Jardine, founder of Jardine Matheson, but now long gone and the buildings re-branded under a Chinese name. However, the Customs House is one of the few buildings to have retained its original function, with its distinctive clock tower which was modelled on Big Ben and completed in 1927. At the northern end of the Bund at the confluence of the Huangpu River and Sozhou Creek, is the Huangpu Park, created out of mud and silt, containing a stone monument to the "Heroes of the People".

Landscaped by the British - its original park rules forbade entry to 'dogs or Chinese'. After protests, regulations were relaxed to admit "well dressed" Chinese, but who still needed a special entry pass. The Waibaidy Bridge crosses the creek here and which was a no-mans land between the Japanese occupiers on the North side and the International Settlement on the South during the Second World War. Here, against a backdrop of the dramatic futuristic - Oriental Tower just across a very busy river, in the more pleasant surroundings of today, tourists posed for photos. Today, its narrow spire was visible in the clear blue sky, but on other occasions, it is covered by mist or smog.

The mid-lake pavilion teahouse in the old Chinese city was recommended to us as being worthy of a visit, but required a short taxi ride from where we were. We had prepared ourselves by having the teahouse name already translated into Chinese characters - because without this - no Shanghai taxi driver has any idea of the English translation, and we might end up walking. There used to be tens of thousands of Chinese characters but the vast majority are now obsolete. To live here and get by, you need a minimum of 2,500, whereas educated Chinese are unlikely to know more than 10,000. The characters themselves are pictograms, each representing a concept rather than a specific pronunciation. Some years ago, it was hoped to replace the Chinese characters with the Roman alphabet by introducing the pinyin system. Eventually it was abandoned, but it left a legacy, which today helps foreigners in pronouncing Chinese words.

This famous teahouse gets its name from a small artificial lake and pavilion which was originally part of the Yu Gardens, constructed during the Ming dynasty and which claims to be the oldest teahouse in Shanghai. The teahouse itself is reached across a zigzag bridge spanning the lake and elegantly decorated in traditional Chinese style. Kate was keen to sample their tea - which was made with pure mineral water and delicate tea leaves, picked from different tea-growing regions. We went inside the pavilion that can accommodate more than 200 customers, whilst outside a band played traditional woodwind and string instruments.

The choice was the very best Chinese teas with exotic sounding names like, "peach of immortality of jasmine - the language of the flower - grand red robe and king of tie guanyin", served by smiling waitresses. We sat at a table on the upper floor and ordered for starters the jasmine tea, whilst three musicians entertained us with music from their string instruments. Practically every visitor to Shanghai comes here and on the wall behind where we were sitting - there hung a photograph of Queen Elizabeth II sipping tea with a former prime minister of China in exactly the same spot. This was a good recommendation, and we were certainly in the right place. In these pleasant surroundings, we enjoyed endless refills whilst watching the elderly locals playing mah-jong and listening to the music.

Our day ended with a visit further west, to an area, which used to be known as the French Concession. When the French were in control the two main arteries were called, rue Lafayette and the avenue Joffre - now renamed Huaihai Lu, which has a multitude of fashionable boutiques. The French also had their own French Club, generally regarded as the most chic of all and having the biggest ballroom and the best food. In the last year before the Communists arrived, the 14th July was celebrated with flowers on each table dyed blue, white and red as well as a huge tricolour hung behind the band. Unlike the well-governed British Concession, this area suffered from lax policing, where gangsters thrived and political activists fermented revolution, because here was the first meeting of the Chinese Communist Party in 1921.

Kate and I dined in the garden of a Cantonese dim sum restaurant, in the warm evening weather and then called it a day.

Monday 6th June

Pudong, where I was staying is on the east bank of the Huangpu River, which historically has been known as the "wrong side of the Huangpu", because in the past, living conditions were appalling, and rife with crime. This all changed in 1990 when a special economic zone status was granted to this former agricultural land. A move which triggered a massive investment of nearly 100 billion dollars - that has turned rice paddy fields, into a sea of cranes which will ultimately become a panorama of skyscrapers, stretching as far as the eye can see. The grandiose plan of the Chinese is to create a city for the twenty-first century here in Pudong, which will be eventually one of the major financial business centres in the world.

There was a temporary hiccup to these plans in the wake of the 1997 Asian currency crisis and construction of the world's tallest building of 94 storeys as its world financial centre were shelved by planners. In its place, the Japanese are in the process of constructing a more limited structure, and there are plans to build the equivalent of the London Eye, which will be twice the circumference of the London one. Currently dominating the skyline is the 421 metre-high, Jin Mao Centre, which houses the Grand Hyatt Pudong, and on its 54th floor is the tallest restaurant in China, whilst close by is the Oriental TV Tower. This city is now the largest building site in the world, working 24 hours a day. It is growing up and growing tall with a fusion of skyscrapers but beautiful old architecture is sadly imperilled!

In the early morning heat as the city's construction workers arrived at their many sites, I went for a stroll along Pudong Avenue and watched the Monday morning rush hour evolve. Along this wide tree lined avenue stood a lone traffic policeman in the centre of it, standing at traffic lights helping to control the flow of traffic with a baton and a whistle. Two stern-looking traffic wardens in brown uniforms firmly controlled the large number of cyclists and pedestrians by authorising them to cross the road when appropriate. On the other side of the road, I noticed twelve high-rise buildings, side by side, under construction, and no doubt being prepared for the future workers of Pudong financial centre, the economic powerhouse of the new Shanghai.

By Train to Shanghai

Today, David Gu had volunteered to act as our guide on the Huangpu River tour, as he recommended that this was an excellent way to view the edifices along the riverbank. David speaks good English from his time working in London and now works for Chris. Having collected Kate from her hotel, we all set off down Shanghai's vital water resource, on board a large tourist vessel, just one of the vast numbers of shipping using this busy harbour, along with a few hundred other tourists.

Here, amongst its busy shipping lanes, a staggering one-third of all China's trade passes through it. As we moved slowly along the side of the Bund - where this stretch of quayside must have witnessed great arrivals and departures before the age of the jumbo jet, when everyone arriving in Shanghai came by ships, which moored nearby. Continuing our journey, we marvelled at the new skyline emerging, as old wharfs and warehouses are being razed to the ground, to be replaced by a whole new deep water port, which is being constructed further down the river, close to the mouth of the Yangtze at Chonming Island. We watched barges, container vessels, junks and sampans go up and down as our vessel continued on its 30 kilometre round trip to the Yangtze. Somewhat surprisingly, the Huangpu River is also Shanghai's chief source of drinking water, although thick and brown, but is no longer used as a burial ground for poor Chinese as it was in the 1930's.

Whilst sitting in the sun on the upper deck, I talked to David about Chinese naval power and the maritime exploits of the Chinese explorers in times past and in particular the recent discovery of an ancient map which was unearthed by a collector of old charts. This is the map, found by a Chinese lawyer and art collector, who bought it from an antique map dealer in Shanghai in 2001 for less than 500 dollars.

This map seems to show that it was a Chinese Muslim eunuch, Admiral Zheng He, first landed on the shores of the New World and apparently shows the Chinese accurately surveyed and settled the world in the early years of the 15th century, decades before the *Sancta Maria* had ever been built for Columbus. Cartographers and historians believe the map could prove Admiral Zheng had rounded the Cape of Good Hope, 76 years before Vasco da Gama, and circumnavigated the globe 100 years earlier than Ferdinand Magellan. And that's not all. He also surveyed Australia, some 300 years before Captain Cook. Some experts now contend that Columbus, da Gama and Magellan used copies of this 1418 map to reach the New World.

Each continent of the world has correct shape, mass, latitude and longitude and position. All oceans of the world are displayed and many major rivers and islands. There are some gaps in the map's scope - neither Ireland nor Britain features, and California is shown as an island. Experts in New Zealand are currently checking it to make sure the map is genuine, but a number believe it is. To have drawn maps of the entire world with such accuracy, experts believe that these explorers must have circumnavigated the globe.

Emperor Yongle, the first ruler of the Ming dynasty, wanted to project China's naval power and in 1402 commissioned Admiral Zheng to undertake a daring mission to the seas, then known to the Chinese as the "Western Oceans". It took

By Train to Shanghai

another three years before the expedition was ready and set off on a voyage which took in 37 countries over a 28 year period. This is believed by some to be the mightiest fleet that ever sailed, with 300 ships and 40,000 sailors. Pride of the fleet was the *"treasure ship"* a stunning vessel about 130 metres long and with 1,000 men on board. During this period, China was far more technologically advanced than other cultures and had no equal at sea. When the emperor died in 1424, China began to look inwards, beginning a policy of isolationism that was to last for hundreds of years.

Our vessel had by this stage reached the mouth of the Yangtze and our conversation turned to pollution and the consequences that China's spectacular economic boom, may result - in the near future - in the death of its major economic and maritime hub further north, the Bohai Sea. Environmentalists warn that unless drastic action is taken to stop industrial pollution of its waters the sea could be dead within the next 12 years. Almost no river that flows into the Bohai Sea is clean. This is threatening the wellbeing of the sea, known as "the fish storehouse", because of the habitat it provides for many rare migratory species.

The Bohai, which is among only 12 internal seas in the world, and the largest in China, has 26 cities in its hinterland, including three of China's mega-cities, Beijing, Tianjin and Shenyang. China's coastal regions have enjoyed the lion's share of the current 8 per cent economic growth, but this is also producing staggering quantities of waste. Along its 4,000 kilometre coastline, there are over 100 ports and the Bohai Sea joins the open sea, between China and the Korean peninsula.

Along its coastline, many beaches have recently closed due to regular "red tides". These are huge algae blooms - which last for days and swamp vast areas of sea with dangerous levels of toxins. These can prove lethal for its famed shellfish - for which the Bohai is famous, and other sea creatures. China's State Environmental Protection Agency (Sepa), now concede, that half of the off-shore sea-water in China has been poisoned and are extremely pessimistic on the marine environment.

On returning to the quay it was time to say goodbye to Kate who was returning to Beijing, but David and I decided that having viewed the city from the river we would go and get a birds-eye view from the top of the Oriental Tower. This was an ideal day, as visibility was good - a clear blue and cloudless sky. The main sightseeing floor of the tower is at 263 metres, which is reached by fast elevator in what seemed like seconds. From here, on this circular floor, it was possible to enjoy and survey this dynamic city from this great height with the Huangpu River meandering through it. Just above this floor, at 267 metres is a busy revolving restaurant, supposedly the highest revolving eatery in Asia, which apparently is always very busy at night time. Declining David's invitation to go even higher to the Space Module at 350 metres, I was happy where I was and could see distances up to thirty kilometres away in the horizon of this historic coastal city - the apogee of the new China.

Tuesday - 7th June

For this, my final full day in Shanghai - Mr Wu had volunteered himself as guide, and suggested a visit to some of the remaining sites not visited, thus far. Mr Wu, who is a businessman living here, even cooked me breakfast with his usual three fried eggs before we set off. In 30-degree heat, it was a short taxi ride to the nearest metro station at Lujiazui, near the Jin Mao Tower. Then it was just two stops on a new line to Renmin Park, in air-conditioned comfort at a cost of 3 yuan, for the single journey. Mr Wu explained this was a quicker route to downtown in the morning rush hour, as traffic jams in the two river tunnels are commonplace.

At the northern end of Renmin Park runs Nanjing Lu, which has a reputation of being the busiest shopping street in China and sometimes makes London's Oxford Street look like a country byway. Mr Wu explained that all roads running west to east are called after cities, hence Nanjing Lu which runs west from here to the Bund and all roads running north to south are called after Chinese provinces, which should offer some help to the harassed taxi drivers, who find great difficulty with the fast-changing city.

The whole area around Renmin Park and Renmin Square was originally the site of the old Shanghai racecourse. Now, only it's clock tower remains as Chiang Kai-shek decided to try and not pander to the Chinese passion for gambling, and converted the racecourse into a sports stadium and afterwards it became a parade ground for political rallies. Opposite, stands the historic Pacific and Park hotels, the latter was the tallest building in Shanghai and when Mao was visiting the city - it was here that he stayed. This is an excellent vantage point to view the developing skyline and one of the newest and most impressive buildings nearby - the Shanghai Museum, which displays all facets of Chinese art and culture.

From here we took a taxi half a mile away to the old city - based around the original walled city of Shanghai and said to date back one thousand years. This was always known as the Chinese City, but was never part of the International Settlement, where only Chinese lived in one vast labyrinth of narrow, uneven, potholed streets, in the 19th and early 20th century, whilst foreigners lived outside it. Though much of it has been rebuilt over the years, here and here alone in Shanghai, the white man, if not excluded, was a pale stranger in another world, peopled by Chinese, going about their everyday life.

In an area known as Chenghuang Miao, we entered a Buddhist Temple named Shanghai Cheh Xi-ang Monastery where a full-blown Buddhist ceremony was taking place. This was led by twelve chanting, bald-headed monks, surrounded by hundreds of burning candles and incense. A lone monk in the far corner slowly and deliberately banged the gong in unison with the chanting, whilst the packed congregation of worshippers prayed and lit candles from an open fire. It was not clear whether this was a daily ceremony, but what has become clear and evident, is that religious fervour is sweeping the country. People need an outlet to express their emotions someway and finding it in Buddhism - now that Communism is waning - but democracy may not have quite replaced it just yet!

The Chinese authorities are aware of this fact and in 1999 banned the Falun Gong movement as it quickly spread by word and mouth and supporters claim that between 70 and 100 million Chinese citizens had taken up the practice. First introduced to the public in China in 1992, followers say it is an entirely peaceful belief system, which encourages the highest standards of moral behaviour and is a traditional practice to improve mind and body which improves health and inner peace. Sadly, the Chinese authorities think otherwise.

They remember well the Boxer Rebellion and in the 19th century – the Taiping Rebellion, which sprang from a religious cult that provoked perhaps the bloodiest civil war in human history. Then the forces of the Qing Empire clashed with those of a mystic named Hong Xiuquan who said he was the younger brother of Jesus Christ and claimed to be the new Messiah. At least 20 million people – and perhaps as many as 100 million – perished!

They also believe that many adherents of the Falun Gong are disillusioned members of the Communist Party from its Maoist days - who need an outlet for the zeal which has not featured in political life since the end of the Cultural Revolution. And worse of all - China's leaders remember that religious sects can grow in power and turn into national rebellions very quickly!

Considering that the Communist government is nominally atheist, there are 100 million Buddhists in China and 10 million Roman Catholics. The Christian Church is in effect state-run, and has no diplomatic links with the Vatican. The Pope is accepted as a spiritual leader only, and has no authority over China.

Signalling their loyalty to the Pope and the wider Catholic Church is delicate for China's Catholic bishops, who are forced by their government to renounce such ties and to accept government restrictions on their Church. All China's Catholic bishops are appointed ostensibly by the Catholic Patriotic Association, acting for the local Church, but in reality by the

Communist Party. This body is not recognised by the Vatican. Much to the annoyance of Rome and against Vatican protocol, the Chinese Church continues to ordain bishops, without first seeking approval of their nominations!

From this place of worship, we walked down a few narrow twisting alleyways, thronged with pedestrians, past dozens of tiny stalls, their hawkers beseeching you to accept a cold drink, or examine a pair of slippers. Dozens of tiny stalls held mysterious cooking implements and walking past, you could smell noodles cooking. Silk hawkers carried their rolls in deep bags slung round their necks whilst professional letter-writers, with their minuscule desk and pots of ink and bundles of brushes, peered over spectacles at you. Here, this ancient centre around Chenghuang Miao still retains a different feel about it - from the modern Shanghai slowly engulfing it.

Shortly afterwards, we reached the Yu Yuan Gardens, when the best time to be here is during the Chinese New Year, because then, these gardens are illuminated with the lights of ten thousand lanterns. Recreated in classical style from the original Ming dynasty design, it features walkways, bridges, rockeries and many pools stocked with fish.

Bill Clinton was here in 1998 as his photograph buying souvenirs, was displayed in one of the local shops, whilst nearby was a restaurant where Mr Wu and I went in search of some good local food to eat. Over lunch, we discussed the history of Shanghai, and he explained that Shanghai has always been a welcoming city. Shanghailanders of every nationality played a part in its frenetic life, sensing that to be here seemed an honoured privilege and all considered the city

By Train to Shanghai

they had adopted as queen of the East. Whilst it may have been welcoming for non-Chinese from the earliest days - the European rulers had been unable to control the number of Chinese who had migrated to Shanghai.

The very first refugees to arrive were Russians, fleeing from Vladivostok, having been evacuated following the Bolshevik victory in 1920. They arrived in style—in three steamers carrying the remnants of the Far Eastern White army under the command of General Glebov. He brought with him not only his entourage, but also a band, which played when he landed at the quay - marking the end of his voyage. By 1948, the Russian community had dwindled to half of the original 25,000, for after the Second World War; the Soviet Union offered expatriates, citizenship and repatriation. Many older people with fond memories found their longings for their homeland too strong to resist and went home to an uncertain future in Russia.

The original Russian refugees had fought a war and lost, but the 20,000 Jews who arrived in 1938-9 were in a different category. They were mostly Germans and Austrians, who had been booted out of their own countries. Although without any money - unlike the Russians - yet were potentially richer, for they brought with them skills which quickly became useful assets in Shanghai. As doctors, dentists, teachers, and engineers, they became integrated into the life of the city more quickly than other refugees. The Jews had lost everything, but their optimism and Shanghai was a city born of optimism.

The city gave these refugees the start to a new life and they became a thriving community, with youth clubs, schools, dance halls, coffee houses, newspapers, bars and ballet houses - all emerged. Shanghai, was a war-ravaged city with the port controlled by the Japanese, who despite being part of the Axis, the Japanese did not refuse the Jews entry to the city, emphasising their belief in religious equality. Their plight was the subject of a film called the *Port of the Last Resort*, revealing some of the joy, but immense hardships that befell this community which all changed following the attack on Pearl Harbour, on December 7, 1941. And, when Germany declared that all Jews were stateless - representatives from the Nazi regime arrived in Japan to negotiate greater controls to be imposed upon Shanghai's Jewish Community.

In January 1942, the Japanese rulers introduced an "emergency measure" saying that all refugees who would work with the Japanese would be treated with friendliness, but the rest would be placed under "strict surveillance so that any hostile activity may be eliminated or suppressed".

The Jews had to move into the established ghetto in Hong Kew, which was controlled by a brutal commander, called Ghoya. It was here that the community suffered immense hardships, at one stage it was estimated that 6,000 were on the point of starvation, whilst, the remainder were faring little better. Their misery in Shanghai came to an end, when the Americans dropped the atomic bombs on Nagasaki and Hiroshima and the Japanese troops fled the city. Crowds swept through Shanghai, tearing down the signs marking the segregation of the city. By 1949, when Mao took control of China, the vast majority of Jews in Shanghai had left the city to pursue their lives elsewhere.

By Train to Shanghai

After lunch, on the way back to Pudong, we stopped off at the Pudong driving range. Here, in an oasis of green, sandwiched between high-rise buildings and protected on the perimeter by high nets, was a golf driving range. As if to emphasise the popularity of golf, every available bay was occupied, so it seems that golf is finally catching up with the Chinese, although how many can afford to play on a real course remains to be seen. My real concern was for the poor ball-retrievers, who walked around under the protection of a flimsy contraption on wheels, which they pushed around while volleys of golf balls whizzed past their ears!

In the evening it was my final opportunity to hear the famous old jazz band in the long bar of the Art Deco treasure, the Peace Hotel, so it was back across the river again - this time to the Bund. My original journey had started with a parade led by octogenarians, proudly wearing their medals and decorations, as they led their country's 60th anniversary parade, on their Great Patriotic Day as they marched proudly up the Nevsky Prospekt, in St. Petersburg, on 9th May.

My journey ends here, with another group of octogenarians, this time in Shanghai, and I refer to the legendary six-piece jazz band, who, perform nightly in the cavernous bar of the Peace Hotel - which just happened to be voted the best bar in the world by Newsweek in 1996. Although a jazz band has been playing here since the 1930's, they suffered during the Cultural Revolution when forced to disband, but re-emerged again in 1980. When they call it old, they really mean it, because the average age is 75 years. The oldest is Cheng Yue Ziang, the drummer, who used to play in the Shanghai Opera Theatre - now 87 years old. The leader of the band, Zhou Wan Rong, -

85 years old and formerly played with the Shanghai Symphony Orchestra. Nightly, at eight o'clock, these guys assemble round an old teak table and entertain their guests - who in the past have included former American Presidents.

During the interval, I talked with one of these musicians who lived throughout the good old days before 1949, under the Nationalist Kuomintang and also under the Communist regime of Mao. I asked him, his opinion of Chiang Kai-shek, the Nationalist leader, who was a pivotal figure during the 20th Century. He replied that the uncharitable might say that Chiang was an out and out traitor and it is difficult to disagree with this. Yet he was not of the stuff of which traitors are made. Chiang knew defeat was inevitable and believed it was imperative to somehow keep the old China intact. In any event, he was planning his future in Taiwan, where he would become the puppet ruler of an ineffectual country, conveniently surrounded by water and which had been transformed into an impregnable bastion. He bribed his high-ranking military officers not to fight and saw no point in wasting his Navy or Air Force in fighting the Communists, which would be more useful intact for the defence of Taiwan.

The musician also explained and lamented how lucky the foreigners were in 1948 whilst the Chinese Civil War raged on, because they were paid in their own currency. This was paradise for them, as they could dine on caviar and champagne at the best restaurants, for one dollar American. Whereas, the Chinese workers earning 3 million Chinese dollars a week, now starved. Chiang made an unexpected visit to Shanghai in April and made a nation-wide radio appeal, saying, "Shanghai will fight to the end. There will be no surrender". In effect it was a ruse to show the Americans that the Nationalists were still in business, in the hope of getting more American arms and aid.

The speech had a disastrous effect on the city's economy, which by then was slowly grinding to a halt. The day before Chiang's speech - one dollar American could buy 1.2 million Chinese dollars. The day of the speech the rate dropped to 1.7 million, and the day after that - it dropped to a staggering 3.75 million for one American dollar. The sad fact was that Chinese money was now worth less than the cost of printing it!

Today, the Chinese currency has been re-named the Yuan and is one of the strongest currencies in the financial markets. As I sipped a cocktail and listened to the jazz, I reflected on my ten days here in China. In a country with a population of one and one-third billion people - the third largest land mass on earth after Russia and Canada, I had only visited three of its cities and did not even see one of its giant pandas - and little of rural life - other than out of a train window - where large swathes of the countryside may still be as they were decades ago.

For centuries, China was a leading civilisation leading the rest of the world in art and the sciences, but in the 19th and early 20th centuries it was beset with civil unrest, foreign occupation, famines and military upheavals. After the Second World War, Mao Tse-tung established a dictatorship, which ensured China's sovereignty but he was responsible for disastrous famines. In 1978 his successor, Deng Xiao-ping introduced market-oriented reforms and decentralised economic decision making. Output quadrupled by the year 2,000 and today is one of the world's economic powerhouses

- on course to overtake the American economy and the world's largest by the middle of this century. It is as if they are racing to make up for lost time and largely on their own terms!

But this has come at a price. Chinese people are taking their own lives in record numbers. More than a quarter of a million people a year are killing themselves, that is 685 a day, whilst three and a half million make unsuccessful attempts. Suicide is now the primary cause of death amongst those aged between twenty and thirty-five. Society is full of pressure and competition, and as the world's most populous country has lurched - from rigid, isolated Communism to capitalism in one generation. The pace of change in a country where mental illness and suicide, remain taboo subjects, leaves many - especially in rural areas - left behind!

As the old jazz band started to play my personal request of number sixty, from their extensive programme – *"Now is the Hour"*- an attractive Chinese girl joined me at the bar. She introduced herself as Lisa and said she was twenty-five years old and worked in public relations. She asked - if she could practise her English and offered me her business card as I ordered a gin and tonic for her and the band played on!

Epilogue

Just as the Trans-Siberian Railway was the first great enterprise of the 20th century for the Russians - we now find that at the start of the 21st Century - the Chinese have built a train across the top of the world!

Having being considered for fifty years, it took until 2001 before work began. It had to be suspended twice to allow the annual migration of Tibetan antelopes and snow leopards. Just as with the Trans-Siberian - construction work was plagued throughout by extreme cold, as well as low oxygen levels and the fragile ecosystem. This is now the world's highest railway - opening soon between China's Qinghai province and Tibet - which will have carriages specially sealed to prevent altitude sickness among passengers. This pan-Himalayan line - costing the equivalent of nearly two billion pounds, will link the city of Golmud, the starting point, and Lhasa, the capital of China's Tibet Autonomous Region - a total distance of 1,194 kilometres.

Crossing a snow-covered Tibetan plateau known as the "roof-of-the world", it climbs to 5,072 metres, which, - China says is a world record. Almost 80 per cent of the line lies above

4,000 metres and one section of 550 kilometres has been laid on permafrost. These lines sit on special rollers and pontoons - designed to keep them in place as the ice melts or refreezes.

The trains will feature a special cold-resistant material, and be supplied with an air-conditioning and oxygen system to provide sufficient air. Also included on the train, is an emergency clinic, which could be used to treat cases of altitude sickness.

What a way to arrive in Lhasa, capital of Tibet!

About the Author

William Gingles was born and educated in Ireland and is a self-confessed railway enthusiast. He has spent most of his adult life working in the City of London and has travelled extensively, having lived in Saudi Arabia and Dubai.

Now retired and living in Pimlico in London, the ideal time had arrived to fulfil a youthful ambition of a journey that was conceived some decades ago, but which passed into middle age without fulfilment and only now was about to be realised.

This journey was on the Trans-Siberian Railway and onwards to China.